# THE GIG SOCIETY

### How Modern Technology is Degrading Our Values and Destroying Our Culture

**Brian Wolatz**

Design by J-P Stanway.

ISBN 978-1-7342420-9-6 (paperback)
ISBN 978-1-7342420-8-9 (hardcover)

Published by Brian Wolatz.
brianwolatz.com

First edition: February 2020.

*To my fellow countrymen, who have seen American
values fall in exchange for an encroaching
tyranny of the ruling class and have waited
for someone to fight and speak for them, and
to my wife, Destiny, who supported my writing
of this book in every way imaginable, often whilst
pregnant with our second child.*

# Contents

# Introduction

I wasn't alive when the Internet was created, and I don't wish that I was. The history of computation and modern technology is fascinating to me, but there's a reason why it's history. I can't remember or imagine a world without the technology we have today, and for that I am grateful. I've always had the Internet, online multiplayer games, and computers fast enough to help everyday people. I remember that even in elementary school we had a computer lab, and each classroom had a couple of those single-unit colored Apple machines.

For generational reasons, a lot of contemporary humor is lost on me. I never knew the time before this era of technology—when books were the primary way to learn things (as opposed to one of many ways), when relationships were built without constant connection (as opposed to the availability provided by messaging applications and text messaging), and when keeping up with people meant talking to them (as opposed to checking their social media). It's not that I don't understand the humor the older generations make about the younger generations' reliance on technology, it's that I can't *get* it.

This morphs my perspective significantly. I won't ever know the world before the Internet and modern technology, so I don't reminisce. I don't idealize or hold on to a past I never lived. It's clear that the technological advancements of the 1990s and 2000s took over parts of our lives and had negative impacts on our society that make some want to go back. But for me, technology's always had the effect on society that it has today. It makes me want to improve it, not dismantle it. It makes me dream of a better future, not pine for a better past.

And there are negative impacts, potentially a lot of them. The ones we do know about are getting worse for us every day. Loneliness caused by a lack of real-life interaction is causing suicide, and the average American's life expectancy is dropping. Technology fundamentally changes the way our freedom of expression and our rights to privacy are interpreted, often in ways that violate them. The recognized potential for gigantic job loss caused by the technologies of artificial intelligence and automation will bring despair to people and widen the gap between the haves and the have-nots.

These are the challenges of our moment, and how we choose to solve them will define our country's culture and economy. If we don't recognize and address the negative impacts, we will lose our national cohesion, liberty, economic security, and happiness. But if we confront the challenges with solutions as modern and complex as the technologies that befall us, then we will find our national identity, secure our freedoms, create an economic system that works for the people and not the profits, and discover hope for the future.

## Threats to Our Society

The Internet's connectivity is its mission and its power. The Internet can gather people under common interest and enable real-time conversations between them, even if they're half a world away. There are discussion boards and groups for every interest, people can watch and discuss events in real time with streaming, and it's all made possible by the Internet.

It's not just that the Internet has the power to connect people, it's that people are actually using that power. There are four-and-a-half billion people with Internet access globally. The consensus over several studies done in recent years is that the average person is spending over six-and-a-half hours a day online.[1] So in the world of connectivity, we ought to be socializing more, making more friends, and utilizing amicable ways of dealing with people who think differently from us.

Except, as we know, those assumptions are wrong. Americans are lonelier than ever before, with nearly half reporting sometimes or always feeling lonely. 43% of American adults say their relationships are not meaningful and that they feel isolated.[2] As our social support framework has crumbled, a quarter of Millennials say they have no close friends.[3] Our national division has increased too, with 77% of Americans viewing the country as divided, up from 65% in 2004 and 69% in 2013.[4]

While there are other issues at play, this is largely the fault of technology. Or rather, I propose, it's the fault of how we use technology. Technology has connected us all but has failed to keep us connected in ways that feel meaningful, or promote understanding and inclusion. In an era where seemingly everyone is doing the same thing (being online), there's no reason why 27% of Americans should feel like no one understands them.

There are reasons why people don't seek connections online, and I don't discredit those. People don't share personal information because they're worried about being doxxed. People limit interactions on social media sites because they don't trust the tech industry to do good things with their data. I don't deny that these are valid oppositions, but I think we can come up with forward-thinking and technical means to put them to rest.

What the older generations often don't understand is that the younger generation doesn't want to return to an old way. It's not that we don't know that church exists, it's that we don't want to get up early on a Sunday morning. We understand that reading a book is better than reading social media, and that it's easier to meet people at a bar than online. We know these options exist, but we choose not to partake in them.

This really only leaves one option: if we are going to spend a quarter of our lives online, and nothing can talk us out of it, then we need to make being online more positive. We need to find ways to make social media social again. We need to figure out how to create happy communities online, where people can make meaningful connections and friends, establish trust in each other, and stop feeling alone.

The proposition is new and requests a radical change in how we conduct ourselves online. The grave threat of American loneliness is causing us to kill ourselves. This is a complicated problem, and of course additional research and study is needed. This solution, or whatever other solution we use, is going to have to involve us changing online culture. We need to be ready to make the cultural changes that are asked of us to stop the epidemic of loneliness and save lives.

## The Internet's Power in Action

I spend a lot of time on the Internet, probably more than I should. I'd like to imagine I have my finger on the pulse of the user bases and attitudes. I've recently seen a rise in content from people admitting that they're depressed and lonely, in some cases even suicidal. I think it's horrible that people are feeling these ways, but expressing it is better than wallowing about, waiting for something to change. Expressing it is a way of reaching out.

For the broader direction I'd like to see the Internet go in, this is great. People are openly talking about their issues, and in that conversation they're looking for connection. Obviously, these people would be better off talking to a therapist than to Internet strangers, but people beginning to talk is key to people broadly becoming social online again.

I think it's no surprise that the rise of the Internet has led to a dramatic shift in the ways Americans view certain issues. For example, 63% of Americans in 1994 believed that immigrants were a burden to the country, but in 2019 62% believe that immigrants strengthen it.[5] A similar flip in perspective exists in America's views of gay marriage, where in 1996 only 27% believed same-sex marriages should be recognized by the law as valid, compared to 63% in 2019.[6] I think the connectivity of the Internet helped open the discussion around these issues and ultimately changed a lot of minds.

We need to use the Internet's power to fight the cultural threats of today. We need to bring back the openness of discussion where we can talk about our issues, including loneliness and depression. I remember seeing a heavily shared Tweet that said something to the effect of "Why does it matter that I can like whoever I want if no one likes me?" This is emblematic of the problem: our cultural understanding of sexual orientation has progressed, but people remain as alienated as ever.

## Threats to Our Economy

The societal threat posed by technology, that it brings loneliness and depression, is new and scary. Clearly, we do not have a good way to deal with that threat yet. The changes of technology do not just threaten our relationships and our culture, but also threaten our economy. Automation poses a threat to America's most vulnerable workers, and surveillance capitalism endangers our privacy. Technological progress should make our lives better. If it does not, we need to evaluate the winners and losers of the economic model to ensure its fairness.

Automation is an issue for workers in that 47% of American jobs are at a high risk of being automated in the next two decades. I fear, as do millions of Americans, that if automation were to happen in an instant right now, that the biggest winners would be the ruling class, and the biggest losers would be the working class. But it doesn't have to be—with the right economic framework, losing jobs to automation could be the start of those workers' reeducation and reintroduction to the workforce. Under the current framework, that wouldn't be the outcome for those people.

Automation should not represent a threat to our economy, it should represent a springboard we can use to achieve justice for the millions of people it will displace economically. We have the knowledge to preempt this economic transition to take advantage of it. By being forward-thinking, we can derive an economic model beforehand that embraces automation, rather than rejects it.

Another fresh challenge our economy will deal with will be surveillance capitalism. Surveillance capitalism is an economic system that uses its knowledge of consumers to the advantage of the business. Instead of businesses needing to trust consumers, surveillance capitalism offers those businesses with something way better: the user's actual data. It is replacing the trust in what the consumers say with trust in what their data says about them.

Unlike automation, I see surveillance capitalism as a complete negative that erodes our values. Surveillance capitalism relies on having an abundance of customer data, usually obtained by years of tracked activity and real-time monitoring. It's a misplaced assumption that Americans are willing to give up their privacy for an economic model that tells businesses not to trust them.

We need to find ways to curtail surveillance capitalism before it grows into something we cannot control. It is a new threat, one that not many Americans could recognize, and we'll need to be proactive in shutting it down. Being put under perpetual surveillance for the good of the economy is a dystopian nightmare.

## America Needs to Lead the Regulatory Charge

Due to its unparalleled values of freedom and individualism, America has a responsibility to the rest of the world to resist the dangers of these economic trends. Without American leadership on how to handle these new challenges, globally we will watch freedoms erode, speech become limited, and privacy get eradicated. We need to set an example and act decisively on regulating modern technology.

Another facet of this situation is that the tech giants that need regulation are American companies. Google, Amazon, Facebook, Microsoft, and Apple are all headquartered in the US. Regulating the tech industry in America will create downstream effects on their business models and culture in the global market.

Surveillance capitalism brings a change to economic models that the entire world is unprepared for, the United States included. It will bring an unprecedented amount of monitoring and surveillance into the lives of all Americans. It seeks to disrupt the right to privacy and turn it into a privilege on a global scale.

Bear in mind that there is no other country on Earth with a legal commitment to the privacy of its citizens like America. We have the Fourth Amendment to protect us from this threat of surveillance from the government, and it's high time we enforce that amendment on businesses as well. The United States must face the challenges of the new economy and regulate them to preserve the rights and dignity of its own people as well as the world's.

Because of the unique status of America as a champion of the rights to speech, privacy, and freedom, we must take up this mantle and lead the world. The world's culture and economy are changing dramatically, and while we're bidding farewell to a lot of old ideas and bringing in the new, let's make sure that we keep what's worth preserving. It's important to promote the American perspective on individuality and liberty as American companies gain power and enact their will globally.

## Identifying How Big Tech Wrongs Us

The purpose of this book is to educate and inform the American people of the way that modern technology has changed and will continue to change our country, and propose legislative action to help alleviate the negatives of those changes. My educational background is in Computer Science with a concentration in Internet Technologies, a minor in Management Information Systems, and a certificate in Systems Development. I've worked as a full-stack (responsible for all categories of technology) software developer and engineer for four years.

I see the threats that the modern tech industry is posing to Americans, but I also understand that there are barriers that prevent meaningful regulation and accountability from occurring. Too often a lack of technical knowledge can impede legislators' abilities to find nuanced solutions or cause the judicial system to fail in holding people accountable. Writing a book which provides essential background on these threats is a good way to increase baseline knowledge in the American electorate.

That's what the first half of this book is largely focused on-discovering and analyzing the dangers posed by big technology. I want to give a face to the evils of the tech industry: what kinds of subversive practices they have, what their economic endgame looks like, and how they abuse their customers' freedoms. Identifying these moves us closer to the point of regulation.

We'll talk about Google, the company with a penchant for authoritarianism and their control over the market; Facebook, the company that can't align its business practices in ways that lets users feel comfortable; and Internet service providers, the companies that made false promises to gain market advantages and monopolize a category of service without helping the American people.

We will also talk about technology in this book: not just events surrounding the tech industry or their business models, but topics like encryption, how data gets moved across the Internet, how data is stored, and the potential for security breaches. Accompanying these topics will be detailed walkthroughs. There are no topics without introductions or words without definition.

## Stop Big Tech's Bad Practices

Naturally following the first part of the book, the second will explore how we can stop the tech industry from being destructive. There are problems not only with the tech industry itself, but also with the framework in which we legislate it. We don't have the right agencies in place, and we don't have legislators bold enough to take these issues on.

There are a lot of ways that we could regulate the threats of modern technology, but I want to keep the focus on ones that maintain people's civil rights and dignity but don't regress or prevent the progression of technology. Technological advancements have a lot to offer society, but we need to do our part to make sure all of society shares in their benefits. The way we can get that done is through regulation.

We need to regulate how private companies gain access to our data, how they use that data, and what rights users have over their own data. We need to examine laws that allow private companies to act in unfair ways against each other and how those laws affect the software market and user choice. We need to limit how private companies exploit government services. We need to ban technologies that pose a threat to our autonomy.

From the perspective of national consensus, I think implementing most or all of my proposed policies would be a homerun. As a country, we agree on these solutions and the corresponding philosophy behind them. We agree that big tech is invading our privacy and we're not comfortable with it. We want the free market of technology to flourish without bad faith actors. We want our freedom of speech preserved.

With just over half of Americans thinking that big tech companies need regulation[7], it's time to start having more discussion about what we can or can't do. There are regulations that people from all political stances can get on board with, as infringements of tech on our lives have become too egregious to be ignored.

## I Am You

In an ideal world, it would not be me writing this book. I've never published so much as a blog post before I found it necessary to start the process. I am the average American: I work 9–5, I have a family and a mortgage, I take care of my pets, and I spend way too much time online. I'm not naturally inclined to put my name on things or push my personal stock.

But the threats of the tech industry can't be ignored any longer, and I don't have the option to wait for more advocates of a free Internet to start speaking up. I've spent practically my entire life living in one place (Omaha), in the middle of the country. The dangers of modern technology are not local to Palo Alto, where the big tech companies reside. They affect me, they affect you, they affect America, and they affect the world.

The time for change is now. We need to get in front of these challenges. Our culture, society, and economy are all changing as a result of modern technology, and Americans deserve to have a say in those changes. We don't have to be helpless; we can use representation in government to guarantee that these changes help us, the average Americans.

The undermining of our liberties and values of individualism is too important not to worry about. These ideas are core to the American identity. If nothing else, I want to be clear that modern technology threatens these values, and we all will be worse off if it is allowed to progress unimpeded. Our generation, our kids' generation, and the generations that follow cannot afford to have their rights dismantled for all tomorrows because we lacked the courage to take on those who threaten them today.

# I

## Modern Technology Undermines Our Privacy Rights

### Technology Should Improve Our Lives, but Is Starting Not To

Fundamentally, the purpose of technology is to improve our lives. Whether the technology was the wheel, the pulley, the lightbulb, the car, or the computer, the ultimate goal has always remained: we develop technology so that our lives may be easier. The idea that we humans can manipulate our natural resources to create technology that improves our lives has existed throughout all human history. Scientific research and engineering have existed in all political and economic regimes.

In a capitalist society, we are driven to create technology that improves lives simply because people are willing to pay for it. An ideal capitalist might tell you that so long as your creation is useful, it is bound to be profitable. We spend our money on new technologies, that money funds technology companies that further invest in innovation and invention, and the cycle self-perpetuates.

Therefore, it's important to reflect and critically think about the technologies of the late 2010s versus the technologies of the early 2000s. Technology companies, it seems, are running out of truly innovative ideas for improvement on their products. Their newest products, such as their respective smart speaker lines, provide nearly no new benefit to society other than taking what was at our fingertips and putting it at the tip of our tongues.

Across the industry, technology companies are finding it difficult to make new products with new features that people are willing to pay for. Instead, their strategies focus on sapping money out of existing customers, innovating new technologies which come with a Pandora's Box of ethical questions, or reworking their products to work better for advertisers and the government. None of these schemes are benefiting the customers, and we shouldn't be okay with that.

## Planned Obsolescence

It was revealed in early 2019 that Apple's 2018 year-end sales had suffered immensely.[1] Earlier in the year, Apple had released their smart speaker, the HomePod. Besides some newer versions of old products, such as the Apple Pencil, Mac Pro, and AirPods, it was the only new product hitting the shelf for Apple.

"Planned obsolescence" is a business practice where consumer goods are rapidly phased out, where products' spare parts are discontinued, features in new products make old products incompatible, or old products otherwise become less viable over time. The goal with planned obsolescence is to force consumers to buy new products more frequently, even if the old products would work fine under normal circumstances.

Apple uses planned obsolescence to retain customers without creating anything new. In their case, they intentionally slow down older devices' performance speeds. This means that, over time, Apple technology will become slower and less efficient. This is not on a relative scale to new products, but their devices individually will start to slow down. Apple accomplishes this by sending bloated software updates to its devices which take up space and purposefully slow down core processes.

Apple's end game is simple: try to force as many users off old technology as possible, thus forcing them to spend money on new technology. If Apple cannot convince users to buy new technology, then new technology must be made more impressive. It must improve livelihood more drastically. New technology should not be purchased simply because the old technology was intentionally slowed down.

This is clearly an attack on consumer rights. In some European countries, like France and Italy, planned obsolescence is against the law. In Italy specifically, both Apple and Samsung have been issued fines for violations as of 2018,[2] and France's consumer protection agency has opened investigations into Apple.[3]

In addition to being fined for intentionally pushing software updates which lower speeds, Apple has also been fined in Italy for not describing its core components to users explicitly enough. End users are required to have information on the maintenance, life expectancy, and directions on how to replace the lithium batteries in iPhones, however, the information provided with the iPhones was not sufficient for Italian regulators.

Because of their lack of creating legitimate improvements to technology to drive sales, Apple is faced with having to do these tricky dealings in order to generate revenue. Not telling customers how to fix their products or by intentionally slowing those products down is terrible business. It's a shame to see a staple company of technological innovation sink this low.

## Tech Industry's Curtain to the Public

Apple is not the only technology company suffering from lack of invention and innovation. Similarly at Google's 2018 conference, a majority of the announcements were centered around improving Artificial Intelligence capabilities. Not new products, nor anything fresh or exciting that will really impact the lives of everyday people. If technology companies aren't releasing products that aim to help people, then what are they working on?

The answer may be more sinister than what we can imagine. The behind-the-scenes social engineering that subtly defined our social media experiences in the early 2010s has had the curtain pulled back. We're aware that technology companies track everything they can about us. We're aware that our data is for sale, and that companies like Facebook have built entire business models off selling it.

Instead of playing the good guys, we learn that the industry is really just evil. It was reported that Silicon Valley employees discourage the use of their own technology to their kids.[4] Yet, they turn around, give us consumers a used-car-salesman smile, and tell us to trust their product. If the goal of researching, building, and using technology is to better our lives, why won't the industry use it to better the lives of their own children?

In 2018, a Google employee named Jack Poulson quit the company. He revealed that the company is hell-bent on stopping internal information from getting to the public. He characterized that managers have made stopping leaks the company's number one priority, and that one point a senior engineer told a large group of coworkers "f— you leakers!" Other evidence supports Poulson's claim. Lawsuits made public allege Google made employees sign extreme confidentiality agreements. Additionally, Google has a program called "Stop Leaks" which, true to its name, is intended for employees to use to report leaking done by others or themselves.[5]

It was also revealed that Google would stop recording certain company-wide meetings after a leaked video from Google's leadership cast serious doubts about the tech giant's ability to remain unbiased politically. The video originated from an all-staff meeting which came shortly after Donald Trump's surprising election victory to become the President of the United States in 2016. The video shows many (both leadership and non-leadership) Google employees denouncing and ridiculing the President-elect. At one point during the video, Ruth Porat, Google's Chief Financial Officer, chokes up and nearly cries after reliving her election night experience—again, at an all-staff meeting.

Poulson claims that similar movements of imposing secrecy on employees are taking place at Amazon and Microsoft. Speculating, it seems realistic that one or two technology companies might be working on something so ground-breaking and innovative that it would require these high levels of secrecy. However, it seems extreme to have such restrictive and broad locks on everything, in seemingly the entire industry.

What the public needs is transparency into technology companies' operations, and those companies seem to be determined not to reveal anything of the sort. This creates a trust problem that the industry itself has a duty to solve. I'm not advocating for every company meeting to be made publicly available. Obviously, sharing heartfelt moments of sadness with your employees as CFO shouldn't necessarily be something broadcast to the world. But the other side of the equation is starved and the system needs some level of public insight.

## Why It's Hard for People to Walk Away

The public is losing trust in the industry. The capitalist solution is simple and universal: If you don't trust your service or think a bad job has been done, simply find another one. However, the power that technology companies have over us is far more than that of a convenience store. Walking away from the technology is not so easy when evaluating the massive reach of companies like Google and Facebook into all corners of technology and the Internet.

Even if you don't have a Facebook account, Facebook still knows everything about you, whether that's through their social media platform itself or their wide array of partnered websites that track your Internet browsing activity (more on Facebook Pixel later). Similarly,

Google enjoys huge market shares in just about every facet of Internet technology. Consumers are faced with no option but to accept the powers that be, for even if they attempt to walk out the door, they leave behind an Internet lifetime's worth of personal information, all to be sold to the highest bidders. In effect, even people who don't use the products of tech giants like Google and Facebook have their privacy violated and data sold all the same.

The end goal of creating technology is to enrich and better the lives of its users. In attaining this goal, the industry is failing. Innovative technology is being released less and less quickly. Instead, companies are swearing workers to secrecy not to discuss their work publicly, and the workers don't want their kids to use their inventions. Lack of transparency is damaging the public's trust.

Nothing that these companies are doing seems to be for the betterment of society. Clearly, we need regulation which allows for users to split themselves from these companies for good, as in, once they decide to stop using the services, the company no longer has a right to the user's data. I'd also advise technology companies to increase transparency. Our intimate personal information is owned by technology companies, and we have a right to know how it is being engineered and utilized behind the scenes.

We want those companies to use our data to better our lives, not to sell it to advertisers. If technology companies really are working for our betterment, why is the door bolted shut?

## Facial Recognition Being Withheld

There are already scary examples of companies building technology that isn't going to benefit humans in general. A good example is that Google and Apple have both built facial recognition technology that is apparently very effective. However, these companies have refused to share it with law enforcement for fear of abuse. This raises several questions from an ethical perspective:

- Did Google and Apple continue developing this technology after understanding the scope of its potential impact? If so, why?
- If Google and Apple understand that the power of the technology is too great to be trusted with the government, why trust it with private corporations such as themselves?
- If Google and Apple understand that the people in law enforcement are flawed and need their power reigned in, have they applied that view of people to themselves?
- If the government had made a technological weapon this powerful, and wanted to use it to control the public, but the government didn't trust itself to use that weapon, would the public cry for its destruction?

The answers to these questions would be very revealing of the internal operations and mentalities of the biggest technology corporations. The lack of transparency is stunning. Big technology companies have created a massive gap between what we can do and what we should do, often not even attempting to ask or qualify the latter.

To the public, this is a cause for concern. Since it has become obvious that technology creators are unable to self-regulate, fears of harmful technology have grown. We are becoming more worried that the negative effects of building new technologies will not be controlled or restricted. This, of course, would be the direct opposite of making our lives better.

## Amazon Rekognition

Amazon is yet another technology company that has built facial recognition technology, though Amazon is less reserved than their ilk. Amazon's Rekognition product allows for any user of Amazon's cloud services to run recognition on a photo. Keep in mind that Amazon has hundreds of millions of dollars' worth of contracts with US intelligence agencies to host information with their cloud services. This is the public description of Rekognition, taken directly from Amazon's website:

> [P]rovide an image or video to the Rekognition API, and the service can identify the objects, people, text, scenes, and activities, as well as detect any inappropriate content. Amazon Rekognition also provides highly accurate facial analysis and facial recognition on images and video … Amazon Rekognition is based on the same proven, highly scalable, deep learning technology developed by Amazon's computer vision scientists to analyze billions of images and videos daily … Amazon Rekognition is always learning from new data.[6]

That description reeks of a clumsy attempt to cover up the blatantly heinous nature of the product. It also raises more questions, such as "Where is Amazon getting all this data to pump into their machine learning algorithms?" Is it using data from other Amazon products? Is it stealing from unknowing Amazon cloud users' personal storages? That's a heavy accusation, but not unwarranted.

An article in The Guardian published in June 2018 pointed out the massive problems with Rekognition: "it's disturbing that the company can offer a powerful platform-based surveillance technology without any public input, oversight or regulation. Amazon should not have free rein to develop and profit from new surveillance technologies without regard for their effects on civil liberties and human rights," the article said. "[Amazon] must stop building the facial recognition infrastructure for law enforcement agencies and the government and be committed to never return to the business in the future … Facial recognition technology poses serious and imminent threats to civil liberties and human rights."[7]

The article continues with a succinct summary of the concern and calls out the need for an equal and opposite force against such technology (i.e. oversight and transparency), which doesn't exist today:

> Given the blurring line between public policing and private security, and between government security agencies and their private contractors, we question whether a moratorium on government and law enforcement uses of Rekognition would go far enough. The security industry has long touted the public safety benefits of facial recognition technology. But a functioning facial recognition system that can consistently and accurately identify specific, targeted individuals requires building a surveillance infrastructure of unprecedented scope and scale, powered by machine learning algorithms and perpetually expanding databases of identity information. The threat that such a massive, automated surveillance apparatus poses to society far outweighs the security benefits it could provide. At the very least, it would require an equally vast system for oversight, transparency and public input, one that neither Amazon nor any government agency has even begun to develop.

It's also deeply concerning that the government, or at least military intelligence, is using these services. Is there no care left in this country for our rights to be protected? Or is our right to protection from unlawful searches not adequate? The article poses it bluntly: "When government practices violate civil liberties, Amazon has a choice to make. Will it blindly accelerate and exacerbate violations of human rights, or will it take responsibility for its powerful technologies?"

We must be wary of any attempt of our government to conduct mass violations of our rights in favor of security. We must dismantle any technical system that enables and encourages that behavior, especially those created by private companies that have no regulation or accountability to the public. As Benjamin Franklin wrote in 1755, "They who would give up an essential liberty for temporary security, deserve neither liberty nor security."

## Bias in Artificial Intelligence

All technologies are created by humans and are thus subject to human bias. Artificial intelligence, as a concept and as a technology, has the most to lose if its functionality and algorithms are corrupted by its creators' biases. For artificial intelligence to replicate the perfect human mind, it must be sufficiently complex to look for the nuances in the world that can re-explain otherwise obvious realities.

An example that comes to mind is how artificial intelligence might see crime in the United States. Specifically, a statistic that I have often seen cited by racist online groups states that black people commit half of the violent crime in the country despite being nowhere near half the population. In order to understand this statistic, one must understand the nuances of low socioeconomic status, the intentional creation of ghettos and redlining, systemic problems in law enforcement which never lets communities recover, the correlation of violent crime to joblessness and family disruption, etc. However, a biased artificial intelligence might make the same mistake that I've seen so many real humans make, taking a statistic at face value, attempting no evaluation or alternate explanation, and accepting that statistic as a basis for its reality.

On a social media platform, having a single biased algorithm that puts "black people" in the same category as "violent criminal" would be harmful, but it would only affect a small amount of automated functionality. For artificial intelligence, whose goal is to replicate the human mind and learn to make decisions on its own, having these sorts of biases could have extremely harmful impacts on our society. It is vital that artificial intelligence production require even more transparency than the production of other algorithms in the Internet.

We are already seeing the effects of bias encoded into artificial intelligence. A commonly referenced example is the facial recognition software's success rate on white faces versus black faces. The software's success rate on white females was 99%; on black females, only 67%.[8] This biased outcome could be a result of a number of failures. It is entirely possible that the artificial intelligence simply didn't study enough black faces to learn the minute details that separate one black face from another. It is also entirely possible, although this is a nefarious accusation, that the learning algorithm itself was skewed to be better at interpreting white faces. In either case, bias on the creators' end undoubtedly led to the failure and perceived discrimination.

Google's artificial intelligence-enhanced feature Smart Compose automatically suggests sentences while typing emails and other messages. The program came under fire in 2018 when a user typed "I am meeting an investor next week" to which Smart Compose offered the next sentence: "Do you want to meet him?", a mistake as the investor in reference was female and the suggestion should have said "her." Google removed all gendered pronouns from the service as a result of the backlash, though it will probably attempt in the future to reinstate gender assumptions. As an article from CNBC claims, "Getting Smart Compose right could be good for business. Demonstrating that Google understands the nuances of AI better than competitors is part of the company's strategy to build affinity for its brand and attract customers to its AI-powered cloud computing tools, advertising services and hardware."[9] The article goes on:

Google's decision to play it safe on gender follows some high-profile embarrassments for the company's predictive technologies. The company apologized in 2015 when the image recognition feature of its photo service labeled a black couple as gorillas. In 2016, Google altered its search engine's autocomplete function after it suggested the anti-Semitic query 'are jews evil' when users sought information about Jews. Google has banned expletives and racial slurs from its predictive technologies, as well as mentions of its business rivals or tragic events. The company's new policy banning gendered pronouns also affected the list of possible responses in Google's Smart Reply. That service allows users to respond instantly to text messages and emails with short phrases such as 'sounds good.'

Human intervention in creating non-harmful artificial intelligence systems is clearly required. As ethics falls to the wayside on other technical matters, it seems as though the public is keen to hold Google accountable to its artificial intelligences' bias. In addition, it is crucial to understand that some decisions should never be made possible by artificial intelligence—issues such as criminal sentencing, military intervention, and hiring decisions—not only because they require a large amount of understanding of nuance, but also because those decisions should be made by publicly accountable individuals, not machines.

Another risk of developing bias in artificial intelligence is understanding cultures that may be less data-flush than the West. The technology industry has been siphoning all the data they can out of North America and Europe for over a decade, which is not the case for areas of the world like Africa, Asia, and the Middle East. Since the algorithms developed by artificial intelligence will be driven by data from the West, it is important to understand that those algorithms may not be accurate in the East. Being mutable based on region may be required, but not to the point that the algorithms would commit harmful discrimination. The technology industry is going to have to balance how artificial intelligence algorithms change outcomes based on variables while not discriminating harmfully, as there is potential for those behaviors to conflict.

## EFF Report on Facial Recognition

A February 2018 report by the Electronic Frontier Foundation highlighted the already existent problems with law enforcement and facial recognition technology. The report claims that law enforcement already possesses the ability to identify individuals on surveillance cameras in real time. In addition, half of Americans have their facial data stored in a facial recognition database accessible by law enforcement agencies.[10]

Facial recognition software exists in a unique space, because it allows for biometric data to identify individuals but does not require authoritative testing to obtain that data. Contrast this with fingerprint recognition software. Artificial intelligence is a requirement in order to determine someone's identity based on their fingerprint, in addition to a mass database of fingerprints to which to compare that person's fingerprint. An individual's fingerprint, however, is not available to the public. People do not expose the outline of their fingerprints, fingerprints cannot be made out on a public security camera, people do not post their fingerprints to social media, etc. Thus, it becomes harder for a private technology company to build out fingerprint recognition artificial intelligence, as the data must come from an authority like a criminal or medical records database.

No such limitations exist on facial recognition software. People post pictures of their faces, they expose their faces publicly to cameras outside, and faces can be made out at great distances. It is not a subtle or hard to gather that piece of data about an individual—it's probably the only biometric piece of data that is so publicly accessible. This, combined with pathetic regulations on technology companies, has allowed "covert, remote, and mass capture and identification of images."

The abuses by law enforcement have already begun. The report claims that the Baltimore Police Department used facial recognition software, combined with data from public social media posts, to identify and eventually arrest political activists protesting the death of Freddie Gray at the hands of the police in 2015. It was political censorship and a direct violation of the First Amendment to target protesters who might have only been guilty of association. To quote the report, "government surveillance like this can have a real chilling effect on Americans' willingness to engage in public debate." This is unacceptable in a democracy.

Because of uncorrected inaccuracies in the ability of artificial intelligence to distinguish black people and other persons of color apart, law enforcement ought not to rely on it as a technology. This is compounded by the fact that there are simply more pictures of people in these minority groups in crime databases than of white people, due to disproportionate crime and incarceration rates. This can have uncontainable impacts on innocent people's lives. If a black applicant for a job is denied because facial recognition software identifies them as a criminal, these harmful law enforcement practices would be to blame.

The power of facial recognition software is expanding too. Artificial intelligence and machine learning are currently poring over millions of records of historical photographic and video evidence in order to train its algorithms. The future of facial recognition software includes embedding it into law enforcement officers' body cameras, the ability to match results based solely on police sketches and being able to identify faces in photos taken at night.

The body camera enhancement is particularly worrying as it would shatter the anonymity of approaching officers and agents. Knowing that all interactions with law enforcement are not only recorded but attributable to the individual could be a violation of that individual's First Amendment rights. The EFF report states, "Using face recognition would allow officers to quickly identify and record specific protesters, chilling speech and discouraging people who are typically targeted by police from participating. Face recognition on body-worn cameras will also allow officers to covertly identify and surveil the public on a scale we have never seen before."

The report concludes with propositions that lay out what kinds of practices law enforcement should undertake and what regulations should be passed to ensure accountability. There should be no scraping of non-law enforcement records to enhance facial recognition matches, this would include publicly accessible information on social media and some governmental databases such as the DMV's. Collected records with vast numbers of faces, such as pictures of crowds or stadiums, should be analyzed only in the case of identifying suspects at the scene. Faces of innocent people should be obfuscated or blurred such that the records could not be used in subsequent investigations.

The report also calls for a return to a justice and surveillance system rooted in the Fourth and First Amendments. Prior to being subject to search or surveillance by law enforcement, a warrant should be obtained from a judge. "Government entities that collect or use face recognition must be subject to meaningful oversight from an independent entity. Individuals whose data are compromised by the government or the private sector should have strong and meaningful avenues to hold them accountable."

Lastly, photos and videos collected by law enforcement that use facial recognition should have clearly defined mandates. This would include systems to let otherwise innocent people know that their data was collected and for how long that data will be retained. The EFF also suggests the separation of biometric data from personalized behavioral data, as this vastly increases the scope of privacy invasion. An example would be storing facial recognition evidence separate from driver's license information, meaning another step must be taken to determine a person's license number from their face. Not only must the separation exist, but clear audit trails must be present to detect misuse of the facial recognition data.

The EFF has wonderful suggestions here that ought to be implemented. The dangers, both in potential and what we've already witnessed, are violations of our rights that are meant to be protected. If the United States is to become a surveillance state, that decision must be made between its people and the government. We should resist the efforts of law enforcement to subvert the checks and balances of our system in the name of mass surveillance. On the same note, regulations are necessary to hold them more accountable and to destroy the structures and technologies that enabled this power grab in the first place.

## Taylor Swift's Facial Recognition Operation

Facial recognition software has been used in non-governmental settings as well. It was reported in December 2018 that pop music star Taylor Swift had used facial recognition software to identify "potential stalkers" of hers at a May 2018 concert. While well-intentioned, the system was a covert breach of her concertgoers' personally identifiable biometric information.[11]

The process for this practice started with a collection of Swift's stalkers and potential stalkers, and photos of them for facial recognition matching. It is unclear what factors drove the decision of who would or wouldn't be considered for these categories, though it is also not hard to imagine. It is nevertheless important to individual liberties that people know when they are being tracked and monitored, whether by a governmental or private entity. These records were stored in a "command post" in Nashville, TN.

Next, a large number of kiosks were constructed. These included video screens which were set to play videos of Swift rehearsing. Secretly, the kiosks were embedded with cameras that would monitor the faces of anyone who watched the screen. This would give a clear view of their faces, and would allow for pictures to be taken and sent back to Nashville for facial recognition matching.

While the concert was setting up and the seats were filling, Swift's fans would be lured into watching the kiosks. This presented a new aspect to the facial recognition process, one that relied on human tendencies facilitated through technical measures to give a more thorough testing of the crowd. For those of us who actively don't want to be secretly surveilled, tracked, and monitored, we'll have to learn to be careful of these honeypot traps seeking to get our attention through secretive measures.

The debate on this topic, should the public ever be allowed the opportunity to have it, will help to find the nuances of the issue. Taylor Swift certainly has every right to deny tickets and entrance to unwanted fans, even if her safety was not involved. On the other hand, those fans also have a right to their privacy and to the collection of their biometric data by unaccountable parties.

The bigger picture of this story involves the contrast between our knowledge and what companies and corporations are doing. We simply have no idea what the inner workings of systems like this are. We certainly don't have any regulations against it. We don't know how many people are using it, how many companies are making it, what the success of the operation was, what was done to identify stalkers, etc. We need more insight and control over these topics, which are frankly a privacy violation and individual rights nightmare.

## Regulating Discriminatory AI

We should implement controls on artificial intelligence that account for the biases and discrimination that Americans encounter daily. It is unfortunate but necessary to point out that civil right movements in this country have been long and hard battles. As a result of those movements, however, we have regulations and laws that prohibit considering certain attributes of a person when making certain decisions. Those provisions should extend into artificial intelligence algorithms as well.

We must consider cases where groups of people are given skewed results from artificial intelligence algorithms as a result of data points which qualify as protected classes under current law. If discrimination weren't a problem, then this would be easy to ignore. Algorithmic decisions should at no point boil down to one's gender, race, sexual orientation, religion, disability status, etc.

This could be particularly harmful, even law-breaking. Something as simple as a man being shown an advertisement for a higher paid job than what a woman sees might qualify as unlawful discrimination. It was demonstrated in 2016 that advertisers on Facebook could control who saw housing advertisements based on their race. The investigation prompted responses from the Congressional Black Caucus[12] and the Department of Housing and Urban Development.[13] The story came from an investigation into how advertisers explicitly control advertisement visibility, but the principles don't change when the advertiser is replaced by a machine. We need to be future-focused about this issue of preventing harmful discrimination.

I propose regulations that block data points representing protected classes from being involved in artificial intelligence algorithms in any capacity. Think of the US Food and Drug Administration (FDA) banning poisonous ingredients. There's no reason that anyone should be "cooking" with them, so get them out of the kitchen entirely.

An alternative proposal I would support would be careful examination of the algorithms to ensure that protected class information is not included at key points. Maybe an advertisement for adoption wants to change its picture based on the user's gender and sexual orientation, so if the user was a married gay male the advertisement would show two fathers, if the user was straight it would show a father and a mother, etc. I wouldn't consider this a harmful use of the data, as this decision is simply to decide what picture to show. It's not a "key point," as with determining whether to display the advertisement at all. But the line could be crossed very quickly, thus necessitating oversight (a regulatory agency) and transparency.

The downside to this is how machine learning will affect artificial intelligence algorithms moving forward. Machine learning seeks to "train" the algorithm to give the best results, constantly messing with variables and analyzing results to see which version of the algorithm yields the best outcomes. For advertisement algorithms, the outcomes are clear: the more clicks and sales, the better the advertisement is doing.

Because of the constant tweaking of machine learning, diligent oversight into how those data points are being used would be impossible. The algorithm could change in a second on its own and be changed again by the time a reviewer had verified that the change was not discriminatory. This would cause the process of advertisement algorithm regulation to become burdensome on the regulators, not the advertisers.

If it could work with transparency, then that would be an ideal solution to fit the advertiser's as well as the consumer's interests. If the process doesn't work, then we should look at outright restrictions on the use of protected-class data in artificial intelligence algorithms. It may be the only way to ensure that laws are followed. Civil rights activists didn't make their progress convincing humans to value equality just to be discriminated against by a machine.

## Smart Speakers

Throughout 2018, smart speakers became the next big thing in technology, and were embraced by the mainstream. A smart speaker is an appliance, like a toaster or lamp, that sits on a nightstand, kitchen counter, or coffee table. The device listens for a query ("Alexa," "Hey Siri," "OK Google," etc.) to prompt it into action. Then, the user can ask it to do a task ("Look up the weather," "Order a new set of headphones"). Nearly every major technology company has a smart speaker product available. This includes the Google Home, the Amazon Echo/Dot, the Facebook Portal, and the Apple HomePod.

Even separate from the line of smart speakers is that we're adding the "always listening" feature to many other electronic devices. For example, the latest Xbox (Xbox One, a video game console developed by Microsoft) comes with the ability to tell it voice commands to turn the Xbox on and off. Apart from a few various other selection dialogues, there is no use for this voice listener other than to know when to turn the device on and off.

As a society, we should stop and think about whether we really want these devices in our homes. These pieces of technology have the ability to listen to every word we or anyone in our houses say, record that information, analyze it, and save it all to a giant database. Yes, they provide benefits to consumers in the form of convenience and access to information, but we need to seriously evaluate the cost of those benefits.

What are the pros? The biggest one is probably the ability to ask it questions. Having a quick, hands-free way to ask what the weather is when getting ready for the day, or to know movie times when planning a date night, is valuable. Having the hottest news headlines read off with just a question is convenient and useful. And at the end of the day, these are speakers. They can act as music players, and with just a voice command, one is seconds away from hearing the song that's been stuck in their head all day, or from turning on a Christmas playlist during the holidays. Smart speakers can start multiple timers, to track every part of dinner on the stove and in the oven.

Apart from these major uses, I'd venture to say that these other features are less commonly used. Smart speakers can also create and save lists, such as a shopping list or to-do list. Smart speakers can set reminders, alarm clocks, and calendar entries. Some smart speakers have the ability to purchase items from online retailers and have them shipped, all hands-free. If a user creates a "smart home" (which requires buying a host of other products), their smart speaker can take control of their house's thermostat, lights, and garage door, as well as other compatible appliances, like a TV or blender.

What are the cons? It's necessary to repeat this one for emphasis: these devices are constantly listening to the users and everyone else in the house. Those recordings are all analyzed, and if a keyword like "Google" or "Alexa" is stated, then the recording is permanently saved in a data warehouse. This is such egregious behavior that I'm surprised these devices still exists. This is a level of surveillance that our Founding Fathers wrote the Fourth Amendment to combat. The idea that the general public would willingly allow these devices into their homes for the ever-so-small increase in comfort is appalling.

The second con to smart speakers is that they provide no new value to anyone's life—at least, not anyone who owns a smartphone. All of these features can be done by any smartphone, from asking a question to setting a timer to ordering things online. There is absolutely no new value added by these technologies, and they don't solve any new problems.

It's naive to think that the surveillance aspect of these devices won't be a point of contention. There was a court case in which two people were murdered in one of their homes. At the scene of the crime was a smart speaker, an Amazon Echo. While the murder was in January 2017, it surged into national headlines in November 2018 when the court ordered, under search warrant, for Amazon to retrieve and supply the recordings of the device from the time period of the murder.

Amazon has yet to respond with whether or not they will turn over the recordings as evidence for the case. When they do respond, it will be a landmark event, as will the reaction of law enforcement agencies. Because of our ill-defined laws and regulations on these topics, these decisions about how the government can use data collected on us by private corporations will be made by the justice branch of our government, rather than the legislative branch.

It will be an interesting case to watch unfold, but regardless of the outcome, it highlights why a responsive legislative body is necessary to tackle 21st century problems. What we need in this case is a decision about whether big tech companies are obligated to effectively change the use of all their smart speakers (of which there are 50 million in the US) into surveillance devices to be used by the government. We need that decision to have been made before this case happened. This conversation should have been had years ago, perhaps even before smart speakers were invented. In this manner, our legislative body has failed us.

## The Tech Industry Can Never Self-Regulate

It would be possible for a harmful technology to exist that appears beneficial but is actually antithetical with American values, and smart speakers are a good example of this principle. In a country where we have specific provisions in the Bill of Rights which prevent our homes from being searched without probable cause, there's no place for an eavesdropping speaker.

Smart speakers base their business model on having a constantly recording device in a private home, collecting data that can be accessed at will by a private corporation. The technology is beneficial to a few people in specific circumstances, but is harmful to many others. In a more direct sense, bias in the building process can be a determinant in whether a technology is useful or harmful to a user. Bias will impact the building of technology, just like the building of anything else.

For example, consider the implications of altering search results based on topic. Take the political issue of abortion. It would be possible to invent a technology that always displayed pro-choice results whenever any abortion term is searched. For users who are already pro-choice, this technology is helpful as it immediately delivers them search results they will agree with. However, for a user who is pro-life, they will find the technology frustrating and harmful, as every term they search on abortion gives search results that challenge their viewpoint.

Artificial intelligence, like all other technology, is faced with these core problems. Its main goal is to increase the quality of life for humans, but it can easily be corrupted by bias, turned into a technology that some users find harmful. It can be used to bolster and empower the spread of false information and the effects of weaponry, given the worst kind of orders to follow.

The fear that big technology companies are about to push the button on creating forever-biased and harmful technologies is not unfounded. Elon Musk, founder of SpaceX and Tesla, said that Artificial intelligence could be "far more dangerous than nukes."[14] Sundar Pichai, Google's CEO, specifically said that public fears about Artificial Intelligence having harmful applications is "very legitimate." Pichai goes on to further argue that it is up to the technology industry to ensure that Artificial intelligence keeps its end goal in mind: to help humanity.[15]

Of course, I disagree with Pichai's second point. I think that the time has come for government intervention and rule-setting. The technology industry, frankly, has had its opportunity to "set ethical guardrails," as Pichai suggests they currently practice. No, Mr. Pichai. It could have done it at any time, and hasn't. It's time to stop depending on the industry to regulate itself.

It could be for a number of reasons. It could be because, as an unregulated capitalist corporation, the need to account for externalities is low. It could be because programmers, engineers, and technicians simply don't want to deal with the extra workload of working around ethically-imposed regulations. It could simply be because the entire industry moves at the speed of light, and slowing down to do things "right" would be a market disadvantage.

The reality is, it doesn't matter why the technology industry hasn't set their own ethics standards, because they've lost the public's trust in their ability to do so. Any regulations they place on themselves will seem light, disingenuous, and self-serving. At a certain point in time, the corporation that pumped poison into the lake doesn't get to decide what clean water looks like.

In perhaps his most hilariously hypocritical statement, Pichai also stated, "I think tech has to realize it just can't build it and then fix it. I think that doesn't work."[16] Does the CEO of Google need a reminder of who made Google Earth, a technology so invasive that it needed censorship and editing for years after launch to stop giving away government secrets? Does Pichai not remember who sent privatized, company branded vehicles down every street in the Western world, taking pictures in every direction?

This is a completely blind statement that highlights everything wrong with big technology companies thinking of themselves as perfectly moral entities. Pichai seems to have buried his head in the sand, oblivious or indifferent to his company's own flaws. He will freely admit that the "build it first, figure out the problems later" model doesn't work for making technology, yet he is the head of the company that has time and time again made this error, and doesn't show signs of stopping.

## Secret In-Home Surveillance

The problem of smart speakers doesn't end with the speakers themselves. Smart speakers are just the most explicit surrendering of our privacy as the tools have no use *but* to spy on us. We also have to think about our phones always listening and our Xboxes always listening. While surveillance is not their whole purpose, they are equally culpable for the data they track and store. Consumers should have an option to purchase these devices without the constant surveillance they force on us. We shouldn't let the technology industry pervert trusted technologies to meet their surveillance capitalist desires.

Not only should consumers have to watch what they say around every device that has a microphone, we must also use caution around devices that don't have microphones. In February 2019, Google revealed that their "Nest Guard" product, which is a control center for their "Nest" security system, all had been equipped with microphones. The product line has existed since 2017, but no branding, technical specifications, or other material ever stated that the product had a microphone.[17]

Google claims that they never intended for it to be a secret that the product had a microphone. But at this point, should we believe them? It's an outright tool of surveillance with the purpose of misleading consumers and tricking them into a false sense of security. Google should realize that people are unhappy with the stated amounts of data they are taking and saving on us, so why would we be ok with secret recordings? It's a complete violation of consumer protections.

The smart speaker and in-home surveillance industry should be considered a bust. We consumers should reject in totality these motions with such vitriol that technology companies get the idea: We don't want their data-sharing deals. We don't want to sacrifice our privacy and data any longer to these slimy, subversive, and evil companies. Google, and any other companies selling non-surveillance products with secret microphones installed, should be prosecuted with every ounce of strength that consumer protection agencies have. The data collected from these devices should be destroyed immediately. Enough is enough.

## Google's Problems with Self Control

Despite what Google's CEO says, Americans can be certain that the most influential technology company won't take self-regulation seriously any time soon. The proof is in the pudding—they haven't started making meaningful ethical decisions yet in their 20+ year existence. Google has had all the power and none of the responsibility. Their leader's own ignorant statements show that they will never acknowledge how powerful, and frankly dangerous, their technologies are, and therefore, why Google regulating itself will never be effective.

Even Google's own employees, in a late 2018 open letter to their employer, wrote that they are losing faith in the company's will to uphold integrity over profits. The letter was written in response to Google considering moving into the Chinese Internet market, a decision that would be profitable but would require censorship in order to appease the Chinese government. The sentiment, however, is still valid. Corporations without regulation have no monetary incentive to care about the impact they have on people and communities. The issues are purely ethical.

...We join Amnesty International in calling on Google to cancel project Dragonfly [the project team exploring the Chinese market]. We also demand that leadership commit to transparency, clear communication, and real accountability. Google is too powerful not to be held accountable. We deserve to know what we're building and we deserve a say in these significant decisions.[18]

Transparency, clear communication, and real accountability. The right to know what is being worked on before it is released. The right to having a say in the decision. To the Google employees who wrote this letter, I say Amen. The mistrust felt toward Google as a company is emblematic of how Americans feel about the entire tech industry.

## China's Social Credit System

A great example of how technology can be used to regress humanity exists in China. In China, the government seeks to use technology as a mass surveillance and censorship tool against its citizens. The Chinese government has created a list of blocked foreign websites, which are not accessible from within China, including most US social media websites. This has been colloquially called the "Great Firewall of China," a play on the actual Great Wall of China. This censorship has greatly limited the Chinese populace from using the Internet to its full advantage, and realizing the progress of humanity in general.

In addition to mass censorship, China also wishes to use its technology to keep tabs on its citizens. This very anti-individual stance tracks a person's activity and rewards or punishes them based on their behavior, both online and in real life. These punishments are enacted via a "social credit system" which tracks every individual person, runs their actions and behavior through an algorithm, and assigns him or her a sort of credit score.

Every user's location being monitored in real time, 400 million surveillance cameras, constant monitoring of online activity—all these information sources feed into the beast of determining one's social credit score in China. Negative remarks about the government or the social credit system itself will lead to a decrease in score. Even low scores belonging to real-life friends or online acquaintances can negatively impact a citizen's own score. The end goal is to have everything located in a single, centralized database for all technologies and government agencies to interact with.

Chinese citizens will have scaling rights and privileges based on their credit scores. High scoring citizens will receive government-subsidized deals and discounts to shops and services. High-scoring citizens will have unrestricted access to buying property, taking out loans, and using transportation. On the other hand, low-scoring citizens will be blocked from doing those activities, their children will be blocked from private schools, and their movement will be restricted, all because an extremely biased and government-serving algorithm determined them to be socially untrustworthy.

Technology can be used for many good things, and historically it has been used for the improvement of humanity. The Chinese social credit system and mass censorship tactics are perfect examples of how technology can be used for evil. Only a regressive society would wish to use the gifts of technology to make people's lives worse.

## Authoritarianism in US Tech

One would be incorrect to assume that the only reason that system is being implemented in China is due to its own authoritarian problem. It's not just China: western technology companies themselves have started creating and using some of these same ideas. The similarities between Chinese leadership and western technology firms' leadership is scary: unaccountable and power-hungry overlords seeking to surveil, quantify, and control every single thing that every single person does.

In terms of a social credit system, Facebook has already started this exact same concept. In their purported fight against the fabled "fake news," Facebook has started to assign a "reputation score" to each user based on the types of links they post. If one posts too many reactionary hot takes, they can expect a dip in their algorithmically determined trustworthiness.

Because a Silicon Valley-based company is rarely alone in its endeavors to violate the public space and user freedoms, Twitter also has a form of behavior monitoring. As reported by *The Washington Post*, it "now factors in the behavior of other accounts in a person's network as a risk factor in judging whether a person's tweets should be spread," an eerily similar policy to what we learned about China's social credit system.[19]

The worst part is, the public will never know the contents of these algorithms. Facebook claims that this is simply because they don't want people to "game" the system to give them a good ranking. Another way to look at it: If Facebook didn't make a subversive user-rating system, then users wouldn't have to worry about manipulating it. Facebook sees manipulative and disingenuous user behavior as a detriment to their behavior algorithms. I see Facebook's manipulative and disingenuous behavior algorithms as a detriment to users.

I'm a firm believer in the phrase "give a man a mask and he'll tell you the truth." I think it encapsulates the need for anonymity online, and why social control in technology would be massively detrimental to our society. As individuals, the ability to speak our minds and own our thoughts is a fundamental right protected by the Constitution. Of course, we still have the ability to conform, but we'll only do so when it's warranted. An individual should never be punished for their thoughts or their innate need to rationalize their world.

Give a person a mask and you remove the risks of them receiving punishment for their opinions. If an individual has non-conformist opinions, one should debate them. Take their ideas to the court of public opinion, stack them up against one's own. People are reasonable; we use reason to make small and large choices every day. To punish people for engaging in natural thought processes is despicable. If the ideas cannot stand the test of public discourse, they deserve to be discarded. To give a person a mask and make them unaccountable to their words is the direct opposite of any so-called social credit system.

We will continue to be covertly manipulated behind the lead curtain of Silicon Valley until these companies learn to make technologies that better everyone and respect the individualism of each person. Humans should have no masters, especially not unelected and unrepresentative ones. Authoritarianism doesn't look any better when it's branded "Facebook and Twitter" than the Chinese "Social Credit System."

# II

## Surveillance Capitalism

Surveillance capitalism is a term invented by Shoshana Zuboff, defined in her 2014 article "Big Other: Surveillance Capitalism and the Prospects of the Information Civilization," and her 2019 book, *The Age Of Surveillance Capitalism*. She defines surveillance capitalism to be the version of capitalism where the most valuable part of the economy is knowledge and information.

She explains that the technology industry is gathering seemingly useless information about the consumer population. The end goal is to map our behavior, to know more about ourselves than we do. With this in mind, predictions and trends will become increasingly more secure, and the capital market will be determined by the price of selling those predictions and trends to fuel the beast, rather than by traditional economic drivers.

Zuboff specifically names five companies as being guilty of this kind of tactic: Microsoft, Facebook, Google, Apple, and Amazon. Among these companies, Google specifically has the largest market share of all operating systems (37% with Android and Chrome OS), web browsers (62% with Google Chrome and Chromium variants), and search engines (92%). The only market share Google is perhaps missing out on would be Social Media, though if YouTube qualifies as Social Media, then Google has the second largest market share there as well after Facebook.

Zuboff describes that the surveillance capital market is interested in more than just what users post, but also in every data point possible about their activity: the time of posting, the words used, the punctuation used, what other programs were running on their computer, etc. Google, undoubtedly, has the most access to this information. Zuboff writes: "Google is to surveillance capitalism what General Motors was to managerial capitalism."

To most people, both technologists and laymen, the term "big data" simply refers to massive amounts of data being collected and analyzed to feed predictive *models* and algorithms. Those people will therefore see big data collection as a byproduct of technology use that can't be stopped. Zuboff argues the opposite, that it was humans who started the practice of amassing big data, and therefore humans can regulate and stop it.

Zuboff analyzes documents written by Google's Chief Economist Hal Varian in her 2014 Journal. Varian describes the four main uses and goals of big data under surveillance capitalism:

- data extraction and analysis
- new contractual forms due to better monitoring
- personalization and customization
- continuous experiments

Data extraction and analysis refers to Google and other companies in the technology industry getting as much information as possible from every transaction done online. This will feed the algorithms and machine-learning enhanced artificial intelligence. Its analysis will drive recommendations for predicting future markets. Everything that these companies make, from smartphones to smart watches, smart speakers to Street View cars, has the purpose of gathering data for extraction and analysis.

The next goal of a surveillance capitalist is to enhance monitors and surveillance of even more aspects of people's lives. An example that Varian offers is a car rental contract. If a consumer is making monthly payments on a car, and misses a payment, the car's data can be accessed to know its location, where the user might be, how many miles were driven, etc. The car can even be blocked from turning on until the car payment is made. All of this data would lead to "new contracts," as in new ways that people agree to services and deals, with more proof of validity being available and more fail-safes for lenders.

A quote from Varian that Zuboff uses in her journal expertly describes this goal: "There is no putting the genie back in the bottle....Everyone will expect to be tracked and monitored, since the advantages, in terms of convenience, safety, and services, will be so great...continuous monitoring will be the norm."

Varian also describes "personalization and customization" as a goal of surveillance capitalism. This is visible even in the modern Internet. Users go to YouTube and expect to see recommended videos related to what they like. The goals of a surveillance capitalist, however, are not just to recommend YouTube videos, they are to entirely map their users' behavior. Surveillance capitalists aim to know what users want before the user does, and this requires algorithms that work on individual levels, not just group and tribe levels. Users won't fit into existing algorithms, they'll each have their own.

The last goal of surveillance capitalists is to continuously experiment. Since data will always be processed algorithmically, it's necessary to have some percent of the results deviate. The resulting behavior influenced by this deviation will be recorded. The ultimate goal is to figure out how to alter content to alter behavior. If behavioral control can be achieved, then the free will of the market is effectively being covertly influenced and the freedom of choice gets replaced by the loss of agency. At a fundamental level, this challenges "the classic neoliberal ideal of 'the market' as intrinsically ineffable and unknowable."

The end result, Zuboff claims, is the "Big Other." This title is a play on the villain of George Orwell's 1984, where "Big Brother" is a government program which monitors all citizens, knows all truths, and has complete control. Zuboff's clever naming refers to the same entity, yet instead of being run by the government, it's run by private corporations. The "Big Other" would surveil everyone in every way possible, and control their lives remotely. It would be, as she puts it, "a new kind of sovereign power."

Changes to our lives, in the radical ways that surveillance capitalism threatens, should not come from a fast-paced industry that usurps the slow-paced government. It's obvious what surveillance capitalists really want: an economic model based on control. Our lives ought not to be controlled by any entity, governmental or privately owned.

The opportunity for regulation still exists. Many of the utopian goals of surveillance capitalists have yet to be realized. The population, however, needs to understand the goals of these people and the potential power they want to have. Zuboff finishes her journal: "deception-induced ignorance is no social contract, and freedom from uncertainty is no freedom."[1]

## Continuous Monitoring for Car Insurance

An example of the second tenet of surveillance capitalism, enhanced monitors, is being fully utilized today. In 2019, State Farm insurance started promoting and advertising a program called "Drive Safe & Save," where clients of State Farm insurance can download an application to their smartphone and, based on their driving patterns, earn discounts on their insurance rates.[2]

The application only needs to be downloaded once, and as long as location services and Bluetooth are kept turned on, it will monitor the trips a driver takes. It will analyze the information to determine if the driver is being safe, and if they are, it will automatically apply discounts to their insurance costs. The specific data points that the application looks at are: "annual mileage, braking, speed, time of day travel, acceleration, and fast cornering."

This is totally in line with how surveillance capitalism will work, and a predecessor to how most contracts will be written in the future if surveillance capitalism is not stunted. While it gives up private data about the user's whereabouts and quite literally puts them under constant monitoring, the user is enticed to sign up under the pretext of savings. However, the insurance agency wins the biggest. They get to learn more about the habits of their drivers and put their drivers under more pressure to drive safely, saving the agency money in cases where it would need to pay out.

The loser in this scenario, and the loser in all surveillance capitalist scenarios, is the individual's rights. People have a right to privacy and dignity, and shouldn't be asked to surrender those rights if they want to save on a discount. I think that people should stand against State Farm on this policy, as well as any company that tries to push constant surveillance onto their clients. Let's reject the idea that our privacy has a price, and discard companies who disrespect it enough to try to buy it.

## The Cost of Privacy

Clearly the data that users generate is worth an incredibly high amount of money to surveillance capitalists, but it's rare that we (the public) get glimpses into the real market value of our data. Facebook paid users $20 a month to download an application which gave complete monitoring of the entire phone's data to Facebook (more on the Facebook Research App later). Facebook considers the cost of one device's worth of data to be $20 monthly. Just for the fun of speculation, let's imagine that Facebook's average 40% profit margin in 2018 is the exact profit margin of this data.[3] This would indicate that a single device's data for a month has a market value of about $33.33 dollars.

This is comparable to what AT&T was offering users who wanted to pay extra for more privacy. From 2013 to 2016, the Internet service provider (ISP) AT&T offered a program called "Internet Preferences," which allowed users to opt out of the companies tracking and selling of user data, paying a higher monthly rate for the same service speeds. AT&T terminated the program in 2016. AT&T claimed the decision was to make their subscriptions "simpler for customers," but cynics have claimed that the true motive was to look more innocent in the eyes of the Federal Communications Commission.[4]

One very troubling aspect about this program was how AT&T tried to sell it as a beneficial service to the poor. Between the unmonitored and monitored Internet services, speeds and consistency did not change. The premium was only for guaranteeing that AT&T would not collect personal and targeting data while the users browsed the web. Poor Americans were more likely to take AT&T's offer, and enjoy the "lower" cost service with no detriment to the service's quality. Personal data privacy simply isn't a big concern to poorer Americans, especially when it costs extra. AT&T did not make any claims about the counterpoint: what should a poor person do when they value their privacy, but cannot afford AT&T's more expensive programs that secure it?

Additionally, AT&T claimed that the individuals who chose to pay the lower cost with the fewer protections are winning twice. AT&T claimed that, since AT&T will be tracking and processing all their data, the ISP is actually giving them a gift: the gift of machine learning and artificial intelligence, which promises whatever data comes through the ISP will eventually create better-designed machines. Following this, those users' lives would (presumably) be better off. AT&T's conclusion is that, by choosing the cheaper option, AT&T users actually got the best of the short- and long-term situations: they save money in the present and help build more comprehensive technology for the future.[5]

The price for AT&T to not track users was $30 more a month, a rate hike from $70 to $100. We should also assume AT&T sought to profit in this deal. AT&T had an average profit margin of approximately 9% throughout 2015, the last year before the Internet Preference program was cancelled.[6] So we can assume that the market value of this forgone information to AT&T was $27.5 monthly. So Facebook estimates the market value of a month's worth of a single device's data at $33, and AT&T puts the price of a month's worth of data for a household at $27.5.

It should be noted the differences between these two data points. The Facebook Research App would have seen every single action done on the phone, online and offline, but would not have seen activity from other devices. 66% of Americans own two kinds of digital devices: smartphones, computers (laptops or desktops), or tablets. 36% of Americans own all three, and the Facebook Research App's power was limited to only smartphones.[7]

Conversely, AT&T's Internet Preference program would see the online activity of all devices on the network, while being blind to the offline activity happening on those devices, and online activity while connected to different networks. Those same 36% of Americans with a great variety of Internet-accessing power would be monitored all the same by the Internet service provider. So long as the devices were connected to the network, the data collection would occur.

Nevertheless, it seems that a portion of our data is worth about $30 monthly to these technology industry giants. The basis of this claim is very shoddy, of course, but I think it is a good starting point. As the maxim goes: "If you don't pay for the product, you are the product." It seems ominous how appropriate this phrase is for our current situation with the likes of Facebook. We each signed up for a free service, and we each ended up being an asset generating $360 worth of data to the company every year.

## Bloatware

There will be times when a computer or phone manufacturer will preload their devices with applications that the user doesn't necessarily want installed. The creators of the device can even make it impossible to remove those applications from the device. These preinstalled and sometimes un-removable applications are often referred to as "bloatware."

There was a period of time when the Facebook app came preinstalled on all Android devices (Google's smartphone operating system), and the users could not remove the application like they could any application that they voluntarily installed. Despite bloatware being a nuisance on computers, especially smartphones, for nearly ten years, there are not major laws against it in any major country.

Android and Facebook aren't the only perpetrators of this behavior. In actuality, Microsoft is probably the worst example, making their Windows 10 operating system come with games like Minecraft and Candy Crush preinstalled. Vlad Sovav writes for The Verge in an article titled "Isn't it time we declared our independence from bloatware?":

> [T]here's little room for disagreement when it comes to third-party additions. Candy Crush Saga on Windows, the News Republic app on HTC phones, and the Oath bundle that Samsung preloads on Verizon Galaxy S9s all serve corporate interests before those of the user....if no one is showing consumers a better option, they just accept it as an unhappy status quo and get on with life.[8]

Agencies like the FCC and the FTC simply just don't care enough, as long as the issue lands anywhere near the other one's court. Thus, we should create a new agency to handle the regulation of modern-day technology, and make clear guidelines separating which practices should be regulated by each commission.

## Infrastructure Imperialism

When private companies create new inventions with no transparency or disclosure, all the important conversations happen after the release. That is far too late, and as a result, the public has lost trust in those companies. The public not having a say in the invasive business practices of the world's biggest companies, and the loss of trust as a result of those practices, should be viewed as far more urgent than a minor inconvenience.

In fact, Shoshana Zuboff, in her article "Big Other," which names the evils of surveillance capitalism, cites the term "infrastructure imperialism" for this kind of intrusive behavior that is performed on public infrastructure like roads and satellites. Zuboff writes: "In Street View, Google developed a declarative method that it has repeated in other data ventures. This modus operandi is that of incursion into undefended private territory until resistance is encountered....Google puts innovation ahead of everything and resists asking permission." Zuboff continues her criticism of Google by stating: "The firm does not ask if it can photograph homes for its databases. It simply takes what it wants. Google then exhausts its adversaries in court or eventually agrees to pay fines that represent a negligible investment for a significant return."[9]

Regulation of infrastructure imperialism could actually be quite simple. Let's say there was a public software tool that allowed for the lookup of a person's address by their name based on government records. A human user might do one lookup every 15 seconds, assuming they are working fast, whereas a robot could request thousands of records a second and save the entire dataset in minutes.

To limit this kind of behavior would be pretty easy: just set a limit that one can only make five requests per minute. The way that humans interact with the service remains unchanged, however, the robot's task of stripping the entire database goes from taking minutes to taking weeks. For Google Street View, one could write a regulation that limits everyone to only taking 100 pictures an hour from public property (I'm just spit balling the numbers). This wouldn't impact how real people use public property, but would cause Google to take fewer pictures of fewer places.

Infrastructure imperialism is an enormous threat to our privacy. The good news is that it is exclusively posed by giant technology companies, since only they would want to have that massive amount of data, and only they have the ability to dispatch resources to collect and store it. By having such a small scope of potential threats, it would be easy for regulators to halt and stop that anti-consumer behavior. The bad news is that those technology companies have already collected that information and will most certainly abuse it to feed into their surveillance capitalist desires, and our regulators are not active enough to try to stop the future use of that data nor prevent those actions from happening again.

## Using Capitalism to Address Ethics Problems

I believe that capitalism has led to revolutions in the ways we work, live our lives, and exist. I am extremely in favor of an economic system where the people own the means of production, innovate, and create new solutions to problems. This doesn't mean that I'm blind to the negatives of capitalism. I don't naively believe that ethical capitalism has ever existed. I'm aware that capitalism is not an economic system that could provide equality to the people on its own.

However, I'm not ready to throw out the whole playbook. As Americans, we've always been able to account for the egregious problems that have been perpetuated or even started by capitalism. The existence of slavery in America, for example, wasn't something new to the world when capitalism became mainstream. Slavery is unpaid labor, and wanting to own something to make perpetual profits from is a capitalist desire, whether the thing to own is a machine, technology, or a person. But America used was still able to defeat the practice of slavery despite being a capitalist country throughout the entire Civil War. Using government involvement in a capitalist system, the American people solved a moral and ethical problem that had plagued humanity for its existence.

The system has worked well to solve our problems. In its near 250-year existence, American capitalism has handled nearly every curveball that's been thrown at it. When we moved from an Agricultural economy to an Industrial economy, there were a slew of problems, ethical dilemmas, and moral questions that we had to solve. We did so in the most American way possible: We debated, brought up points and counterpoints. Experts weighed in. We solved ethical dilemmas about issues like child labor laws and wrote the appropriate regulations.

If the transition into the next economy makes ugly and unethical systems like surveillance capitalism viable, then we must be proactive about debating the issues and coercing the economic system into outcomes that truly benefit people. While I do think surveillance capitalism is a stain that needs to be removed, due to its unethical reliance on the invasion of personal freedoms, I don't think that capitalism itself is worthy of replacement. Rather, I think using the regulatory powers within a capitalist system are the best ways to solve the dilemmas posed by surveillance capitalism.

## Meritocracy and Capitalism

A meritocracy is a system which rewards participants based on their skills and talents, not based on external factors such as social status or identity. When applicants for a job are compared in a meritocratic system, they are evaluated based on their accomplishments and abilities. Meritocracies are similar to capitalist systems in that both rely on the existence of competition, winners, and losers to validate themselves.

Meritocracies are not perfect on their own. They do not account for all factors when judging participants. Meritocracies do not necessarily factor in background; they simply care about the end result of what people have accomplished. This is a weakness, especially along socioeconomic and identity divisions, as underprivileged groups feel disadvantaged when compared directly to people who have achieved more but with much less resistance and obstacles. Indeed, meritocracies do tend to over-reward privileged individuals. Even if that is not a stated or explicit function, it is nonetheless a result of a flawed system.

These blind spots are very similar to capitalism's perpetuating of class structures, and abuse of externalities. For example, in capitalism, there is no incentive to "care" about the environment. If money is to be saved by burning down a rainforest, then the rainforest be damned. In meritocracies, if hiring a lesser-skilled employee from a marginalized group means passing up on a privileged (but more accomplished) candidate, then the marginalized individual is going to be rejected. Or, in more dishonorable circumstances, the hiring manager could actually hold biases against the underprivileged person. The system just doesn't account for every potential nuance.

Thus, calls for the expulsion of capitalism in recent years have been mirrored by calls for expulsion of meritocracy. The rules for the world of building technology are written by people who want to abolish these systems. For example, Coraline Ada Ehmke, the author of "The Post-Meritocracy Manifesto," rewrote the Linux operating system's Code of Conduct in 2018, changing the rules and behaviors of how software developers interact with each other, while engineering the world's biggest open source operating system.[10]

These calls are not baseless, as I've conceded. These systems are not perfect. Underprivileged people have received unequal dividends from these systems, and we shouldn't ignore that. To act as if that's sufficient justification to attempt to dismantle entire systems is reckless and ill-advised. The solutions to the stated problems can be far simpler and equally rewarding. We shouldn't give up work quality in favor of representing more people. Instead of believing the false dilemma that underrepresented groups necessarily produce worse results, we should focus our efforts on increasing inclusive behaviors that reduce the barriers of entry and increase representation altogether. If faith in these systems is to be restored, then proof that these systems can fix their problems autonomously is required.

These feedback loops have become more prevalent in recent years: Political, social, and economic systems are receiving well-deserved criticism for their injustices, and these criticisms at times include calls for outright destruction. To ignore the benefits of the system's existence is just as irresponsible as to ignore the potential negatives of the newly proposed replacement systems. Thus, we should focus on taking progressive action to acknowledge and fix the existent problems, without sacrificing the structures to those who wish to tear them down.

There are certainly threats posed by the emergence of surveillance capitalism in the new economy. Any economic structure that is based on the existence of the "Big Other" is going to have to be dismantled or majorly hindered if our rights and freedoms as individuals are to be preserved. However, the existence of those problems on their own do not merit the destruction of the current economic system, instead, the solutions to those problems can come from within that very system.

# III

## Google: Don't Be Evil, Unless It's Profitable

### Google is the Face of Authoritarian Tech

When they restructured their corporation in 2015, Google changed their company motto from "don't be evil" to "do the right thing." While it's a semantic nitpick, it describes Google's authoritative influence extraordinarily well. What kind of non-evil corporation would drop such harmless phrasing from their corporate literature? The answer is clear: In terms of dishonesty to users and autocratic ideology, no company better represents the technology industry than Google.

Google enjoys gigantic power from their market share in nearly every corner of Internet technology, and abuses this power to unfairly promote itself and engage in antitrust activity. Google subverts user expectations and surveils users, even those users who turn off key services. Google uses its enormous power to influence elections.

All of Google's behaviors are intentional and directly tied to either amassing more power or abusing the power they already have. Google has positioned itself to be the number one company for the emerging Digital Economy and took an unethical route to get there. Google has an idea for how the Internet and new economy should operate, and it's out of line with American values.

### Google Takes Over the Web Browser Market

Web browsers are an undervalued but gigantic part of how we all experience the Internet. Web browsers have to read and process code, manage network requests, and manage reload, back, and history functionality. Web browsers have to keep the user's information secure and play defense against potentially malicious content sent from websites. Web browsers enact security protocols before exchanging information over the Internet. Web browsers have an enormous role and power in how the Internet works, from the amount of data that pours through them to the way their interfaces define our experience; and Google is getting close to total market domination.

In late 2018, it was announced that Microsoft would no longer be actively developing its Internet Explorer or Edge browsers. All Microsoft products from then on would use Chromium, a version of Google Chrome that borrows its core functionality, but is open source and different enough from Chrome in terms of style and superfluous features. However, when Chrome makes updates to its core features, such as security, it needs to update those features as well in Chromium.

"[Microsoft] can't ever meaningfully fork Chromium and diverge from its development path, because doing so will jeopardize that compatibility and increase the cost and complexity of incorporating Google's changes," experts warn that Microsoft's move will "hand over the Web to Google." There is particularly concern for the impact that Microsoft's decision will have on the web's security, giving more power and control of the protocols web browsers use to Google, which "has on a number of occasions used its might to deploy proprietary tech and put the rest of the industry in the position of having to catch up."[1]

In the past, Google has placed their own invention in the forefront and making everyone else conform, for example, with the development of Hypertext Transfer Protocol (HTTP). "Back in 2009, Google introduced SPDY, a proprietary replacement for HTTP ... SPDY was adopted by other browsers and Web servers over the next few years, and Google's protocol became widespread. ... SPDY was subsequently used as the basis for HTTP/2 ... While SPDY did initiate the HTTP/2 work, the protocol finally delivered in 2015 was extensively modified from Google's initial offering. ... The same story is repeating with HTTP/3. In 2012, Google announced a new experimental protocol, QUIC ... HTTP/3 uses a derivative of QUIC that's modified from and incompatible with Google's initial work."

Security protocols are not the only universally adopted Internet technologies that Google is trying to change. "Google AMP ('Accelerated Mobile Pages') is a cut-down HTML combined with Google-supplied JavaScript designed to make mobile Web content load faster. This year, Google said that it would try to build AMP with Web standards and introduced a new governance model that gave the project much wider industry oversight."

We must be wary of the encroaching influence of individual companies to define technical models that its competitors must adopt. To have these practices is to act as an industry monopoly, something that should be regulated. Google-based products will soon account for 80% of the desktop web browser market share and two thirds of the mobile web browser market share.

Of the desktop browser share, a plurality of the remaining 20% belongs to Mozilla Firefox, at just 9%. Mozilla Firefox is an open-source technology made by a non-profit organization. As such, the values it espouses are more in line with individual freedoms and less in line with the profits to be made from mass data collection. That being said, Google accounts for 88% of Mozilla's revenue, coming from deals made with Mozilla to promote Google services within Mozilla products.[2]

Every website and web developer will be catering to Google's demands and specifications. They'll have to, if 80% of their clients are using those browsers. Google's practices will only become more authoritarian as their market shares grow wider and their power remains unchecked. Not even the technically savvy and politically aware individuals will have a choice but to accept Google web browsers as the greatest and fastest, as a result of Google rewriting the

Internet's protocols and technologies to its own liking. Google effectively owns the access points of the Internet.

## Google's Abuse of Its Market Share

Google owns Google.com, the world's most popular website and search engine. In the search engine industry, Google has a market share greater than 90%. Google answers over 2 trillion search queries annually, a rate of approximately 63,000 search queries per second. Google has a stranglehold on the distribution of information over the Internet.[3]

Google's use of this power has been criticized heavily. Google has often been accused of favoring its own services and products over competitors in search results. This kind of bias and antitrust activity is unacceptable for a company of Google's size.

In 2012, it was revealed that the FTC was preparing to recommend that Google be sued over its antitrust behavior. However, in 2013, the FTC voted not to engage in prosecuting Google for antitrust activities. This action was seen as a slap in the face to many who felt cheated by Google's self-serving algorithms.[4]

A couple years later, in 2015, as part of a Freedom of Information Act (FOIA) request, the media was able to attain some of the report which would have recommended Google be punished. The report was 160 pages long, but the one given to the media through the request was half that length. The report claimed that Google "used anticompetitive tactics and abused its monopoly power." This doesn't mean that Google didn't change anything about their practices, it just means they weren't punished.[5]

One of the questionable practices in the report was how Google was pulling data from websites like Yelp, a user review website, to supplement their own search results. For example, if a user searched Google for "Little Caesars on Main Street," the top search result would be the business's Google's reviews (submitted to Google by Google users) combined with Yelp's reviews (submitted to Yelp by Yelp users). This meant that Yelp's entire business model was undermined, as users were getting their information without going directly to Yelp's website.

Google then increased the pressure on Yelp by telling the website that their only recourse was to opt-out of being shown in Google's search results at all. Again, this was Google abusing its power, as Yelp knew about Google's market share of Internet searches. The FTC characterized this as an "all-or-nothing choice" that was losing in every scenario for Yelp. As a result, the FTC suggested that Google make a concession: let companies like Yelp be listed in search results without taking their information directly. This concession was enacted by Google.[6]

Another concession was made regarding how Google ran its AdWords program. Google's AdWords program is their targeted advertising platform, where advertisers buy ads. Google was accused of being discriminatory to advertisers who wanted to use more than one advertising platform for their ad campaigns. Google removed these restrictions at the FTC's request.

The United States' FTC deciding not to sue or reprimand Google for antitrust violations wasn't the end of Google's uphill battle with regulation. Google is an international corporation and must abide by more laws than those of the US. In 2016, the European Union claimed in a formal complaint against Google that its packaging of Google software on their Android operating systems was a violation of antitrust laws.

The basis of the claim was that Android devices would come with Google's search software, which was anticompetitive against other search providers. For reference, the Android operating system on mobile devices enjoys a market share of about 75% worldwide. Android is the most popular operating system in the world, even beating out desktop operating system giant Windows. After two years of discourse, the complaint received closure and Google was fined $5 billion by the EU in 2018.[7]

## Google's Subversive Tactics to Collect Data

Google has a problem with treating users one way publicly and a different way behind closed doors. Google's revenue and market influence is heavily centered around data collection, so Google often resorts to subversive trickery to collect the most data possible. "There's no such thing as a free lunch," "if you don't buy the product, you are the product"—these are wise words that most Americans probably know. Still, too frequently companies like Google play us for fools and sell us on their no-cost services.

Google's Android devices come with the ability to "control" parts of the phone's services and hardware. Some of this is obvious whether there's foul play at hand. For example, turning on the flashlight on an Android phone—it's pretty obvious when the flashlight is on or off. Other features, like location services, are not as obvious. Google does offer users the ability to "turn off" location services, but there's no visible beam emitting from a user's phone to the sky indicating their movement is being watched.

Because Google has the ability to tell users one thing and do another, it takes that opportunity and runs with it. In 2018 it was revealed in an Associated Press (AP) report that Google continues to track their users' locations even when the location services of their devices are turned off. The company's page explicitly describes the opposite: "You can turn off Location History at any time. With Location History off, the places you go are no longer stored." As the AP report revealed, that was a lie.[8]

In a statement made after the allegation, Google claimed that the "Location History…is entirely opt in, and users have the controls to edit, delete, or turn it off at any time, we make sure Location History users know that when they disable the product, we continue to use location to improve the Google experience when they do things like perform a Google search or use Google for driving directions."[9]

That statement shows either a complete disconnect with the user base or an admission that Google is ready to lie even further about their services when called out. If users had known that they were still being tracked (as Google claims) when location services were explicitly turned off, then it wouldn't have been breaking news to reveal Google was doing that. Of course, this isn't the case. Instead of owning up to the subversive tactic, or actually changing the practice, Google continues to lie and claim that "everyone knew about this."

Another allegation was made against Google Chrome's Incognito mode feature.[10] The feature is designed to be a "tracking-proof" way to browse the Internet on the world's most popular Internet browser. When Incognito mode is launched, the following message is displayed:

"Chrome won't save the following information:
- Your browsing history
- Cookies and site data
- Information entered in forms

Your activity might still be visible to:
- Websites you visit
- Your employer or school
- Your internet service provider"

It seems, by the wording of this, that anything Google knows about a user is going to be off-limits in Incognito mode. After all, Google is stating here that nothing is going to be saved, except by the network being used and the traffic to the websites being used. To a layman, this effectively reads as a "no tracking here" sign. To more informed people, however, this message reads that a user's online persona is going to be treated the same as it would without incognito mode, but their own personal computer won't save anything. This disparity highlights the huge gap for Google to overcome to start making more digestible and informed statements.

This is an opportunity for Google to be more transparent to their users. Google could clearly say "everything a user does online in Incognito mode will still be tracked, monitored, and stored the same as normal browsing. Incognito mode does not hide user activity across the Internet, it simply stops users' computers from saving information about their activity," but Google doesn't.

The lines between what's "Google" and what isn't "Google" can be difficult for an average user to understand. For example, if a user is on an Android device (Google operating system), running the web browser Google Chrome, and performs a Google search, then they're using three different Google products. Any one of these could be playing by its own rules, but the expectation can't be on users to know that. It is very easy to be confused and think, "Well, Chrome is Google, and Chrome said it won't save anything in Incognito mode. Therefore my Google searches aren't being tracked."

To someone who doesn't understand the complexities of technology, this conclusion is logical. However, the repercussions of putting more trust in a company so unworthy of trust are massive. This is Google's swindle, Google's scam:

Step 1: Own every layer of technology.

Step 2: Don't educate the user base about what piece of technology does which actions.

Step 3: Use that confusion to selectively turn off small parts of small technologies, creating a sense of security among the user base that they aren't being tracked/monitored/surveilled and are in control of their technology.

Step 4: Exploit that trust to obtain as much data as possible.

## Google Appeases Political Activists

Google also uses its power to influence politics. Many criticisms have been made against how Google handles political issues. With a monopolistic market share, thousands of software engineers, and worldwide influence, Google Search is undoubtedly a powerful tool. Used for political purposes, it could drastically impact public perceptions of politicians and behaviors such as voting.

Google has been criticized for its showcasing of certain political viewpoints over others. In 2018, a writer for the magazine Slate named April Glaser published an article claiming that YouTube's search results for the phrase "abortion" showed too many anti-abortion videos. In response, the YouTube team "de-ranked" those videos in favor of pro-abortion videos.[11]

Glaser alone took full responsibility for the change in content, claiming YouTube had listened to her and made prompt change. Glaser wrote that the matter was important because "more than 1.8 billion people look for information on YouTube every month, and that could easily include someone who is considering getting an abortion." Glaser also made claims that the pro-life videos were not scientifically accurate, but those claims were disputed by the creators of those videos.

Make no mistake, what Glaser did was political activism. By making changes in response to her activism, YouTube was supporting her and her political viewpoints. Regardless of personal positions, YouTube has an obligation to present information in a transparent and neutral manner. Videos that violate YouTube's terms of service should be removed. Every other video should be fair play to be selected by the algorithm and presented to the user.

However, there is no information displayed to a user performing a search that "these results were manually picked and are not an indication of their popularity or appeal," even though that's the honest interpretation of what happened. YouTube's team clearly showed their ability to intervene and change their information to appease pro-choice advocacy. YouTube, and through them Google, has taken a side on this issue, and chosen to give that side more representation of information.

Only because of the news cycle are users informed about Google's bias on this issue. In six months' time, however, it will be hard to remember which issue Google took a side on and which they didn't. The most frustrating part is the lack of transparency, YouTube can be manually manipulating the search results for a number of political topics with videos that support their side, and the user would be none the wiser. The public is only aware of this instance because the individual who requested the change started bragging about her activism. What about what happens behind Google's or YouTube's closed doors?

## Google Tells Lies about Its Manipulation

The April Glaser case also opens up a huge can of worms of legality as it contradicts other statements that Google has made. The article by Glaser getting YouTube to manipulate search results was published on December 21, 2018. Just 10 days earlier, on December 11, 2018, Google CEO Sundar Pichai testified before the US Congress that no search results are manually manipulated.[12]

The question came from California Congresswoman Zoe Lofgren: "So it's not some little man sitting behind the curtain figuring out what we're going to show the users, basically a compilation of what users are generating and trying to sort through that information?" And Pichai gave his fateful response: "Last year we served over three trillion searches...so this is working at scale so we don't manually intervene on any particular search result."

In the case of the "abortion" search results, it was the exact case the Lofgren described: a human being (maybe not a "little man") manually altering what YouTube is going to show users on a particular search, "behind the curtain" in the sense that there's no disclosure or accountability to that person's actions. Pichai was willing to deny this under oath in a Congressional testimony, while political activists are writing articles about their victories in getting Google to alter results to their ideology.

This shines a light on the transparency issues that the public faces with technology giants like Google. Pichai's willingness to say under oath that there's no manual search intervention and Glaser's statement that she convinced Google to manually intervene on a search result are obviously contradictory, and need explanation. How can the public be expected to trust statements about how Google operates and uses its power when Google won't clear up confusion and provide clarity?

## Google Influences Electoral Politics

In the heat of the 2016 presidential election, many technology companies engaged in non-transparent practices to further their political agendas. Twitter, for example, made never-before-seen use of its "Trending" section to inform potential voters that Hillary Clinton had been cleared of an FBI investigation into her, just two days before the election.

Google was no exception to these irregular behaviors during this tense time in the United States. Google specifically partnered with a group called "Voto Latino," Spanish for "Latin Vote." In a leaked email coming from just one day after the election, a Google employee named Eliana Murillo claimed that, despite Democrats losing across the country, their collective goal of getting Hispanic-Americans out to vote was a success. Murillo's role at Google was called "Head of Multicultural Marketing."

Murillo's email does celebrate things worth celebrating. Groups that aim to get minority representation at the polls should be happy when that gets accomplished, and we should celebrate representation in democracy. However, there's more to Murillo's message than just happiness about Hispanic-American voting numbers.

Murillo points out that Hispanic voting numbers were significantly up in swing states across the United States, including Arizona, Nevada, and Florida. Specifically, she noted that "Arizona was a key state for us." She claimed that Google had used its financial power to give money to Voto Latino, which promoted Hispanic-American voting and gave rides to polls. She also claimed that she had directed Google's power "to ensure that millions of people saw certain hashtags and social media impressions with the goal of influencing their behavior during the election." She even went as far as to describe these activities as a means of Google giving a "silent donation," which could have legal implications depending on campaign finance laws.[13]

What was once a sincere message about promoting democratic activity quickly turned into a biased, partisan view of efforts made to covertly influence the election. Voto Latino is largely anti-Donald Trump, who won the presidential election. Voto Latino claimed that they'd be prepared to get out one million more Latino voters by 2020 in retaliation to Trump's 2016 victory.[14] In addition, Voto Latino has made public statements denouncing the 27% of Hispanic-American voters who voted for Trump and vehemently opposes his agenda.

Google should clearly not be partnering with such biased groups in order to promote participation in democracy. It is undeniable that other, less activist organizations exist which Google could partner with to get out the vote in underrepresented demographics. Certainly, Google employees bragging about abusing Google's power to biasedly influence "millions of people" concerning the election is troubling, and their use of influence to try to sway elections in one direction shouldn't be taken lightly. No one tasked Google with promoting participation in democracy, so if they are going to do it, they should do it without bias in a transparent manner.

## Google and Filter Bubbles

Another charge that's been levied against Google is that it creates "filter bubbles" for users. These bubbles are metaphors for the technological barriers and filters which "block" certain types of information from reaching certain users. Thus, users "live inside a bubble," and are only exposed to Internet content that is formfitting to their opinions and biases.

Whether or not they acknowledge it, consumers love the filter bubble. Cognitive dissonance and confirmation bias are two mental processes that humans are burdened with. Filter bubbles play a role in both: there is no cognitive dissonance in a world where there's no exposure to dissenting opinions. Similarly, all the content put in front of a consumer is pre-checked to fit their narrative and worldview, so the information consumed contributes to their confirmation bias.

Google is a key player in creating these filter bubbles, as they have the most data saved to draw algorithms from. Essentially, these filter bubbles are using the same data that the technology industry uses for personalized advertisements, such as age, political party, and location. Except this time, instead of reporting back with a series of products to offer, the result is a non-challenging answer, subdued and reduced by the need for bias. Unlike the other issues that Google causes, the consequences of creating filter bubbles will be more social than anything else.

We are increasingly apt to retreat into our tribal ways when faced with adversity and challenges. This, perhaps, has been one of the greatest drawbacks to the age of global connectivity made possible by the Internet. Humans need tribes—we need groups, posses, cliques.

For whatever reason, we lost them. The Internet's distractions have caused us to lose time spent in person with friends and family. Our reclusive homes encourage us to run away and hide from confrontation. Our move away from the rural communities in the industrial age meant leaving our home towns and connected families. Rising secularization is leaving our places of worship empty.

But in the loss of these connections, the technology industry offered us a way out. Companies like Google offered us our safe places, where we could interact with people like us, conversing about topics on which we all already agreed. It was once described to me that "memes are just inside jokes you share with the Internet." Nothing could better describe the way we lost our real friendships.

In the late 2000s, discussion on the Internet was vastly different than how it exists today. In the typical Internet forum, threads (or "original posts") were created, and comments on these threads would send the thread back to the top of the list. This meant that the threads and posts generating the most discussion were the ones that stayed up the longest, generating the most views, whereas posts that generated low amounts of content and discussion were simply exhausted of energy by the tenth reply and left to die off.

On the other side of the Internet, entire websites were dedicated to sharing memes and images. It was known that there wasn't much content to be talked about or discussed about these, so the order of visibility was often just a sequential line based on submission time. These two models worked, in their own separate ways, to foster the best Internet experience for their purposes.

However, around 2011, a new form of Internet website was gaining popularity. "News aggregator" websites like Reddit and Digg used mechanisms of "likes," "diggs," and "upvotes" to determine which content was the worthiest of visibility. This meant that dead content, such as an image or a joking post, would be as visible as a 1,000-comment discussion post, so long as the number of likes was equal. Additionally, Reddit and Digg relied on splitting their websites into subcategories for the best user experiences. On Reddit, these are called subreddits. A subreddit called "science," for example, would be used to make posts, link articles, and have discussions related to science.

The long-term effects of this model are completely segregated communities in terms of content and ideology. By using the likes system, users can essentially promote any content they agree with to the top visibility. Conversely, they can also dislike content that they disagree with, lowering that content's visibility for all other users. In this way, users can effectively create their own ideological echo chambers, where all they see it content they agree with, and hide from visibility content that causes them cognitive dissonance and challenges their beliefs.

For bonus measure, it's entirely done by the users themselves. No need for any Googlesque algorithms! Humans' desperate need to avoid confrontation while still being connected and tribal, without a doubt, led to the rise in use of websites like Reddit. This is supported by evidence, too: Reddit has become the world's sixth and the United States' third most visited website as of 2018.

While this self-segregation is inherent to a website like Reddit, it shouldn't be the norm across the entire Internet. A user's political alignment on Reddit shouldn't necessarily follow them to Facebook or Twitter, at least not without those websites independently determining that user's politics. Google's filter bubbles make sure that a user's Internet preferences follow them to whichever corner of the Internet they travel, and I believe this is to the detriment of our political discourse and culture.

It's clear that people getting into filter bubbles and refusing to try to get out isn't just the fault of Google, but that doesn't mean Google can't do better. Google does put people's behavioral data through their algorithms to make determinations of the user's beliefs and ideologies, perhaps more than any other company. Google does make advertisements and content recommendations to users. What I'd suggest is that Google be less static and more relaxed with their determination of a user's ideologies and politics, and to ensure the restraints are loose enough for a user to not be confined and sheltered while online—the user should choose their biases, not Google.

Google should not be the one to determine whether a user is shown content that might challenge their worldview. If people choose to go exclusively to places online that cater to their ideologies, that is fine, but the choice to understand an opposing viewpoint is paramount to having engaged and holistically educated users. Google shouldn't take the choice away from people, or automatically push users deeper into an ideological rabbit hole for fear of them losing interest in a site or advertisement.

## Google's Dangerous Data Mixing

Google's tracking of users has subtly increased over time. It's no surprise that Google inventions like Google Assistant, a voice command engine, increased the amount of voice recording and monitoring done by Google. Products like Fitbit, a wearable wrist device that monitors physical activity, have Google software in them, which means that Google has more access to our physical and biometric data. Not only has Google rolled out products like Google Assistant and Fitbit's software to increase data collection, Google's also started going back on promises to not increase the scope of their surveillance.

In 2008, Google acquired the Internet advertising network DoubleClick. This caused growth in public curiosity and concern about the way many advertising platforms would interact with user data. Where companies like DoubleClick were tracking web browsing behavior and patterns on a broad scale, Google would theoretically be able to supplement that data with user-specific and personally identifiable data.[15]

The concern was that, in mixing personally identifiable information with advertiser's data, too much confidential data would be spread too carelessly. It's a security risk. Suddenly, to DoubleClick I'm not just a white liberal Nebraskan who likes video games, I'm Brian Wolatz, I have a Computer Science degree, here's my address, etc. Google co-founder Sergey Brin reassured users that this would not be the case in 2007, stating privacy was the "number one priority when we contemplate new kinds of advertising products."

For eight years this was the case. Google's policy on sharing information with DoubleClick read: "We will not combine DoubleClick cookie information with personally identifiable information unless we have your opt-in consent." This policy gave excellent transparency into how the companies interacted and shared their data, while providing assurance and security for the end users.

However, this all changed in the summer of 2016. Google crossed out the previous phrase and rewrote it: "Depending on your account settings, your activity on other sites and apps may be associated with your personal information in order to improve Google's services and the ads delivered by Google." Suddenly, any separation of powers and information between Google and DoubleClick was nixed. DoubleClick isn't even mentioned by name anymore—it's just another provider of data.

This has become the standard among Google's practices. Google makes ethical and morally sound policies when they're in the public eye, then renegotiates those policies with themselves and cancels them when the public's back is turned. In this previous example, privacy advocates had been arguing against the marriage of personal data with web trafficking data since 1999. The Network Advertising Initiative was formed in 2000 to provide formal dissent to invasive online advertising practices and to "establish ethical codes."

Google tore down that wall of separation without public debate and without consensus. There is no excuse to think Google didn't know that the public would not collectively be on board with this decision. If Google really thought mixing personal data with behavioral data wouldn't be an issue, then they wouldn't have made public statements condemning it and codified policy which made it impossible. To think this was an agreeable position, they would be willfully ignoring institutions dedicated to combating this decision for decades.

Google is unregulated and unaccountable. We the people absolutely need to regain our voice in these decisions about the way our lives are run by technology. The more we sit on our hands, the more Google makes decisions on our behalf. And unfortunately, the more Google is tasked to make decisions in our best interest, the more it doesn't.

Let's make it clear that Google is making decisions in the pursuit of profit that they know will be unpopular the public. Let's get the regulatory agencies involved. And if the current ones don't want to get involved, or think the issues are out of their purview, let's make new agencies that do have the will and power to help. When a company with little regard for its customers gets more power and becomes more abusive with each passing day, refusing to challenge it is not a solution.

## Google's Public vs. Private Attitude on Change

Google is incredibly open about these problems internally, but refuses to make concrete, unwavering stances publicly. In a leaked 2018 Google internal slide deck (very ominously named "The Good Censor"), Google admitted to many of the accusations levied against them: they shadow ban content (banning without explanation or announcement), they use subversive tactics to reroute attention, and they change their Terms of Service (and with them, their values) at the drop of a hat.

The leaked release admits that "tech firms are performing a balancing act between two incompatible positions." On the one side, the industry is attempting to "create unmediated "marketplaces of ideas'" that "prioritize free speech for democracy," where "all values, including civility norms, are always open for debate." On the other side, tech firms are also trying to "create well-ordered spaces for safety and civility" that "favors dignity over liberty, and civility over freedom" and "censor[s] racial and religious hatred."[16]

The release admits that these values are inherently contradictory, and characterizes the first as a "commit[ment] to the American tradition," whereas the latter is a "100% commit[ment] to European tradition." It admits that the balancing act started in the "pro-freedom" side and is now further in the "pro-censorship" side. If Google is so ready to admit they want to shift from American values (or "tradition"), why aren't they willing to bring that debate to the public space? If Americans wanted the "European tradition" of rules and censorship, why would we have declared independence from those exact rules and traditions 250 years ago?

Even though Google admits in the same release that there's been challenges to being fair in the practice of moderating information, the technology industry continues to favor moderation and censorship. Simply telling Google that "these practices are antithetical to American values" is not enough, because Google already knows that - they acknowledge it internally. What Google needs to be told is that the incompatibility is not okay. Not only are their practices conflicting with American principles, changes to their practices are needed if they're going to serve the American people.

# IV

## Facebook: The Ongoing Privacy Disaster

### Facebook's Trust Problems

We can't know the true depth of the privacy violations committed by the technology industry. We can assume that companies like Google, companies that have their hands in every aspect of the industry, probably have the most data stored and mapped. Despite the faults of others, Facebook, which is quite literally just a social media company, has done a spectacular job of making themselves to be the face of privacy violation.

Whereas Google will ease off after being accused and slither back into the shadows, Facebook takes the brunt of their offenses when exposed. In the age of more public dissent and awareness, Facebook is consistently the first kid found in hide-and-seek. This, certainly, has negatively impacted how their billions of clients view them, even if it is unjust in relation to other companies.

It's not just the clients who are beginning to question Facebook, but their employees as well. While naturally there are employees who dismiss the negative press, citing the media's "economic incentive to slander [the company]," there are others who, more anonymously, have sought to vent about the company's practices. One employee asked a question that should be asked of no company with Facebook's power: "Why does our company suck at having a moral compass?"[1]

It speaks volumes to Facebook's integrity. In the world of technology, the laws are simply not there. No external agency or regulator is going to tell a technology company like Facebook how to operate. There is no push for moral imperatives to be followed, except internally. As said by John Wooden, "The true test of a man's character is what he does when no one is watching." As we know, no one at all watched these companies for almost two decades, so in a way, we really have seen their true colors.

## Facebook's Paranoia Culture

Facebook employees were only able to speak critically of their company under anonymity. A service called Blind was used to report and discuss this anonymous-yet-verified activity. Blind does not publicly reveal user identities, but does verify its users based on email addresses. Thus, it was the tool of choice for Facebook employees to talk openly about their company's culture.

For fear of their phone activity being monitored, Facebook workers have started using burner phones in order to have honest and open conversations with each other about their mutual employer. The burner phones are a symptom of the company's culture, which has a "a growing sense of paranoia."[2] Who would have guessed that a business model dedicated to tracking, monitoring, and recording every possible thing about its customers, saved on an individual level, would have created a feeling among employees that they're being tracked?

These revelations about Facebook's culture are recent, but the paranoia has always been there. In an inadvertently revealing photo of Mark Zuckerberg's personal laptop, it was shown that he covers his built-in webcam and microphone with a piece of tape.[3] The shared photo prompted users to ask: "if the CEO of Facebook doesn't think his basic privacy is secured, should I?" The naysayers would declare that "of course" Zuckerberg takes those precautions, as he is a CEO and a likely target of hacking attempts.

At the time of the photo, in June of 2016, most of the commenters thought Zuckerberg was taking a precaution against aggressive governmental surveillance or hackers. The public had known, at that point, that government agencies like the National Security Agency had surveillance mechanisms that could access the feed of any webcam or microphone, even without showing the devices were turned on. These revelations were gifted to the populace thanks to Edward Snowden as far back as 2013. There was also a similar fear that malicious hackers had similar capabilities.

Naively, we didn't know that the entities doing the most spying on us ordinary citizens were the ones with which we signed user agreements. Private companies performing mass data saving of their users was well underway by 2013, and certainly by 2016 surveillance capitalism was getting out of the booster seat. If we had known this information then, seeing Mark Zuckerberg's laptop camera taped would have indicated that we should be scared of the corporation, not the cop or the robber.

There are so many entities that are willing to surveil us. The government, the hackers, and all the big tech companies. Mark Zuckerberg feels like he needs to physically alter his laptop to avoid being tracked. Facebook employees are using burner phones and other anonymous ways of communicating. At what point should we start taking the threat of monitoring and tracking as seriously as a Facebook employee does? At what point should Facebook's paranoia culture become the world's paranoia culture?

## Facebook's Censorship

Although Facebook is generally associated with issues of privacy violations, Facebook is no stranger to the censorship game. Facebook takes part in the conspiracy to silence groups of users with the big technology coalition. Facebook played a large part in the post-2016 war on fake news, creating a team which was honorably self-named the "war room" to oversee which news stories were buzzing, and determine which ones needed swatting.

During the 2016 US presidential election, much of the reason voters did not trust the Democratic nominee Hillary Clinton was due to the remarkably concisely named issue of "her emails." Of course, this short naming convention disregards the seriousness of what was actually multiple issues. In total, Hillary Clinton was cursed with three different email scandals. The first one being her unsecured private email server in her home which contained classified information and was repeatedly hacked. The second email scandal was her campaign chairman's emails being leaked to and published by WikiLeaks. The third scandal was emails from the Democratic National Committee (DNC) being leaked to WikiLeaks which proved that the DNC had rigged the presidential primary in Clinton's favor.

The release of the leaked emails was incredibly damaging to Clinton's candidacy. WikiLeaks was under the orders of their leader, Julian Assange, who held the political viewpoint that a Clinton presidency would have been horrible. WikiLeaks made sure their leaks were released at key periods during the primaries and the last months leading up to the election in order to be the most damaging to her campaign. However, at two separate occasions, Facebook filters blocked the link to WikiLeaks's website after leaks were published.

The first time was one day before Super Tuesday, on February 29, 2016,[4] and the second time was one day before the Democratic National Convention, on July 24, 2016.[5] Both times, Facebook claimed that the censorship was automatic. Both times, WikiLeaks asserted that Facebook was lying.

Facebook's censorship of these leaks shaped how millions of Americans perceived them. The WikiLeaks website is actually fairly easy to use, if one has the patience to read through thousands of normal documents in search of a few damning ones. But Facebook's banning of links to the source material, in addition to journalists like CNN's Chris Cuomo (wrongly) saying it's illegal to view the documents,[6] made Americans more likely to pursue media coverage of the leaks instead of the leaks themselves.

Though I have no way of knowing, I'd would bet that Facebook manually removed the links to WikiLeaks's documents. In their removal, Facebook actively contributed to political censorship that would have given valuable insight for people trying to make important decisions about the country's leadership. Facebook should reevaluate the use of its power. They have billions of customers worldwide, including hundreds of millions of Americans. What right do they have to use their power to ban the dissemination of information to the American electorate?

## Facebook Sends Suspect Data Points to Advertisers

In 2016, Facebook came under public scrutiny when it was revealed that they were selling information about users that included their "ethnic affinity."[7] This raised questions about the practice of advertisers targeting users based on something as blatant as skin color. In some cases, like the advertisement of jobs or housing, this practice may even be illegal.

It would also be illegal to discriminate the advertisements on the basis of sex or gender, under the same laws. In 2018, the American Civil Liberties Union (ACLU) and the Communications Workers of America filed a formal complaint against Facebook to the US Equal Employment Opportunity Commission that Facebook was violating the 1964 Civil Rights Act because it let job advertisers limit an ad's audience on the basis of gender. The complaint says that job advertisements can be selected to only appear to "men, women, or all." The complaint says that at least four companies have already used this option to recruit workers.[8]

In the 2016 case, Facebook claimed to have rectified the situation by changing the naming convention from "ethnic affinity" to "multicultural affinity." But that's hardly a fix, and it's still important that users are not discriminated against unlawfully, whether online or in person. The issue was never with the adjective "ethnic," but the fact that Facebook was opening the door for advertisers to discriminate by even telling them the users' skin color in the first place. If racism and sexism didn't exist, then we wouldn't need civil rights laws that protect those classes of people from discrimination. If racism and sexism magically ceased in online activity, this conversation wouldn't be necessary.

Legally, it's hard to construe a situation where Facebook is in trouble. Facebook has and will continue to claim that it's just passing along information to the advertisers. While Facebook can encourage non-discriminatory practices, it can't be held liable to enforce them all the time. Placing the onus of regulating content away from the platform and toward the content creators is good practice, and is completely protected under the 1996 Communications Decency Act (CDA).

Also, having a single data point of a user's racial identity isn't the only way to determine a user's race from Facebook's data set. A combination of other data, such as location, music tastes, political alignment, and other cultural indicators could create a fairly statistically accurate painting of the user's skin tone. This means that Facebook wouldn't even need to outright tell their advertisers what race the user is, racial information could be deduced regardless.

Perhaps what's more uncomfortable than having an "ethnic affinity" data point is that advertisements are going to become much more individualized going forward. In fact, this is one of the end goals of surveillance capitalism: to have each user's behavior pinned down so well to know their every taste and desire, then, advertise it to them. Americans have learned to accept advertisements being targeted at some level. We know not to expect a car commercial on Nickelodeon, and we know not to expect a toy commercial on ESPN. Even on a racial level, we don't criticize T.V. channels like BET for playing advertisements targeted at black Americans. The idea that the advertisements I see on Facebook are different than what my neighbor sees, even though it is the same website and medium, could be the more unnerving aspect of the advancements in targeted advertisements.

Google's advertising engine used to let users "opt-out" of what sets of data advertisers are sent. Users were able to pick which parts of their personal information were sent to advertisers. For example, I would be able to specify to advertisers that I am a white, mid-20s Omaha native, but not that I am male or a computer scientist. A 2015 study tested these options, creating fake accounts with the exact same online behavior, and only sharing the fake account's gender. With all other things equal, sharing only gender with advertisers, the study found that men were targeted for high paying jobs at a much higher rate than women.[9]

This meant that Google needed to rework their contract with advertisers to ensure that its users were not being treated unfairly on the basis of sex. But by implementing these changes, Google was caught in a no-win situation. Google could be proactive about censoring certain sexist advertisements, but this would forfeit their protections offered by the CDA as a neutral platform. On the other hand, they could allow sexist advertisement to continue, essentially standing idly by while illegal discrimination occurred.

Cynthia Dwork, a computer scientist who does research at Microsoft and at Harvard University, wants to understand what it would take to algorithmically create a fair advertisement system. She wants to understand what it would mean to be fair. In an example, she says, high-achieving minority students might get targeted with advertisements for a math degree, while high-achieving white students might get targeted with advertisements for a finance degree. While the algorithm might be based in scientific reality, that white students are more likely to go into finance than math and vice versa, this is not an acceptable reason to target advertisements. Instead, she claims that "culturally aware systems are necessary, ... better understandings of actual, fair similarities can be deduced."

However, these concerns for harmful bias come from the scientists and researchers, not the advertising industry itself. Even knowing it may be causing harm, it's doubtful that the marketing industry would cease using these highly detailed data points because of ethical reasons. Dwork noted her concern: "Without a mathematics to capture values of interest to society, such as fairness, we quite literally do not know what we are building.... I'm concerned that the theory will be too late to influence practice, and that 'values' will too often be viewed as 'getting in the way' of science or profit."[10]

## Facebook Advertisements Harass LGBT Users

Like sex, gender, and race, Facebook also has data points which indicate whether or not a user is homosexual or transgender. This has caused them to receive a considerable amount of flak from the LGBT community, and has led to very discriminatory advertisements being presented to LGBT Facebook users. This is incredibly frustrating for closeted LGBT people, who may not be ready to share their identity with the outside world—much less a bunch of advertisers they don't know and definitely don't trust.

In 2018, young LGBT users reported that they had seen advertisements on Facebook promoting "sexual purity" and "gay conversion therapy."[11] Gay conversion therapy operates under the belief that being homosexual is a treatable condition, and attempts to apply a therapeutic fix. Gay conversion therapy advertisements targeted at young LGBT people essentially tells a group trying to understand themselves that there is something broken in them. Facebook responded quickly and resolved the error, but would this error have occurred if Facebook wasn't sending LGBT information to advertisers in the first place?

The problem doesn't only exist in advertisements. Other users have a vast amount of power to reveal information about each other, even sometimes without the intention. In 2012, a gay couple who was not publicly out yet, was added to a LGBT "Queer Choir" Facebook group. This update was not initiated by them, but rather by one of their choir friends, but nonetheless it ended with their public outing as LGBT due to Facebook displaying group membership publicly.[12]

Similar to the problem with race, however, is that Facebook does not even need to know a user's sexual orientation outright to start making guesses. Through simple data analytics, Facebook can use a user's own data against them. For example, a 2017 study showed that a user who likes (likes being the specific action on Facebook, not the general verb) Lady Gaga, Human Rights Campaign, and True Blood is statistically more likely to be gay.[13] If the user's data on likes is sent to advertisers, there's a good chance those advertisers will draw a similar conclusion.

LGBT Facebook users are not out of luck. Those that want to keep their sexual orientation secret can "cloak" this part of their identity by deleting just a few likes. While this may seem disingenuous, a 2017 study proved that by removing on average 4.6 Facebook likes, LGBT users started getting fewer LGBT-related advertisements.[14] Of course, due to the proliferation of big data storage, their orientations and identities will probably never be a secret from Facebook again, but at least that information is less shared to advertisers.

Considering Dwork's work from the previous section, how can we make advertisement systems which can make culturally-aware decisions but also not be harmfully or illegally discriminatory? Is it even possible to create automatic systems of any kind, such as artificial intelligence, that can know its users' protected class information but be trusted not to use that information negatively? In the case of things that matter like job opportunities, protected class information should simply never be an input into the algorithm.

I would also suggest creating laws to require advertisement platforms like Facebook and Google keep logs and track which advertisers are advertising important things on the basis of protected class information. This would help regulators ensure that the advertisers are not being unlawfully discriminatory in their target audience for advertisements. This solution would also allow those platforms to remain neutral in the content they host, which would let them keep their protections under the CDA. And as always, if there are no regulators or agencies with the will or technical know-how to enforce these advertisement standards and review how companies are using the advertisement platforms, I suggest creating and empowering one.

## The Facebook Research App

Facebook's business model is starting to fail them. The company has relied on collecting as much data as possible on its users since its inception. However, users are starting to be more conservative in the things they post online. There's a certain level of ignorance required to maintain the level of collection that Facebook did for years, but the younger generation has learned better.

Like LGBT social media users "cloaking" their interests to be less predictably queer, users everywhere are starting to censor themselves online. There's fear of losing out on future opportunities in life due to a poorly timed joke. Young people especially are doing this,[15] and it will definitely put them at a comparative advantage over their peers in the future. Being offensive and rude online may still happen, but it's becoming less frequent to find this harassment posted under real names.

Facebook is actively pursuing the goals of surveillance capitalism and trying to map human behavior into data sets. To Facebook, users engaging in self-censorship online is essentially a corruption of data. To Facebook, users purposefully lowering their activity on Facebook-monitored applications is lost data. And for a surveillance capitalist, that data is key.

In 2019, it was revealed that Facebook had started paying 13- to 35-year-olds to have a highly intrusive application on their smartphones. This application, ominously called the "Facebook Research App," monitored every single aspect of the phone and sent the data to Facebook's big data stores. Text messages, emails, phone calls, browsing history, location tracking, photos, videos, etc. were all available for Facebook to take from the user's device.[16]

The worst part about the application was that it seemed to be a copy of Onavo VPN. Onavo VPN was a virtual private network bought by Facebook, after which Facebook reworked it into a highly intrusive data collection app. After the public learned of the changes to Onavo and subsequently protested its existence, Facebook made it unavailable and removed it. This was in 2017, and the "Facebook Research App" had been around since just a year earlier, in 2016. Even portions of the code are exactly the same; the "Facebook Research App" has files of code that quite literally start with the letters "ONV."

Just so the timeline's clear: Facebook was forced to take down one invasive application due to public pressure. Then, almost right away, they started paying users—some as young as thirteen—to download a "new" application with the same monitoring, tracking, and control as the application they were just told, resoundingly, that the public was not okay with. This is on par with Google ignoring entire groups advocating for the separation of private and personal data and simply doing what they pleased when no one was looking.

The "Facebook Research App" was so invasive and controlling that Facebook purposefully subverted the Apple requirements to have the application on iPhones. Instead, Facebook gave the application's users directions on how to subvert Apple's application installation process and give the Facebook Research App complete control, essentially by putting the device into a "developer mode." Because of this violation, Apple decided to block Facebook from having any access to this developer mode. This will hurt Facebook's ability to develop, create, and test the main Facebook app for iPhone.

Take a moment and realize that Apple, the company which has had decades of public image woes due to their use of cheap outsourced child labor, the company that in 2018 was paying for Chinese teenagers to build the iPhone X, came down harder on Facebook than the US government ever has.

Facebook gave thirteen-year-olds $20 dollars a month to essentially sell out their digital lives. Where is the protection for our children? If the government can't write laws in protection of kids because they don't understand technology or the American values of privacy well enough, then the government is utterly useless on these issues. This industry should not be the Wild West, with giant technology companies committing heinous crimes and being hypocritically upset with each other. This should be a user-focused industry with the intent of making technology that improves our lives.

As we've come to expect, Facebook offered no apology, even in the face of such negative public dissent and outcry. Sheryl Sandberg, Facebook's COO stated: "This is a Facebook Research app. It's very clear to the people who participated. It's completely opt-in. There is a rigorous consent flow and people are compensated. It's a market research program."[17]

Even if we were to accept this explanation, we must know that it is based on falsehoods. Evidence was shown of the "rigorous consent flow" being bypassed. As security researcher Will Strafach said, "this hands Facebook continuous access to the most sensitive data about you, and most users are going to be unable to reasonably consent to this regardless of any agreement they sign, because there is no good way to articulate just how much power is handed to Facebook when you do this."[18]

## Facebook Offering Swaths of Private User Data

It's especially important to remember that Facebook will sell anything and everything it can about its users. Even when users set their Facebook privacy settings a certain way with the goal of protecting their privacy, it only impacts how *other* Facebook users can see their information. It has no bearing on what Facebook will track about the user or what Facebook will tell advertisers about the user.

Perhaps the most aggressive violation of this trust was when Facebook was caught selling user's private messages to giant corporations like Spotify and Netflix. No one would have ever expected that a private Facebook message sent from themselves to another person would ever be a commodity sold by Facebook. In other cases, as in the cases of Amazon, Microsoft, and Sony, Facebook offered to give over users' emails and the emails of their Facebook friends.[19]

If the companies that bought the data are to be believed, it would appear that Facebook was the company with the prerogative to come forward and offer these services. In the case of Netflix and Spotify, Facebook wanted the companies to create features that allowed for seamless interaction with Facebook—for example, a Spotify user messaging a Facebook friend the link to a song without leaving the Spotify application.

While Facebook may, yet again, be able to explain an enormous privacy violation with the best intentions, it doesn't mean the company is off the hook. Multiple other software vendors are wondering why Facebook didn't make similar offers to them for integration and coupling of services. At worst for Facebook, they may be in violation of some antitrust regulations for giving preferential treatment.

It is incontrovertibly a Federal crime to open someone else's mail. Meanwhile, Facebook reserves the right to sell private messages simply because the messages were sent on their platform. Facebook has a problem abusing power that it's not going to solve on its own. These practices are evil, they are abusive of the trust people put into their platform, and if our government understood technology the way they understand paper envelopes, these practices would be illegal.

## Cambridge Analytica Scraped Facebook Out

When we consider how much data Facebook has, and how nonchalantly they treat that data, we should be concerned. Facebook essentially stores every bit of information it can on 2.2 billion people. Facebook has no problem just handing out this information to advertisers for money, and it has no problem giving out pro-bono special access to user data to other high-profile technology companies.

In 2015, the U.K. political consulting firm Cambridge Analytica scraped the publicly available personal information of 87 million American Facebook users right off the platform.[20] Under the guise that they were an advertisement company — which to an extent they were — Cambridge Analytica requested and received highly detailed information about nearly 90 million people. Then, instead of using it in transit to post advertisements, Cambridge Analytica simply saved the data to their own databases, to be used for their own data algorithms and analysis.

In 2016, Facebook found out about this practice, and sent a simple letter to the firm asking them to delete the data. Facebook told the firm to send back the letter signed with acknowledgment that the data had been deleted. Former Cambridge Analytica worker Christopher Wylie recalled in a US Congressional hearing: "It requested that if I still had the data to delete it and sign a certification that I no longer had the data.... It did not require a notary or any sort of legal procedure. So I signed the certification and sent it back, and they accepted it."

I don't blame Cambridge Analytica for what they did, as they were utilizing an advanced algorithm to determine which users to display advertisements to. That's exactly what political consultants do. Facebook offered the firm plenty of individualized data on its target market, so it should come as no surprise why Cambridge Analytica would save that data and use it to further enhance their algorithms. The concern has to lie with Facebook's data practices.

Facebook accepted that the stolen records of 87 million people had been erased by a private firm based on a signed piece of paper. This level of scrutiny in private business dealings is unacceptable. How can a company be so indifferent about the massive amount of data they collect on the public? Is it a matter of lacking ethics, or not understanding risk?

## Facebook Uses Plugins to Track Users

In recent years, Facebook's public image has tanked. In 2018 alone, CEO Mark Zuckerberg's net worth went down $20 billion, as he owns 13% of the company.[21] Data privacy issues concerning what data Facebook tracks, how that data is collected, what kind of buyers Facebook entertains, and security issues revolving data breaches all guided the path toward the low level of public trust that Facebook currently has.

The discovery of Facebook's methods of gaining data on its users has created ethical controversy. Facebook uses any means necessary to gather data and information about its users. This includes far more than the posts its users write and pages they interact with on Facebook's own websites.

Facebook offers a variety of web interfaces that third-party websites can use. These can be found in the style of a simple "Share" or "Like" button on a news article, accompanied with the Facebook logo. The implication is that it would be shared/liked by the visitor's Facebook profile. However, in order to complete this action, the third-party website would have to know which user is looking, so when "Share" is clicked, it knows which profile to use.

This is accomplished by what's called a plugin. It is very likely that a user's computer or phone knows their Facebook login information, or is currently logged in to a Facebook session (to check, just go to Facebook and see if it is already logged in). When a user goes to a website with a Facebook plugin, that plugin will validate and identify the user based on their device. This seems innocent, but like I said earlier: Facebook will record and save any data it possibly can on its users.

Sometimes the plugins are able to do much more than just simple Like and Share functionality. One of Facebook's plugins allows for a comment section to be inserted in a third-party website. I know from personal experience that it can be incredibly disorienting and Orwellian to see my own Facebook profile picture on a website that's not Facebook. It shatters the veil of privacy to see the information being shared between the sites firsthand.

Another one of Facebook's plugins allow for full Facebook pages to be displayed and interacted with on a third-party application or website. This essentially gives the entire Facebook website and application—a user's friends, profile information, pages they visit, etc.—to them when they're not even on the site. Facebook uses these plugins, in all of their forms, to track users as they navigate the entirety of the web.

The simple, virtually meaningless services that Facebook offers in return for the insane amount of data sharing and collecting is imbalanced. The end user is getting next to nothing in return for this data transaction. What benefit do they experience seeing a "Like" button on an article they're reading? Has a Facebook comments section ever been full of valuable information, especially one embedded in a third-party application? The explanation is simple: Facebook wants to know what its users are doing around the web at all times, even when they're not on Facebook. Facebook offers these freebies to third party websites as bait to get into their roots and track their users.

## Facebook Pixel

This whole suite of plugins provides limited benefits to users. However, there also exists tools that provide absolutely no benefits at all to end users. If and when a company decides to advertise on Facebook, one thing that they can do to give themselves a competitive advantage is to add Facebook Pixel to their website.

Facebook Pixel combines all the dreams of an advertisement platform. Without the user having any knowledge of the transaction occurring, Facebook will monitor individual actions taken on a third-party website. This means that the user doesn't even have to see a Facebook comment section or Like button on the page: Facebook is still tracking their every move.

The information is abundant and virtually unlimited. For example, an online store can report which specific products a user clicks on, hovers over, and scrolls right past. This level of detail and granularity is probably absent even from the store's database, which would house data on the user's orders, order history, and payment information. Facebook Pixel is truly a nightmare of a product for anyone who doesn't want to be tracked online, since there will be no notification or indicator in any way that Facebook is currently monitoring the user between one website and another.

For Facebook and the third-party website, Pixel works great. On Facebook's end, they get loads more individualized data and the third-party companies can even choose to share with Facebook the logged in user's name, phone number, address, and gender. On the third party's end, Pixel gives them analytical and data processing tools to give the website insight into how to improve, as well as statistics on how advertisements are doing so the website can optimize those.

It should be stated that Facebook Pixel is not the only tool like this. Similarly, Google has a product called Google Analytics which has the same features: unannounced, highly specific tracking of how customers use websites, with a suite of analytics tools for the third party to use. Users need a way to protect themselves from this kind of monitoring and surveillance; they need a way to opt out. Even adding in some kind of noticeable disclaimer would be a step in the right direction, because right now these secret and invasive programs are giving more power to the companies that can't be trusted with it and violating users' rights to privacy along the way.

## Facebook Secret Tracking and Non-User Profiles

One might wonder, however, if not having a Facebook profile would absolve them from any of these problems. The short answer: no. Because websites share so much information with Facebook, it is certain that Facebook knows who the users are even if they've never owned or created a Facebook account (or did own one but deleted it).

None of these practices are regulated by law, because we don't have a reactive Congress. Facebook claims to keep browsing data on non-users for 90 days before deleting it. The theory behind this is that 90 days' worth is enough data to target advertisements to these users, but without a permanent account there is no use in keeping it more long term. This is another example of a technology company making up rules as they go and acting as if the public implicitly agrees with these behaviors.

However, if a non-Facebook user has voluntarily shared any information with Facebook (without rescinding it later), then Facebook will permanently store the data just like it would for a user signed up on Facebook. Additionally, any sort of data that Facebook receives with a non-user's information, such as a Facebook user uploading their smartphone's contact list which includes the non-user, gives Facebook permission to permanently store that non-user's data. Again, this is not real permission, just permission as Facebook has defined it for themselves.

This is scary for a lot of reasons. It means that Facebook probably has a better idea of every American's personal details than the government does - even those that don't use the platform. It also speaks to the level people are willing to give away their privacy without even checking to see who owns information about them and who is tracking it. If a user's never been on Facebook, is it their responsibility for making sure Facebook isn't tracking them? What gives Facebook that kind of power?

The good news for non-users is that, at least right now, they can ask and Facebook will delete their permanent data as well as any information about them that would have led it to permanently store information. And again I iterate, these rules are completely up to Facebook's discretion: They can be changed at any moment. There are no laws regulating any of this behavior or guiding Facebook's policies, although there definitely should be.

# V

## Censorship in the Digital Age

### Online Platforms Ban Legal Speech

The issue of banning has nothing to do with rule sets and everything to do with bias. Many online platforms leave vague and unclear rules about which topics, tones, and beliefs are allowed to be expressed on their platform. Typically, online platforms have two overarching rules to all speech on their platform: one against the inciting of violence, and one against hate speech.

The first common rule, the one against inciting violence, is well-founded and is actually criminal in the United States. In Brandenburg v. Ohio, it was ruled that there is an exception to the First Amendment (the right to freedom of speech). Speech that is "directed to inciting or producing imminent lawless action and is likely to incite or produce such action" is not protected speech and can be prosecuted.[1] Online platforms have a basis in law for banning this kind of speech.

However, just because the rule is based on law does not mean that online platforms have a duty to ban it. In fact, online platforms have the exemption specifically to not ban it under Section 230 of the 1996 Communications Decency Act. In the United States, online platforms that platform and host illegal content cannot be held liable for the sharing of the content itself. Instead, the user who posted it must take responsibility.[2] This means that any online platform that hides behind the curtain and bans content that is "illegal speech" isn't actually doing themselves any favors, since the platform itself could never come under legal fire for hosting that content.

The second common rule is one against hate speech. The definition of hate speech varies, but in non-specific terms, hate speech is speech that incites the hatred of others based on factors such as religion, nationality, race, gender, sexual orientation, and disability. These factors are typically seen as protected classes in the United States, and thus, any speech against them should be categorized differently. Hate speech is a real category of speech, the problem always comes down to the one doing the categorizing.

I believe that hate speech itself completely falls under the umbrella of protected speech. Protected classes in the United States are typically only protected from discrimination in legal agreements, such as employment, landlord-tenant relationships, etc. There is nothing provisioned in United States law which protects protected classes from hate speech they might encounter, and the Supreme Court even declared that it is legally protected free speech.

This makes any rule banning hate speech to be categorically different than a rule banning the inciting of violence: one is illegal under United States law and one is not. Further, any consequences of hosting both kinds of speech would never be the responsibility of the platform itself, under United States' Internet laws. This means that the decision to ban both is always the ideological reflection of those who run the platform.

## Online Censorship is Anti-American

What's scary is how disconnected this sentiment is from American ideals. The First Amendment specifically protects offensive speech and hate speech, but nearly every online platform bans it in droves. The First Amendment wouldn't have to exist if hateful and offensive speech didn't. If everyone's opinion was pre-approved and non-controversial before it exited their mouth, or was guaranteed to promote tolerance, peace, and acceptance, then there simply would be no need for the First Amendment.

But that's not the case, we know that people say controversial things all the time. People challenge the status quo, write provocative articles about their politicians, and express themselves in ways that make others feel uncomfortable. The First Amendment wouldn't need to protect any kind of speech if everyone simply agreed with everyone else's worldview and politics, but in reality people find disagreements in these spaces quite often. We need the First Amendment to protect ourselves from a conformist state of the world. The First Amendment exists to facilitate the "question everything" mentality that challenges the mainstream mentality.

In 2016, Pew Research conducted a poll which posed the question to Americans: "should citizens be able to make public statements that are offensive to minority groups, or should the government be able to prevent people from saying these things?" Every category of respondent (race, generation/age, political party, and education) gave a majority response of in favor of the citizens' ability to make those offensive statements. There were trends down in some categories; for example, Millennials only agreed with the first statement 58% of the time, down from Generation X's 70%, Baby Boomers at 71%, and the Silent Generation's gigantic 80%. The overall response was clear: There is no category of Americans that doesn't have majority support for the freedom to say offensive statements.[3]

While the majority of Americans in every category are in agreement about the freedom of speech, online platforms are taking a completely opposite approach. Nearly all of them ban hate speech as they interpret it. Online platforms that don't have anti-hate speech rules, like Gab (a social media platform dedicated to free speech), are blacklisted by technology companies that typically offer necessary support to social media platforms.

It seems that the technology giants have intentionally created rules that represent anti-American ideals. This is a rather infuriating circumstance, especially considering that the law tells those companies that they don't have to be quick or heavy on censorship. The law explicitly says that those companies need not be held liable for the content they host, yet these rules about content posting still exist.

## How the Unregulated Free Market Creates Unwanted Power Dynamics

It is, of course, important to note that these companies are not public entities. The rules that they create and enforce are created and enforced at their own discretion. It's a beautiful attribute of our free market. The online platforms have a duty to represent themselves in a way that looks good to consumers and other companies that want to do business with them.

All is fair in the free market, so banning controversial opinions or users can be incredibly effective at creating a more attractive platform. A company may not want to buy an advertisement if it may be displayed next to a post that degrades homosexual people. A company may not want to interact with users on a site where those same users can share pornography. However, an NHL team definitely wants their merchandise pushed next to a post discussing a hockey tournament.

These problems can be hard to control, especially since signing up for these websites is simple, and posting is stupidly easy. Thus, simple and vague rules are created, and the censorship begins. Accounts are banned, posts are deleted, and the platform looks cleaner as a result. It is easy, perhaps too easy, for these companies to get away with mass censorship without a care for the public's opinion. When power has no responsibility, everyone suffers power's wrath.

When the companies have as much power as they do, however, there is a legitimate cause for concern about how they use that power.

When these companies have the power to control public opinions, censor members of the public, and gather potentially blackmail-level incriminating evidence against them, fair play simply must be enforced. The draw of power is too alluring to be self-controlled.

Because every platform is private and acts on their own rules, there is no baseline for how we expect these companies to act. If another company wants to buy a $10 million-dollar ad campaign on a platform, but doesn't want that platform to host any anti-Christian opinions, there is nothing from stopping that platform from starting to unfairly apply their hate speech rules to users who post anti-Christian content. That platform is of course free to do this, and doesn't have to alert a soul to what they've done—even though their actions are anti-American and don't do the First Amendment justice.

There even exists a shady practice called shadow banning. A shadow ban is placed on a user which drastically reduces the amount to which a user's content shows up to the public discourse. Only people who explicitly follow or subscribe to the shadow banned user will see their content, while anyone who doesn't know of the user will never see a post of theirs. In addition, the user is not alerted of this restriction on their posts' visibility. This is an incredibly subversive and sneaky action to take against a user, but of course, it is completely within the rights of online platforms to do so, without notice to the affected users.

There exists too much power, in theory and in actuality, within these platforms. The amount of traffic that only a few platforms entertain constitutes the need for oversight. These platforms should be held responsible, for their abilities have the power to sway elections and public opinion, all with their user base and the public being none the wiser.

## Hate Speech Rules are an Affront to American Unity

Hate speech rules on online platforms hinder trust in the platform and make the platform a player instead of a referee. In addition to being intentionally vague for the purpose of mass censorship, hate speech rules are also not applied equally at all, ruining faith in their effectiveness. If rules like these are going to exist, which I don't think they should, then they need to be applied fairly. Anything less is political censorship and acting under bad faith.

There are many one-off examples of online platforms using hate speech to remove content from one side but not the other. A common one people may remember comes from August of 2018. When an American journalist Sarah Jeong was announced to be joining the *New York Times* editorial board, she was discovered to have made racist tweets toward white people. As a form of protest, conservative commentator Candace Owens tweeted the exact same tweets as Jeong, except swapping out the words "white" with "black" and sometimes "Jewish." Owens' Twitter account received a suspension for hate speech; Jeong's did not.[4]

This is a good example of why companies like Twitter have no business being a referee. When it's clear that a good many tweets could be removed under the same premise by which other tweets are removed, and there seems to be no effort to fix the discrepancy, people rightfully begin to question the motives of these companies. When some racist tweets go unremoved, and others made in protest to those tweets do get removed, it feels like Twitter is sending a message of endorsement to one form of racism and denouncing another.

Rules like these need to be abolished or become better regulated. An online platform with a huge user base, like Twitter, should not be able to pull the curtain over its processes, especially when the results of those processes become so detached from the mission statement. If the specific race being targeted is going to be a factor in these decisions, that makes Twitter liable to many existing anti-discrimination rules. I can see why Twitter would want to keep a lid on the process, but when the American public feels censored and discriminated against, something must change.

I suggest doing away with anti-hate speech rules entirely. This doesn't mean that people wouldn't have the ability to do things like block others or unsubscribe to certain feeds. But those decisions would have to be made by the people who consciously don't want to see that content anymore. Having the platform itself involved in creating unsupervised processes and removing content and users on the basis of unclear rules is not a sustainable method for unifying online discourse. It only breaks us apart and makes us angry with each other.

## Twitter Policing Arguments Derails Argumentation

Another way Twitter abuses its rules against hate speech is to ban voices in hotly debated topics. If Twitter wants to say that race realism (the idea that races have enough physical differences to warrant discrimination) is hate speech, so be it. The science on this has been discussed for hundreds of years and almost always leads to the conclusion that race realism is incorrect and need not be entertained. What isn't decided science, however, are topics relating to transgender people.

There currently exists a cultural impasse in feminism, where the issues of transgender women are being debated as true issues of women or not. Some feminists specifically argue that trans women ought not to be involved in the feminist movement for not being "real women." Personally, I think this is wrong and would qualify as hate speech, as it is very offensive to trans women, but I'm a cisgendered male.

The issue is that the science on these topics hasn't been settled yet. Or at least, it hasn't been settled for a long period of time. The issues that come from how transgenderism intersects with existing social movements are relatively new to our culture. The initial science looks to be against the side of the trans-exclusionary feminists, but at this point in time, it is too early to declare one side the politically and/or scientifically correct winner.

The fact that these are new topics hasn't stopped Twitter from banning trans-exclusionary feminists from their platform for hate speech. I have a problem with this for two reasons. First, no one should ever get banned for hate speech, because that's anti-American and pro-societal bubble dictated by the platform.

Secondly, I don't think that Twitter should be the deciding entity of who is right and who is wrong. Especially in an argument this new, it seems like Twitter is caving in to pressure, trying to be politically correct before the underlying cases have been made. If I ran Twitter, I'd simply say "throw it to the sharks." Let them have a good faith debate, bring up facts and evidence, and decide who is correct among themselves.

Instead, Twitter forced one group into the echo chamber and the other into the cage. Twitter now categorizes misgendering (calling a trans person by the wrong pronouns) and deadnaming (calling a trans person by their former, or "dead," name) as examples of hate speech on their platform. Following this perceived victory, the transgender community started becoming more vocally abusive to the way that they talked about their nay-sayers on Twitter. This prompted Twitter to start banning some transgendered users as a result of their own hate speech for how they talked about their ideological opponents.

The debate about who was in the right and wrong to say certain things was actually brought to the UK Parliament in May 2019. On the one side, the transgendered community argued that the other side was denying their existence and validity and that was transphobic hate speech. On the other side, the anti-trans group said that, as a group of mostly women, that they were being targeted for their opinions in ways that resemble misogyny.[5]

But one thing was abundantly clear: this was no longer an ideological debate. This was not a good faith attempt to convince others of one's side. This was a food fight where each side was trying to get the other banned off social media to try and silence their opinions, and it was all made possible because of Twitter's hate speech rules and their inherent problems of fairness.

These restrictions on what could be called hate speech made it impossible for arguers to accurately describe the problems they were wishing to discuss. These forced truths are damaging to debate and are anti-progressive. Progress should come from science, not a doctrine. But such is the state of the post-truth world. People have a right to come to their own conclusions with their own evidence. Further, they have an obligation to the public to engage dissenters and have truth-finding dialogue with open minds - lest they be cast out as ignorant.

## Reddit Censorship

Twitter is not the only online platform to have engaged in this form of spotty censorship. Reddit, an online platform known for its ability to filter users based on topic, has battled to apply rules fairly. Reddit has only a few sitewide rules, such as rules against inciting violence, hate speech, and real-life identity disclosure. Reddit's content, for the most part, is policed by volunteer moderators dedicated to watching over their communities, or "subreddits." However, when moderators fail to enforce Reddit's rules, Reddit has been quick to shut down their communities completely.

There exist transparency problems in Reddit's operations as well. Seemingly without appeal, right-wing conspiracy subreddits are shut down instantly. The most prominent conservative subreddit, one dedicated to memes and news about President Trump, had special rules placed on it to stop it from appearing in sitewide aggregation lists (much like the "trending" sections of other online platforms).

Not knowing the process of banning decisions and appealing has really hurt Reddit's ability to credibly address its own community, with people upset that some communities got banned and other people upset that other communities have yet to be banned. When Reddit was started, it took it upon itself to have a doctrine of absolute free speech.

As Reddit learned over the years, this wasn't entirely possible, as some content is too controversial for a top Internet site to host.

In June 2015, Reddit hired Ellen Pao to replace resigned Chief Executive Officer Yishan Wong. Pao's arrival came with a banning of five hate subreddits, including one cleverly titled "fatpeoplehate." Pao's views on censorship were seen as a massive step in the wrong direction for the website by its users. For this reason, among others, Pao resigned her role as CEO after just a month.

However, in many ways the damage had been done. Reddit had joined the league of online platforms that were willing to commit to censorship of hate speech, a departure from their original credence of absolute free speech. Even after Pao's departure, the culture at Reddit remains tense, at least for communities with less palatable topics. Communities with questionable content are constantly in communication with site administrators to ensure that they aren't axed.

Since Pao's departure, Reddit has banned communities dedicated to shoplifting, right wing conspiracy theories, involuntary celibacy ("incel"), selling guns, racism, and videos of people dying. In some cases, like the banning of GunsForSale, Reddit wanted to avoid any legal repercussions for potentially exposing a loophole in federal law. In most cases, Reddit used its rules of banning content that "incites violence" as the official reason for removal. However, it is atypical for Reddit to provide official statements as to why certain subreddits are banned, and explanations for removal reasons typically come from the moderators of the banned communities relaying what the Reddit administrators told them.

Reddit was supposed to be one of the places on the Internet where free speech would be maintained. As it grew in popularity, and grew to have fewer visionary leaders, it's modus operandi changed to start including some exceptions to the rules. Of course the applications of these rules aren't fair or transparent, but that's what we've come to expect from online platforms in general. All across the Internet anti-hate speech rules inspire hypocrisy, kill discussion, and instill a culture of despair where creators try to gain an edge in a system rigged against them.

## Trending Sections

Nearly every social media website and news aggregator has built-in features which pick out and promote content to users. Using Reddit as an example, when one first goes to the website they see a list of posts and links which have all been posted fairly recently and are popular. Even someone without an account will see this content. What they won't see, however, is the plethora of content that was filtered out to not be shown as the current hottest items, nor the decision-making process into how those items were or weren't selected. While that seems like it wouldn't be a problem, many platforms have had trouble with upholding neutrality on their "trending" lists—so much trouble that oversight may be necessary.

Take YouTube's Trending section. "Trending" appears as the second option in a list to the left-hand side of the screen on the homepage of YouTube. When clicked on, the user is shown a list of videos that have recently been uploaded. The content generally consists of highlights from sports games, new music videos posted by popular artists, new trailers for anticipated movies, and new videos uploaded by popular YouTube creators.

The idea of trending, to the uninformed user, would be to show a list of the most popular, recently uploaded videos to YouTube so the user can stay up to date on the Internet and understand what's received the most traffic. Informed users, however, know that the page is not all that it appears to be. By going to Google's support page for YouTube's Trending section, it appears that there are a couple other rules in place, other than simply being a new video with a lot of views.

The aforementioned support page describes what it takes to get onto the Trending section:

> Trending aims to surface videos that:
> Are appealing to a wide range of viewers.
> Are not misleading, clickbaity, or sensational.
> Capture the breadth of what's happening on YouTube and in the world.
> Ideally, are surprising or novel.
>
> Trending aims to balance all of these considerations. To achieve this, Trending considers many signals, including (but not limited to):
> View count.
> The rate of growth in views
> Where views are coming from (including outside of YouTube)
> The age of the video.
>
> … We combine these signals to produce a list of videos that showcases what's happening on YouTube and in the world. The Trending system tries to choose videos that will be most relevant to our viewers and most reflective of the broad content on the platform.

The second section, which describes the metrics used to determine what is trending, is reasonable. Of course YouTube would use view count, view growth, external references, and upload date for that decision. The first section, however, which describes the other criteria which a video needs to meet in order to make the list, is not reasonable. It is the epitome of what these online platforms use to subvert the expectations of the user's experience.

By writing these rules in such a vague and broad way, YouTube has simultaneously given itself the power to exclude a vast number of videos and freed themselves from having to justify those videos not making the list. Seasoned users of online platforms have grown to expect this kind of behavior, but to the untrained or unobservant users, the experience is quite the opposite. To these users, the Trending section is a completely procedurally generated list of the most popular videos that have recently been uploaded.

There is no giant banner that hangs underneath the Trending section which boldly proclaims that every video on the list has been vetted by a group of conflicted and biased employees of YouTube. There is no disclaimer about the discrete process used to determine the section's videos. The process itself isn't even clearly defined to the public—entirely to the benefit of YouTube and to the detriment of the user's experience.

Even the support page, which does list the rules of Trending in its own vague manner, requires some investigating to find. Without the curiosity to imagine something strange going on with the Trending page, or the information being presented to them, how many people would know of the vague rules and processes that define the section? How many people who go to Trending frequently understand the filtering and gaming that goes into choosing those videos?

In the age of declining cable viewership, and all the missed profits, YouTube Trending is used as a way to get views on classic cable shows, particularly late night and talk shows. Nearly every one of these cable programs uploads clips and full episodes of their programs to YouTube. In some cases, such as with *The Tonight Show* and *Jimmy Kimmel Live!*, those videos end up being featured on YouTube Trending. Similar evidence exists that low-view, definitely-not-trending videos uploaded by the NFL channel have made it into YouTube Trending, inspiring criticisms and accusations.

It's critical that social media platforms like YouTube represent themselves in clear and transparent ways to all users on their platforms. If YouTube allows payment or exchanges for the ability to get onto their promotion pages, then surely they are responsible for disclosing that in some manner. Whether that "sure responsibility" is a codified legal responsibility or simply a downtrodden moral one, it exists, somewhere.

## YouTube Trending Has Bias Problems

In addition to accusations of paid involvement from some companies, there are also people who have accused the platform of not playing fair among YouTube creators. To be clear, I'm referring to people who upload exclusively to YouTube, unlike the NFL YouTube channel which hosts its content on YouTube as well as cable and other online platforms.

In January 2018, YouTube creator Logan Paul uploaded a video in which he filmed a dead body in Aokigahara, a forest in Japan (known colloquially as "the Suicide Forest"). The video was grotesque, disrespectful, and inhumane. It also was completely unsuitable for children, or as YouTube would describe their Trending section, "appealing to a wide range of viewers." Not only did the video's content include the dead body, it also included the body in the video's thumbnail.

Paul had a status amongst YouTube for generally making safe, non-controversial videos (a majority of Paul's content is his daily video blogging). When the video was uploaded, it quickly became the number one video on YouTube Trending. While the video was eventually removed by Paul, and he faced a large amount of deserved public criticism for uploading such shocking and disrespectful content, it highlighted questions many people had been asking about the Trending section.

Certain YouTube creators, who had never been featured in YouTube's Trending section, began to question the vetting process. The lack of transparency around the process became a critical question, as the process which seemed to always discriminate against certain creators had let a video featuring a dead body slip through the cracks. Some of YouTube's creators allege that these decisions are always biased against them, and vice versa for other creators like Paul.

Felix Kjellberg, the Swedish YouTube creator who operates the most-subscribed YouTube channel "PewDiePie," said this about YouTube's Trending section: "They should honestly just rename it 'YouTube Staff Picks,'"[6;7] again alleging bias in the selection process. Keep in mind that this selection of videos is the second menu option on YouTube, meaning it is a place where uninformed or new users will likely go. The page also does not indicate its potential misleading or non-transparent selection process, which is further subversive of what the user would expect.

The problems with YouTube's transparency in their algorithms go beyond getting onto the Trending section. The Verge reported that a great deal of YouTube creators have taken up arms about the platform's algorithms, claiming that the platform doesn't allow them to take breaks or go on vacation lest they pay heavy costs due to their channels losing momentum. This has led to a massive burnout among YouTube creators. The Verge also reported that YouTube's manual process of "demonetizing" content, in which creators won't receive money for views on controversial, vulgar, or offensive content, was equally frustrating for YouTubers. These processes also suffer from a lack of transparency and oversight.[8] YouTube search engines have also been manually manipulated to lower visibility on certain views on political issues in favor of promoting opposite views, such as in the previously discussed case where pro-life videos on abortion were pushed out in favor of pro-choice videos.[9]

YouTube's processes, algorithms, and procedures are massively failing to meet the trust requirements of its users. YouTube, as a dominant social media platform, should make substantive efforts to regain the confidence across its user base that it acts in unbiased, completely algorithmic, and fair manner. One way to accomplish this would be to show the public, or even just regulators, the inner workings of the company's secretive operations to prove they are not manipulative nor biased.

## Twitter Trending Problems

YouTube Trending is not the only "aggregator" of online trends that people use to help keep informed on hot topics. Twitter too has a feature called Twitter Trending which has received an extreme amount of criticism as well, and Facebook also used to have a Trending section that was removed after it faced criticisms of bias and censorship.

Twitter's Trending section was perhaps the first of its kind. Since Twitter always relied on Tweets carrying Hashtags, it was easy to aggregate topics in concise naming conventions—since the users were already doing it. Even as early as 2011 Twitter Trending got accused of censorship, in the case of the #OccupyWallStreet hashtag not making it to the Trending section. This caused outrage, and for the first time, users had to deal with a non-transparent algorithm on a social media not rating their posts to their liking.

The problem has persisted. During the 2016 US presidential election cycle, it seemed that the new scandals and disturbing information we learned about each candidate would never cease. In July, WikiLeaks released emails which incriminated the Democratic National Committee (DNC) in rigging their primary election in favor of Hillary Clinton, an establishment Democrat, against the further left, anti-establishment candidate Bernie Sanders.

The emails were damning. To save face before the election, the chair of the DNC had to resign her position. After the election, the DNC was forced to pay out a class action lawsuit to Bernie Sanders campaign donors, since the emails proved that the election had essentially been rigged. While the Internet was zestfully reading the emails, the hashtag #DNCLeaks became trending on Twitter. Soon after, it was removed from the Trending list, sparking outrage amongst users and accusations that Twitter had engaged political censorship in favor of a candidate.

This wasn't the only time Twitter abused its Trending section's powers during that election cycle. Famously, with less than two weeks before the election, then-FBI Director James Comey reopened an investigation into candidate Clinton. When he cleared her of the investigation just 2 days before the election, Twitter made an unprecedented move: they manually entered a topic and a description into the top of their Trending section.

The trend was inserted with the topic "FBI Director Comey," and a description of "F.B.I. Director says Clinton won't be charged over latest email scandal." Typically in Twitter's Trending section, the topic is a short set of words or a hashtag that got picked up by a lot of traffic, such as "Donald Trump" or "#NotMyPresident." There's no realistic way that enough people spelled out the phrase "FBI Director Comey" to tweet about the incident. Further, the description area is used to say how many tweets or users are using the topic. In this case, that data wasn't presented, instead it was overlaid by a description of the topic, which is almost never presented.

This was a completely subversive maneuver done to educate as many people as possible about Hillary Clinton's exoneration. People logging in to Twitter, unaware of Twitter's gaming their own system, might have believed people were talking about that topic the most, since the topic was number one on the Trending list. It's dishonest, and it was incredibly biased as well.

Let's be clear about how important news aggregator lists are. Twitter's Trending section is such a cultural and social indicator that people have built entire websites and archives to documenting it hour by hour for years on end. It is a powerful tool that could be, and often is, used for evil. If a powerful person wanted to reduce visibility into a story, getting it off Twitter's Trending section would be a good place to start.

Of course, Twitter has never released the actual process in which they select Trending topics, so to them, there was no foul play. The American people need to start expecting more from these companies—we need more oversight into how these powerful tools work to make sure they are used to benefit us, not to sneakily push topics and remove unappealing ones.

## Facebook's Trending Section

Facebook has come under fire for their Trending section as well, so much so that they actually removed the feature altogether. The problems Facebook faced were twofold: on the one hand, Facebook's automated processes let misleading and false stories to become Trending, and on the other hand, their manual intervention in the processes were shown to be too biased. Over time, users grew to not trust the tool, and Facebook removed it for being less and less useful.

As with many issues surrounding Internet censorship, Facebook's woes started in 2016. In a report published by Gizmodo, Facebook workers admitted to suppressing conservative news stories from appearing in Trending. Topics such as CPAC (Conservative Political Action Conference), Mitt Romney (former Republican nominee for President), and Lois Lerner (IRS official criticized for biasedly targeting conservative groups and voters) were stopped from being added to the Trending section even though there was high conversation traffic. In addition to blocking conservative news, Facebook also put selected stories into the Trending section, even if the traffic on those stories/topics was low.[10]

The people who did this were known colloquially as "news curators," and their responsibilities were to maintain the list and to offer support for it, for example, writing concise summaries of the content. I speak in the past tense because the whole section of the website is no more. The curators worked around the clock, always watching and monitoring the list. In this way, the bias of the list could change hour-by-hour, just depending on who was making the decisions. That being said, the number of conservative curators was "a very small handful."

Another way in which bias was applied from the management-level was through the banning of conservative news sites. If a story originated on Breitbart or The Washington Examiner, it would have to be published by CNN or *The New York Times* before it could be posted to the Trending section. This not only made conservative news less likely to make it to the section, but also made the interpretation of the story more left-leaning, since the link would be to CNN's coverage of Breitbart's story instead of Breitbart's original story itself.

It's important not to attribute to malice what could be attributed to stupidity. It's very possible that Facebook's management team was looking for ways to remain competitive with other online platforms' trending sections, for example, Twitter's. By creating a means to insert news stories, the ends might not have been societal media manipulation, but rather just to keep up with stories that have picked up elsewhere but not yet on Facebook. This is all likely, but in the face of the actual admitting of bias, it is harder to believe.

Many efforts were made, both by the management and the workers themselves, to make sure Facebook Trending was not representative of the truth, but rather a fantasy world where only left-leaning opinions, stories, and biases are valued. These efforts and results lead to probably the dastardliest subversive efforts to disguise biased and distorted news as neutral and organic. There was never a disclaimer on Facebook's Trending section. There was no indicator that the list had been altered, censored, filtered, or changed to remove certain topics and manually add others.

The level of influence that these decisions had means that the window needs to be opened. The people need to know what goes on behind these closed doors. Upwards of two billion people use Facebook. It is unbelievable that this kind of lying and twisting of reality was able to happen without disclosure for so long. I am happy that Facebook shut down the section. It might be the only example of a social media company showing self-control over the power they have.

It is time to pull back the curtain on these manipulative and subversive tactics. Online platforms have shown that the algorithms they use are too flawed to be outside the public's oversight. Transparency must be increased, and if it isn't, we'll live in a world where we're only shown subtly filtered results and fake trends. Either the algorithms must change to be less prone to bias, or the people need to be alerted that something as harmless as a trending section could be a manufactured and fake list, not indicative at all of what it claims.

## Mass Banning of Ideological Opposition

It was revealed, in advance of the 2018 US midterm elections, that Google, Microsoft, Snapchat, Twitter, Facebook, and others were invited to meet in secrecy to discuss strategy for the election. The (leaked) email, which betrayed the meeting's secrecy, described the meeting as a follow-up, indicating that a previous secret meeting had occurred with no intent to inform the public or Congress.[11] Keep in mind, many of these companies' owners were being pulled in front of Congress in 2018 to talk about their practices, specifically in regard to allegations of election interference in 2016.

It's easy, given that we know these companies are meeting secretly, to understand why there are so many similarities of how they operate. It's easy to deduce why they nearly never take different stances on the social and ethical issues posed to them, and why their internal operations are all similarly opaque and subversive.

The nature of the technology industry limits the viability of the free market. When analyzing how a new company might start up, there are a lot of factors that are specific to the world of technology. For example, no one expects that when a new online shopping company starts, that the company will have to rebuild the Internet and connect the 3.2 billion Internet users on their own. Instead, the actual access to the Internet is fairly well-maintained as a free right. It's a given when planning a company that those resources will be there.

There are plenty of other features which the company might expect to be available as well. For example, they will expect to be able to pay someone to host their website on their servers. They will expect to be able to use code languages to build the website. They will expect Internet service providers to fulfill requests to their website's address. They expect that their consumer's devices, the hardware, the operating system, the web browser, etc. will all be free to integrate with.

Further, they may expect to be able to brand themselves on social media. This means they expect Google to allow them to have a YouTube channel, Facebook to allow them to make posts, Twitter to allow them an account, etc. They might also expect a payment processing service, like PayPal or Patreon, to facilitate online financial transactions (pretty important for our fictitious shopping company).

The problem with the technology industry is that sometimes the cards don't line up. Amazon might very well see the company as a competitor to their online shopping services, and they might decline the company access to use Amazon Web Services to host any website. PayPal might decide that it will not be processing the company's transactions, for one reason or another. The problem with the technology industry is that so much of what a layman might see as a given is actually owned by private entities (usually within the existent group of big technology companies), and those private entities have rights.

This is happening with the introduction of Gab (Gab.ai) to the online social media sphere. Gab was created as a reaction to the social media atmosphere of the 2016 presidential election. After seeing that many social media sites, like Facebook and Twitter, were banning conservative content, Gab was created as a "free speech" platform. The website marketed itself as a Twitter alternative without any complicated or biased algorithms that sought to silence users and posters of specific political leanings.

Now, I won't defend the user base or content that is hosted on Gab. Nearly all the content is far-right, a good portion of it anti-Semitic, Nazi-praising, and racist—all of which I despise. However, I will give the company props to the fact that they have succeeded in their mission. In the three years since its launch, there doesn't appear to be a single case of unjust banning of users, deletion of content, or shady algorithmic workings. The kind of cases which diminish our trust in traditional social media seemingly daily.

I would never go on Gab, but my reasoning is the users and content, not the administration.

Since its launch, Gab has run into quite a few of the aforementioned theoretical problems. They've had trouble finding other tech companies to integrate with, due to its user base's opinions. Like I said before, some of what is said and discussed on that platform is abhorrent. For example, the 2018 Pittsburgh Synagogue shooter was a frequent poster of anti-Semitic content on Gab. Gab was fully cooperative with the police force in their investigation of that user.

Apple and Google removed the Gab application from their App Store and Play Store, making it impossible to have the application on any Android or iOS device. It has been banned on the Microsoft Azure and Joyent hosting platforms, meaning they'd have to run and own their own servers for their website to "live" somewhere. Domain register GoDaddy banned them, meaning that they'd have to find someone else to perpetuate their web address to Internet service providers. The payment processing companies PayPal and Stripe both banned Gab, so they didn't have a way to process financial transactions. The blog platform Medium banned them, the e-commerce service Shopify banned them, the list goes on.

The reason cited for banning is always hate speech. Just to be clear, Gab as a company has never said anything or done anything hateful or racist or anti-Semitic. The problem is that the technology ecosystem believes that kind of speech should be removed, and Gab does not. All Gab does is host content, and refuses to be the arbitrator of truth on what is hateful and what is truthful. It simply does not even play the game, and that difference in ideology is enough to cause a mass banishment of the platform from the technology world.

Another problem with the banishments is that they always seem to snowball. It never appears as if each company sits back and makes their own decision independently. It honestly feels like collusion. I can understand why an event like the Pittsburgh Shooting would cause companies to think twice about the companies they integrate with, but other banishments have been less prompted.

On August 6, 2018, the right-wing conspiracy theorist Alex Jones and his company Infowars experienced one of these banishments. Jones, through Infowars, delivers a daily radio show/podcast discussing politics, usually from a far-right perspective. In one day, he and his Infowars accounts were all removed from YouTube, Spotify, Apple, and Facebook.[12] Each company had an individual response (all citing hate speech) posted along with his banning in a decisive twelve-hour period. Ask yourself how this was possible—that 4 huge players in the technology industry all were prepared to ban and make a statement on one single person on one day?

It feels ironic to ask these questions, given Jones's background as a conspiracy theorist, but it is necessary. How is this not a blatant showing of antitrust in the technology world? This legitimately does feel like conspiracy. Are there even any laws that exist that would prevent this abuse of power? Given my knowledge of the limited laws that the private tech companies operate under, I'd venture not.

Twitter completed the social media purge a month later. Just like that, a right-wing radio host had gone from a-okay with every social media company's community policies to being in ban-worthy violation. It's worth reiterating that there was no "prompting" event for Jones's banning, no crazy statement, no call for violence, etc. which is different in a sense to the banning of Gab which did mostly take place after the Pittsburgh Shooting.

In a 2016 speech, US Senator Elizabeth Warren made claims that Google, Apple, and Amazon use their powers as technology companies to "snuff out competition." In Google's case, she cited Google using its search engine power to "harm rivals of its Google Plus user review feature." She claimed Apple had placed limits on other music streaming applications on Apple devices, making it harder for them to compete with Apple Music. Lastly, she said that Amazon double-dipping as a bookseller and a book publisher had led to their own books being favored at "the detriment of other publishers."[13]

So I don't blame those companies for playing nice with each other—they have a mutually beneficial existence. It's then easy to follow why they might arrive at the same conclusions on the ethical problems that exist in the industry. However, when those conclusions differ so vastly from what the public wants, or when they impact our lives so greatly and quickly that the public doesn't even get a say, therein lies the need for regulation. When those companies cannot be trusted to act in good faith and provide a level playing field for competition, therein lies the need for a referee.

## Newt Gingrich Promotes Felonizing ISIS Website Visits

We must hold politicians' feet to the fire who don't understand the seriousness of Internet censorship. No form of political censorship is acceptable, all of it is a violation of our First Amendment rights. It is unfortunate that there are some political figures who see Internet censorship as beneficial, and believe that Internet monitoring of citizens is justified.

Newt Gingrich, who was the Speaker of the House in the 1990s, was invited to be a guest on Fox News in July 2016. On the network, he claimed that anyone who even visits problematic websites should be thrown into jail. "Anybody who goes on a website favoring ISIS, or Al Qaeda, or other terrorist groups, that should be a felony and they should go to jail. Any organization which hosts such a website should be engaged in a felon. It should be closed down immediately."[14]

The former Speaker and Republican presidential candidate is offering two ridiculous solutions. The first solution is that anyone, presumably any American, should serve jail time for even venturing to a website owned by terrorists. What if a member of the media goes to the website to research their political positions? What if someone online clicks on a link to the webpage, unknowing of its content? Should all these people be jailed?

Newt, again presumably, is operating under the assumption that simple exposure to these ideologies will automatically persuade individuals to join them. I think this is a dangerously low expectation to have for the American public. We live in the enlightened West where we have conversations about controversial topics daily. No ideas are off limits to the course of debate, and Newt's solution would only punish people for engaging in political discourse.

Newt's second solution is charge anyone who hosts or facilitates these websites with felonies. This goes back to the fact that websites need some support from other companies in order to be accessible. This support includes hosting/server companies, Internet service providers being willing to give access to the website, browsers needing to support generating the website, etc. Under Newt's statement, all these companies could be charged as felons.

It should be noted that companies don't always explicitly know what they are supporting and hosting, at least not content-wise. If a company currently using Amazon Web Services to host their servers suddenly wanted to change all their websites to say "JOIN ISIS," it wouldn't be on Amazon to constantly be monitoring that content. Similarly, if ISIS uses a free open source project, such as Babel (a Javascript compiling project/tool), it is not Babel's prerogative to know that ISIS downloaded their software and is using it.

At this point, it's worth calling into question Newt's understanding of the Internet. How many companies does he believe are implicitly involved with hosting a website? If he understood the breadth of his punishing solution, I doubt he'd maintain his position. Or maybe he is that authoritarian.

Also, we must examine his commitment to the freedoms of speech and expression granted to us Americans by the Constitution. Certainly, if someone were to state publicly their ideological support for ISIS or other terrorist groups, they should not be punished by law (assuming that they are not breaking laws regarding the incitement of violence). The people who bore witness to this declaration should also not be punished by law. Why should this interaction play out differently over the Internet?

I do commend Newt for proposing reactionary regulations on technology companies for what he perceives to be violations. I don't think Newt is making the right choices, however. He should find a rediscovered faith in the American people to sift through and discard wretched and extreme ideologies, like those of radical terrorist groups. Newt should suggest more informed policy changes, not zero policy changes.

This specific case of political punditry represents the many risks that come when people with power fail to think critically about the problems posed by technology. It's emblematic of a wider problem where the residual effects and ongoing philosophies are ignored for quick solutions. As we'll examine in the next section, lack of technical understanding among our political class is not fully to blame. There are politicians who do understand the amount of power that technology holds, but want to harness it for the suppression of Americans rather than their freedom.

## Ted Lieu Asks Social Media Companies to Censor Speech

Ted Lieu is a member of the US Congress, a Democrat. He's an actor from the other side of the aisle (than Newt Gingrich) who also needs a more established faith in American ideals and the American people. In late 2018, Lieu made an incredibly deaf statement about limiting the speech of Americans. Lieu said he wished he could take away the freedom of speech from some people but understood that he's constitutionally prohibited from that censorship.

> I would love to be able to regulate the content of speech. The First Amendment prevents me from doing so. And that's simply a function of the First Amendment. But I think over the long run, it's better that the government does not regulate the content of speech. I would urge these private sector companies to regulate it better themselves. But it's really nothing that I believe government can do. And so that's been my position all along.[15]

There are a couple things wrong with Lieu's commentary. First, he should recognize that the First Amendment is not a nuisance, but a fundamental right of being American. No one should ever wish for the ability to regulate it, especially not a politician in a position in power. I think Lieu is basing his comments on a false, negative perception of Americans and their ability to engage in discussion and discourse without the aid of the aid of an outside force.

Secondly, he recognizes that technology companies in the private sector have the ability to perform the political censorship he wishes he could. This is correct; those companies do have that massive power, but Lieu makes a hard turn in the wrong direction by asking them to engage in more political censorship. Instead, he should realize the importance of giving these companies less power and more responsibility.

Again, Lieu should realize that the First Amendment isn't an inconvenient obstacle in the way of the progressive utopia. The First Amendment protects the fundamental American right to freedom of speech and expression. US based companies should be held more accountable to the First Amendment, instead of being encouraged to use their power as a means to bypass it. I completely disagree with Lieu's approach and attitude toward fundamental American values. Educating politicians on the power of modern technology is only part of the battle, we also have to ensure that those politicians try to limit that power, not encourage its power to be used for authoritarian and suppressive purposes.

## Examine the CDA to See Who It Benefits

The freedom to assemble and collectively organize, protest, and defend ideology is a civil and political right. For Americans, it is a right protected by the Constitution. We must account for the fact that the means in which collective organization and activism for the public has changed in the digital age. There is no difference between the town square of old and the Internet forum of new. Chat rooms, discussion boards, and forums on the Internet have become the new means of public assembly.

It is absolutely crucial that the United States enforce that its citizens' freedom to assemble is guaranteed even if the mode of organizing is different. The ability to share, discuss, and debate political ideologies is too important of a price to pay for the convenience of technology. Of course there will be hateful, disgusting ideologies that will be openly discussed and expressed. The way to fight is through discourse and debate, not through censorship and bias.

The 1996 Communications Decency Act (CDA) allows Internet service providers and Internet platforms to play a third-party observer role in the content on their services by ensuring that they will not be held liable for any obscene or illegal content hosted on their platforms. A very key portion of the law allows for these ISPs and Internet platforms to act in good faith in regard to censorship.

This is contentious, however, since it ambiguously allows for these services to censor and remove some unclear content while not demanding strictly for fairness, only to act in good faith. Internet platforms have run with the idea that they can censor and remove without fear of government oversight or intervention. They learned long ago that the line between good and bad faith censorship doesn't exist. It's all for the taking when oversight is non-existent.

What followed was political censorship on massive degrees. In 2018, a Pew Research study revealed that 72% of Americans believe it is likely that social media platforms engage in political censorship when the site itself determines the views objectionable. This number is divided by political party: 85% of Republicans and Independents that lean Republican, and 62% of Democrats and Independents that lean Democrat.[16]

What's more, the companies seem to evade being put into the spotlight that has come with the accusations of political censorship. One must ask, why? If the process of political censorship is okay, and nearly three-quarters of Americans think those companies do it, what's the harm in being transparent about the processes? I think the answer is simple: under the CDA, their protections from liability come under the condition that their services act in good faith. A deep dive investigation into the algorithms would reveal the biased nature and cause them to lose their protections.

I think that the United States should do an analysis of the ambiguous clauses of the now-23-year-old CDA and how they impact the operations of Internet platforms and Internet service providers. The clauses seem to promote good faith and reasonable control over the content hosted, and they give a very powerful incentive for this offering: a lack of accountability for hosted content.

For the technology industry, it's a dream come true. It's a win-win, as the industry is no longer liable for the activities of their users coupled with an extremely low amount of oversight. However, the United States shouldn't write laws for the values of putting profits over people, and it shouldn't write laws that promote low oversight for the country's critical communications platforms. If the laws aren't benefiting the people, then there's no reason to keep them.

Another Pew Research study, this one from 2015, polled 38 countries and found that the United States is the most supportive country of free expression. 71% of Americans believe that we should be able to say what we want without government regulation, 69% believe that we should be able to use the Internet without government regulation. To quote the study: "Americans don't necessarily like offensive speech more than others, but they are much less inclined to outlaw it."[17]

It's worth pondering, then, if an unaccountable government was engaging in subversive tactics to politically censor its citizens online, would we sit back quietly? My guess, based on the vast support for Internet freedom indicated by those polls, is that we would not. What are the differences between a government using its power for this reason and a small collection of equally unaccountable private corporations using theirs?

# VI

## Doxxing

I am against private corporations gathering obscene amounts of personal details about people without the person's knowledge or consent. Similarly, I am against the Internet practice known as "doxxing." To "doxx" means to gather and create documentation of the details of somebody's life, their personal information. The word "doxx" is used because it sounds like "docs," which is short for documents. Colloquially, the verb "doxx" is used exclusively in the context of over-the-Internet research of investigating specific people in order to learn the most about their real-life and online identities as possible.

To practice doxxing, all one has to do is to expand their search of information past a single post or online platform. The goal is to find a user's entire Internet presence and the totality of their accounts across various platforms. Once that is achieved, the next step is to find out their real-life, personally identifiable information, including full name, address, phone numbers, and employment information. This becomes easier and easier with more associated accounts to pry through.

Once the party doing the doxxing has attained all the personal and online information, the goal is then to cause malice. This can be done in a number of ways. The doxxing victim can be spied on, over the Internet and in real life. Certain information can be used as blackmail against them. The victim, their family, friends, and employer can be contacted and harassed. Sometimes the doxxer will engage in "harmless" actions, like ordering pizza to the victim's residence (even though these actions are far from harmless).

Doxxing has been a problem for as long as the Internet has been utilized for social reasons, but the government response to doxxing incidents has been low. Government and the law might be hesitant to step in since the actual data collection isn't illegal. If a user chooses the same account name for a dozen different online platforms and games, there's nothing illegal about deducing that those accounts belong to a single individual. From there, it only takes a public revelation of just a couple personal details, on one of the platforms, to find out everything else.

Is this always wrong, though? Certainly not. The Internet is opt-in, and in this case, that's a bit of a negative. For a user who goes online and chooses not to be careful about the spread and publicity of their personal details, the end result is that information creating a breadcrumb trail literally to their doorstep. However, my position is that doxxing should be illegal. To be specific, the discovery, research, collection, and storage of personal details of members of the public without their consent or knowledge should not be allowed.

I'd argue that ignorance about the issue is the highest risk. Sure, users may not be voluntarily sending their address in online video game chat rooms. They may not know that a comment about their profession and the city they live in could lead to the same information being used to deduce their identity. In lieu of laws that would prevent people with bad intentions from using that information, education about online privacy must be a priority.

## The Youngest Generation Knows Better than We Did

I should note that I'm speaking more about Internet novices than users who grew up with the technology. In a leaked slide deck, Google claimed that the youngest generation of Internet users engage in self-censorship online. They understand that anything said online can be traced back to them and they don't want their personal opinions or hot takes to come back to bite them later in life.

The next generation will go through the most thoroughly vetted background checks in the history of America. Since there are no laws surrounding the abilities in which people and companies can use publicly accessible information, there could exist a "reverse-doxxing" service in the near-future. That would look like a service that takes basic identifying information, name, address, phone number, etc. (which is typically the end goal of traditional doxxing) and turn it into a data set of everything that person's said online on every platform.

We've already seen the desire for this level of background check. Anecdotally, I was told to do Facebook searches for candidates when I was a hiring manager. The direction was simple—my boss told me to "make sure they weren't the 'eff the world' type." The action, however, was invasive and not a very good judge of character.

It is nice to know that the youngest generation of Internet users takes the phrase "nothing gets deleted off the Internet" to heart. As a young social media user, I certainly didn't. When I was coming of age, my MySpace and Facebook pages were full of angsty, edgy commentary that would have scared away any potential employer. Let's say that my hormones called a few more of the shots than I would have liked. I can easily imagine losing my first employment opportunity due to a modern-day social media background check.

In the early days of social media, there was a lot of trust in the platforms to keep one's information private. As we would learn, this was incredibly naive. Nonetheless, the culture of openness and sharing in posting will probably never be matched again. The current generation knows more about the negative effects of open-book social media posting and, wisely, restricts themselves online.

## Social Media Background Checks

Are the youngest users of the Internet actually censoring themselves, or are they simply being careful about which content is posted to which account? It's not impossible to imagine that users, avoiding the social ostracism or restricted opportunities of publishing their true feelings, are using alternate and anonymous accounts to post their true feelings online. This is purely speculation, but is not outside of the realm of possibility.

It will be interesting to see how background checks will change in the future. As young people learn to better navigate around traditional pitfalls that lead to successful doxxing against them or failed background checks, will professionals start to do the social media and Internet life background checking? If young people are learning to sit behind unconnected and anonymous accounts, publishing as little information about themselves as possible, how does that change the interactions we have online?

As we continue through the post-truth era of "fake news," it will be important to hold everyone to the same standard. Fake news is any news that's made up for the purpose of propaganda; false stories, hoaxes, and disinformation all qualify as fake news. A 2019 study revealed a correlation between age and likelihood to share fake news articles: older Internet users are more likely to share unverified and false stories.[1]

Will we see a backlash against the older population as Internet background checks reveal sharing of fake news? Certainly, if we (as a society) are willing to hold a 14-year-old's character accountable to the amount of F-bombs on her social media accounts, we should also be willing to hold a 50-year-old's character accountable if she shares blatantly manufactured news articles on her online platforms.

Personally, I think that social media background checking is wrong. It introduces a lot of unwanted bias into the hiring and employment process. Especially when there's no real goal and the employer is using social media to try to judge an applicant's personality. There's a lot of risk in assuming employers can make it through that process without having a biased reaction.

Additionally, there is legal risk as well. The 1964 Civil Rights Act prohibits employers from making employment decisions based on protected class information. What if, during a social media background check, an employer found out that an applicant was gay? Or that an applicant has a disability? In some states, employers are legally prohibited from even asking those questions during the interview process for a reason—to protect the applicant from discrimination. But it's perfectly acceptable if a hiring manager finds out via a Google search? That seems unacceptable.

As the young generation learns how to navigate the openness of the Internet without fear of backlash, and the older generation digs in to social media naively as my generation did, we will start to see these large disparities. I hope that employers recognize how unusable social media background checking is and not hold anyone accountable to it. However, knowing that this advice will be ignored by some, I ask that the applications and expectations be fair for all parties, and bias left at the door.

## Celebrities Losing Jobs for Tweets

Even in modern times, celebrities and public figures have had to eat crow over their social media postings, often from years past. It's fair to say that we didn't enter the world of political correctness until 2014, at the earliest. That's not to say that political correctness didn't exist before then, just to say that it wasn't as publicly noticed and policed.

That hasn't stopped activists from going back in time and retrofitting rules against the non-politically correct speech to time periods where awareness was much lower. In 2018, Disney director James Gunn was fired after tweets were brought to light that made light of pedophilia. That same year, Kevin Hart was removed as M.C. for an award show after tweets of his surfaced that were deemed homophobic.

I don't pretend to be the judge about the damaging effects of the contents of those tweets. I won't say if they were jokes, and if they were jokes, I won't say if they were funny. At the time, however, these tweets were not worthy of the outrage. Unlike the racist *New York Times* board member, these people were not under scrutiny of getting a promotion or rising in the public eye. They had been in their positions when they made the tweets, and seemingly nothing important prompted their uncovering.

I will also make the clarification here that this wouldn't exactly qualify as doxxing. Since these people live in the public eye, and have directly tied their accounts to their professional lives; "finding out" who made the comment is a very easy task, as is holding them accountable. However, it is important to see this issue through the eyes of everyday people.

There is a danger in looking at the past through the lens of the present. If we took every person's words of the past and judged them out of context, we'd have some very strange results. Abraham Lincoln, often ranked as the best US President, made comments about black people (a majority of which were slaves at the time) which would be way over the line today. That doesn't, and shouldn't, stop us from looking back at his stances on slavery as the progressive ideals that brought our country to a Civil War over slaves' freedom.

So be courteous to others and give them the benefit of the doubt. People and language change. I don't expect anyone to go back through their social media histories and edit their thoughts from the past to express them in today's lexicon. Not only because I want people to see how petty that would be, but also because it's an unsustainable model for discourse in the future.

## Doxxing Vigilantes

What drives people to engage in doxxing habits and social media scrutiny? Is it always done in bad faith? I'd say no, since wanting to do an extensive background check on a potential hire wouldn't be in bad faith. I'd imagine that most doxxing, however, is done out of bad faith, meaning that the starting point is an anonymous account or profile and the goal is to connect it to its real-life owner.

Some doxxers are vigilantes, and only doxx people that are being evil, with the goal of bringing them to justice. In 2013, a video of a cat being abused was posted to the (notoriously harsh and unwelcoming) image board 4chan. Taking justice into their own hands, 4chan users doxxed the abuser in the video, and quickly found the abuser's home address, cell phone number, Twitter, age, and sister's Facebook page. They reported the abuser to the police, and the cat abuser was given a jail sentence and a fine.[2]

Most people would probably not consider this to be a clear-cut point of righteousness. Like most vigilantes, the investigators willingly enter moral gray areas in order to come to their findings. The end result was beneficial, but what could have been done if just the video was sent to law enforcement investigators? Would they have found the same results and caught the culprit all the same? My guess is yes.

Following that, was a mass, public breach of this person's private details warranted? We can all agree that justice was necessary, but in this case the vigilante 4chan users will be in permanent possession of the perpetrator's personal details. We have a justice system designed to administer fair punishment, but online vigilantism leads to permanent consequences.

## Doxxing Gone Wrong

It's also possible for the results of the doxx to be completely wrong. In the animal abuse example, luckily, the correct culprit was identified and reported. In 2013, after the Boston Marathon Bombing, a similar rage-fueled search across the Internet engulfed Reddit. The end result was not as pretty. Members of Reddit incorrectly identified multiple people as the terrorists, including Sunil Tripathi, a student who had gone off the radar and shared a close resemblance to one of the bombers.

After users posted his online accounts and real-life information to Reddit, Sunil's family was harassed and bombarded by members of the public and of the media in professional capacities. Sunil's name was cleared later, when the police (correctly) identified the actual suspects they were after. Sunil, however, had been battling depression, and this baseless attack on his family caused him to commit suicide a week later.[3]

Following this example, I stand further in my ground that doxxing should not be allowed. There is no case for private citizens to be secretly collecting mass data on one another, other than the fact that it's not illegal. There's no good that can come from it that couldn't be done by professionals, especially when it leads to harm to others (in the form of baseless accusations).

## Public Doxxing

Against people in the public eye, doxxing is often used as a form of revenge, protest, or blackmail. The concept is pretty simple: In a normal doxx, the doxxer wants the victim's information so they (the doxxer) can harass them. However, in a public doxx, the doxxer wants to publish the victim's information, to amplify and spread the harassment across a group of users. Since public figures rarely exist without controversy, finding a number of potential harassers takes little effort.

As an example, in 2018, the country's attention was gripped by sexual allegations made against a potential nominee for the United States Supreme Court, Brett Kavanaugh. A number of circumstances made the situation tense and difficult to come to clear solutions on.

Kavanaugh was nominated by a Republican president and was to be confirmed by a Republican-majority Senate, so the burden to dissuade support for Kavanaugh fell onto the Democrats.

A heated debate swept the country. There was very little supporting evidence and very little exonerating evidence, which means people retreated to their tribalist natures and aligned with their parties. As the weeks went on, the Democrats delayed his confirmation vote into the early weeks of October, about a month before the nation was to vote in the 2018 midterm elections.

Amidst all the tension, one congressional staffer for the Democratic party took action into his own hands. The staffer posted the personal information of three Republican Senators to their Wikipedia pages. Since Wikipedia is open to the public, the changes became public for the world to see. The staffer was caught because the Wikipedia edit was located to have been from a Washington, D.C. IP address. The staffer's goal, undoubtedly, was to give an outlet to Americans frustrated with these leaders to harass them.

The three Senators who had their addresses, phone numbers, and email addresses doxxed were Lindsey Graham, Orrin Hatch, and Mike Lee. All three served on the Senate Judiciary Committee, which held a first round, 21-person vote on Kavanaugh before his full 100-person Senate vote. The information was gained via the staffer's access to Capitol Hill data sets and computers. After the information circulated the Internet (and the damage had been done), the edit was reverted.[4]

It is worth noting that, in this case, the doxxer was charged. Additionally, and rightfully, his termination from Capitol Hill was swift. His full list of charges was as follows: making public restricted information, witness tampering, threats in interstate communications, unauthorized access of a government computer, identity theft, second degree burglary, and unlawful entry. But these charges don't substantiate any argument that doxxing laws are solid. Most charges are specific to the situation at hand.

It should be clear that the lack of anti-doxxing laws meant that the staffer was mostly charged with stealing the information in the first place. If there were more robust anti-doxxing laws (or really any at all), the staffer would have also been charged with storing and posting the information to the world. If this hadn't been a high-profile case with the entire country's attention, it's unlikely that the doxx would have been charged at all.

## Other Examples of Revenge Doxxing

There have been other examples of public doxxing used as protests and revenge. One of the first times doxxing was used politically was in 2011, when the hacking group Anonymous published personal details of 6,000 law enforcement officials. This was a response from Anonymous after it was announced that investigations into their hacking activities had begun.[5]

Similar to the Anonymous group's doxx, the Internet leak publisher WikiLeaks published the personal details of 9,000 current and former officers of the United States Immigrations & Custom Enforcement (ICE) agency. The agency is typically associated with their efforts to combat illegal immigration into the United States.

In 2018, the nation was swept in an outrage over the treatment of children attempting to seek asylum in the United States. These children would attempt to immigrate into the United States with their families, and upon arrival, the families would be separated as the parents had to face criminal charges hearings without the children. The treatment of the children was reported as indecent and inhumane, with some media organizations equating the centers to Nazi Germany's concentration camps.

As a form of political protest, WikiLeaks made their publication. In their own words, WikiLeaks described the publication as "important public resource for understanding ICE programs and increasing accountability, especially in light of the extreme actions taken by ICE lately." The information was gathered using robots to scrape LinkedIn profiles that mentioned employment with ICE.[6] In this way, the information was gained in a manner more in line with what doxxing typically is: the retrieval of voluntarily posted information by private entities for nefarious purposes to the victim.

Of course, anti-doxxing laws should prevent these behaviors. Ideally the laws would prevent third party applications that do not have the user's consent from saving personally identifying information about them independently. This would have made the savings of those addresses and locations illegal and would have prevented the doxx from being carried out legally as it was.

## CNN Blackmail Doxx

Doxxing can also be used as a form of blackmail and political censorship. It shouldn't be news to anyone that President Trump has had a rough relationship with liberal and mainstream media organizations seeking to profit off his reactionary presidency. In particularly, Trump was and continues to be extremely cutthroat with the news organization CNN. CNN, meanwhile, consistently writes and reports negatively about Trump.

This has caused a rift not only between Trump and the CNN anchors, but also a rift between Trump's supporters and CNN's viewership: Trump's base always validated in their opinion of his mistreatment, and CNN's audience always validated in their opinion of his buffoonery. Trump's supporters, however, consistently took to the battlefield of the Internet, posting memes and inflammatory comments about CNN, and it would be a while before CNN would do something against Trump supporters in retaliation.

This form of "meme warfare" is not an alien concept to those familiar with online political discourse. Leftist organizations such as

Shareblue, Correct the Record, and Occupy Democrats actually pay workers to create memes and post anti-Trump content for a living. Memes are especially effective as they can contain a political message in a concise manner, often with the added benefit of humor and imagery.

In 2017, a Donald Trump supporter on Twitter posted a GIF of Donald Trump fighting CNN. The video was taken from a WWE wrestling match, a wrestling entertainment show that Trump appeared on regularly before his political career. In the unedited video, Trump tackles Vince McMahon, WWE CEO, and repeatedly punches him in the head. The edited GIF has McMahon's head replaced with a CNN logo, implying that Trump is beating up CNN.[7]

In terms of meme content, this GIF wasn't particularly shocking, violent, or new. However, President Trump retweeted his supporter's GIF, posting it himself to his official presidential Twitter account. This sparked all the outrage one would expect, from "this is inciting violence against members of the media" to "this shouldn't be the behavior of the president." Essentially, all the criticisms we've grown accustomed to hearing.

The situation became infinitely more complicated when CNN found the user who had created the GIF, tracked him down, and forced him to write an apology under threat of being publicly doxxed. The user, who admitted to creating the GIF (according to CNN), released a public statement onto Reddit which denounced violence against the media and apologized for the "racist, bigoted, and anti-Semitic" content that he had posted before (this must have been a reference to other content, since the Trump-beating-CNN GIF does not appear to showcase any racist, bigoted, or anti-Semitic beliefs). Additionally, the user described his content as "a prank," "satire," and "trolling." He went on to iterate his respect for the journalism community, claiming that he never meant to inspire hatred.

The first offense was that CNN privately doxxed this user and spoke to him, which inspired him to publicly apologize. However, it is possible that the apology was coerced. Here is additional comments made by CNN about the incident:

> After posting his apology, [the user] called CNN's KFile and confirmed his identity. In the interview, [the user] sounded nervous about his identity being revealed and asked to not be named out of fear for his personal safety and for the public embarrassment it would bring to him and his family.

> CNN is not publishing [the user's] name because he is a private citizen who has issued an extensive statement of apology, showed his remorse by saying he has taken down all his offending posts, and because he said he is not going to repeat this ugly behavior on social media again. In addition, he said his statement could serve as an example to others not to do the same.

> CNN reserves the right to publish his identity should any of that change.[8]

If anyone is still wondering whether private, elite organizations are in complete control of our lives, just read above again. CNN essentially used this single anti-CNN meme as a means to threaten and blackmail the user into taking down "all his offending posts," "showing remorse," and vowing not to "repeat this ugly behavior."

How can an organization recognize the dangers of doxxing ("fear of personal safety" and "public embarrassment"), yet still threaten to impose such consequences on private citizens for not conforming to their thought policing? CNN has no jurisdiction over this man's life, and as a free citizen protected by the Constitution, should not be compelled to censor his political speech and activism. This is evil on the part of CNN.

Reading CNN's statement, the fear from this man is tangible. CNN even says "he sounded nervous about his identity being revealed." CNN, a deeply biased news organization, is now playing the arbiter of truth in determining which posts on the Internet are offensive, which memes are ugly, and which comments are bigoted. That should scare us all.

CNN explicitly stated that they wish to use this example to preemptively censor users in the future, stating the user's "statement could serve as an example to others not to do the same." Talk about an Orwellian statement. Revised, the whole statement reads as "We, a private company, threatened this private citizen for being against us. We are only refraining punishment due to him abandoning his First Amendment rights in favor of our own speech rules. All other private citizens should learn to behave the same before we threaten to punish you, too."

Is this the kind of world envisioned for us when the First Amendment was written? A world where we are forced to act a certain way under threat of our lives being threatened by a corporation? These are real questions we need to answer as a country. CNN's last statement says that it "reserves the right to publish his identity." What if they didn't have this right at all? What if no one had the right to do that without consent from the person whose information is being published?

## Antifa's Alt-Right Database

In the growing era of populism around the world, some people have been subscribing to more extreme and reactionary beliefs. On the political right, an ideology has formed called the "alt-right," short for alternative right wing. This far-right ideology, generally, believes in neo-Nazi ideals, white nationalism, and fascism. Meanwhile, on the left, movements have grown for extremist ideologies such as Marxism and Bolshevism, and the creation of groups like antifa (short for "anti-fascist").[9]

Fighting the alt-right has become a goal of many leftist voices, influencers, and politicians. At times, tactics have strayed from the path of debate and discourse. There are times where, in lieu of peaceful approaches to combating the radical alt-right, antifa has acted uncivilly. This is why antifa is sometimes labelled a terrorist organization or deemed as hateful as the alt-right.

Violence on both sides of the political aisle is abhorrent and should be replaced with methods that respect our individual rights. An August 2017 alt-right rally led to the death of Heather Heyer, who was protesting the event, at the hands of alt-right extremist James Fields.[10] An April 2017 political rally led to the beating of three Donald Trump supporters by an antifa member armed with a bike lock.[11] These acts of violence are all despicable and condemnable.

In some cases, for fear of platforming their ideologies, leftist political figures have decided to not debate or engage in political discussion with members of the alt-right. This sends the wrong message, it makes the anti-extremist position of the left appear to be unsupported and weak. Instead, leftists should be willing to engage in these discussions with solid backing of their own positions.

Even if the conversation gets tiring, it is still worthwhile to prove the case against hate and extremism. The idea that platforming the alt-right will lead to more members of the alt-right doesn't hold true if the dissident makes a solid case. If the alternate option is to have the alt-right spokespeople platformed in a manner in which they have no opposition, this will only make the movement look stronger and more appealing.

In the realm of politics, there should never be an opinion deemed correct. No position is safe from the critique of skepticism, no idea should be implemented without dissent having a platform. This hasn't stopped the extreme left from declaring political, ideological, and moral victory over the alt-right. This premature declaration of victory has caused the political left to ignore the spread of alt-right ideology, thinking the movement defeated.

Leftists have taken this assumed victory in stride. By considering themselves the de facto victor, the extreme left has begun its next act: retribution. Rather than respect the freedoms given to the individual members of the alt-right, the extreme left is hell-bent on violating their freedoms of privacy, speech, and expression.

Megan Squire is a professor of Computer Science at Elon University. Her specialties, according to her faculty page at Elon, include databases, data mining, and data security. In late 2017, Squire was leaked the personal information of 4,800 members of the "League of the South," a white nationalist group that supports the Confederate party that was defeated 150 years ago in the Civil War.[12]

Squire began an all-out doxxing campaign against these 4,800 individuals. She googled their pictures, discovered their vocations, and combed through their Internet footprints one by one. Being an expert in databases, she then created her own database to hold the information, which she named "Whack-a-mole." Whack-a-mole is, to date, the most robust repository of information on far-right extremists. All of its data came from leaks and doxxing.

Squire began coordinating with the Southern Poverty Law Center (SPLC). The SPLC's mission is to monitor and identify hate groups in the United States. She gave out the doxxed information to "analysts" at the SPLC and the individual who had leaked her the original list of names. Her goal in doing so was to seek real-life consequences for the doxxed individuals. She hoped the SPLC would contact employers and seek to get the members fired, and that the leaker would post the identities online for the public to run its course on the alleged monsters.

As of 2018, Whack-a-mole contains the personal data of approximately 200,000 alt-right and other hate group-aligned members of the public (Squire monitors 400,000 accounts but estimates just half represent real people). None of these individuals are aware that their data has been stolen from them and stored by a private entity. The database has been called the "antifa's secret weapon against far-right extremists." Yet Squire insists that she's innocent, calling herself "peaceful" and claiming that the operation is completely legal.

Squire is not peaceful. This tool is not peaceful—it is damaging. The only reason to have this centralized resource for identifying problematic people is to harass and endanger them. No one made Squire or the Southern Poverty Law Center the arbiter of who is hateful and who is not; no one elected these people to fulfill this role for society. Certainly, no one would ever allow them to be judge, jury, and executioner in this completely biased manner with no oversight.

Whack-a-mole takes vigilante justice too far. However, there are no laws regulating the use and storage of personal details of people without their consent or knowledge. There are no anti-doxxing laws. It would be easy for Squire to claim that her own actions aren't violent and therefore she is okay, but she does actively hope that members of the extreme-left will use her tool to harass, target, intimidate, and cause harm to members of the alt-right.

To Squire's credit, she has shown some restraint. Whack-a-mole is not public, it is owned by Squire herself, and the information from it is only given to "trusted" people, such as members of antifa and the Southern Poverty Law Center. Squire has admitted to restraining herself from making the project public after the aforementioned deadly 2017 alt-right rally. Another time, she passed the doxxed information of a university student to his school. Upon learning that they had decided not to discipline him, she decided to not pursue further release of doxxed information, trusting the university's decision. Squire is still an ideological supremacist and an authoritarian, but at least she keeps her cards to her chest and wages silent wars.

Unwisely, Squire uses the tragic death of a single person (Heather Heyer, killed by the alt-right in Charlottesville) to fuel her moral fire and continue her dangerous project. The American public has long debated how much death and destruction is cause for subverting our expectations of a private life. During the 9/11 terrorist attacks, roughly 3,000 Americans perished. The US government used these deaths to justify the private data monitoring and collection of the entire US population: just under 300 million. This was a decision that caused debate in the public, as some people thought the reaction was overboard.

The death-to-monitored ratio of the American public after 9/11 was 1 to 100,000, meaning that for every one individual that died, 100,000 were deemed worth monitoring. Squire's ratio is nearly double that: for every one individual that has died, Squire monitors 200,000. Squire's decision to do so is an extreme reaction.

Squire's defense is that she is aware of the risks of her having the data, and its hypocrisy. She claims "... it's the same as how Facebook is hypocritical in claiming to be 'just a platform' and not taking responsibility for hate." Squire claims that, by acknowledging her own hypocrisy, she is more ethical than others who have made technology who were unaware of the problems it would cause and unwilling to solve them. I would imagine the most ethical action would be to destroy systems that one recognizes to be evil, even if they stand to benefit from its implementation.

The ultimate problem with Squire's project is that it seems to be so irredeemable. Squire claims that Whack-a-mole exists to fill in holes that law enforcement "misses." It's possible that Squire could claim that Whack-a-mole prevents violence or the spread of hate, but is there any evidence to suggest that has happened? It appears that the database is simply used as a tool of angry retribution, true to the name, to "whack" individuals who don't have the same politics as Squire.

Squire herself has been doxxed as a result of her actions. She's had her information and identity distributed publicly. Her employer has been contacted. She has been threatened. Everything that she puts others through, she goes through herself. However, she claims it is worth it to endure because "that's what taking a stand is." It is peculiar that she is so willing to see herself as "taking a stand against the Internet bullies who doxxed me," because that is essentially what she is: an Internet bully who doxxes people.

I don't agree with doxxing in any case, and especially not on the massive scale that Squire has implemented it. I disagree that it is a worthwhile effort to doxx people in the name of combatting far-right extremism. Instead, we should focus on winning the battle in the eyes of the public. Instead of using subversive and unethical methods of gathering personal information to blackmail people, the left should be public and vocal about why they oppose these extremists. Unfortunately, the moral victory over right wing extremism is not yet won.

Zoe Quinn is a video game developer who was at the center of the 2014 Gamergate controversy. Quinn was relentlessly harassed, doxxed, and stalked online after details of her personal life brought ethical questions about her career in the video game industry. After Quinn's personal experiences, she questioned doxxers very appropriately: "Are you calling for accountability and reform, or are you just trying to punish someone—and do you have any right to punish anyone in the first place?"

## Covington High School Doxx

Very often, doxxing powers are abused and encouraged by the media. In early 2019, during a pro-life rally in Washington, D.C., a group of teenage boys got into a verbal altercation with various other protesters, including a Native American group and a group called the Black Hebrew Israelites. A video clip emerged in which one Native American, an Omaha tribe elder, is chanting and beating a handheld drum, while the group of mostly-white and male teenage boys surround him, smirking at his actions.

The video clip went viral. The boys, many of which were wearing red pro-Donald Trump hats with his campaign slogan "Make America Great Again," were vilified. The mainstream media and their cohort of perpetually-enraged leftists called out the perceived injustice, attributing blame and the fault of insensitivity to these young men. Most mainstream media outlets covered the altercation, with headlines along the lines of "White Trump Supporters Mock Indigenous Man."[13]

Within hours, calls for the doxxing of the villainous high schoolers began. Shortly following the call for the doxx, their names, personal information, and high school were all plastered over the Internet. Although originally found by Twitter users, the mainstream media outlets published the boys' information. After the angry mob that doxxed the boys found out their personal details, they acted upon themselves to call the school and demand reprimands and action be taken. However, by not waiting to take a breath before unleashing the destructive force of doxxing upon someone who they ideologically oppose, the Internet's mob did not even hesitate to see if the boys were even in the wrong.

Of course a two-minute video from a day-long rally could be taken out of context. Details later emerged that made it clear the Native American man was a career-activist, and a longer video showed him entering the crowd, rather than the crowd surrounding him. These details exonerate certain actions and attributed evil done by the high school kids. Secondly, a video emerged showing the Black Hebrew Israelite group calling the young men faggots and calling the black men of the high school group the n-word minutes before the altercation with the Native American man.[14]

As Reason's Robby Soave put it: "Journalists … got this completely wrong."[15] This opinion was retweeted on Twitter by Jake Tapper, a CNN news anchor.[16] But the destruction had done its course. The teenagers' names were shamelessly printed all over the Internet. The name of their high school was included in several articles published by the mainstream media. For doing nothing but brandishing a smirk while being harassed, these young adults will forever be haunted by this.

It's undeniable that the Mainstream Media's complicit behavior in the doxxing of these individuals plays a role in condoning doxxing. Identifiable details make a story richer. When the Internet mob doxxes people's personal information, the media must not see that as permission to publish it themselves.

There are too many risks for the Mainstream Media to publish these doxxed details. For one, it incites vigilantes to harass and cause harm to the ones they see as in the wrong. For two, there is a good chance that the information gathered on the Internet is wrong. This negligence can lead to damage to people's lives when they were in no way at fault or even involved. In the case of the pro-life marchers being harassed, this was definitely the case.

The media must learn to control itself, take a step back from the madness, and reflect on what is good journalism. Writing an article over a two-minute video clip without looking for a longer, more contextualized version and spreading misinformation is the exact opposite of journalistic standards.

# VII

## Dangers of the Digital Economy

The United States' economy is changing. We are moving into what is being called the "mobile," "digital," "gig," or sometimes even the "shared" economy. We are transitioning into an economy where our labor is no longer tied to physical action and capability. Technologies have the power to truly reform how humanity spends its time, and our economy will certainly change as a result. But how will the United States fare in the new economy, and what actions can we take to make sure that the economic transition doesn't lead to our downfall?

The digital economy is characterized by utilizing technology to improve business processes and consumer livelihood. Using modern technologies like artificial intelligence, precise-location mapping, big data storage, the Internet of things, and virtual reality, the digital economy seeks to find new ways to automate, coordinate, and conduct business.

But there are risks to this transformation. Using these technologies will further infringe on our rights, drive power upwards, and put many working class people out of jobs. We need to minimize the risks and maximize the benefits of this new economy.

### Location No Longer Impacts Work

Starting with the move from the agricultural economy to the industrial economy, the places we work have become increasingly less significant. Where we work tends to not have a large impact on our skill sets as it did in the past. 150 years ago, a worker's location might indicate what kind of farm they worked on. Even in the industrial age, certain manufacturers and industries dominated local markets. The American car manufacturing industry settling in Detroit has had a lasting, profound effect on the type of work done in that region.

Today, location is not as much of a barrier of entry to participate in the economy. We're all connected on the Internet and can learn the same types of skills online, and in many cases, we can also perform a job from anywhere in the country. Many jobs are now offered to remote workers, so moving is no longer necessary to take advantage of career opportunities. This is partially evidenced by American moving rates consistently falling.

This has certainly led to us losing a level of connectedness to our neighbors and our communities in our local area. It's also changed the dynamic of the workplace, where face-to-face interactions are less common; in fact, employees who work remotely say the number one thing they miss is casual conversation with coworkers. For career progression, working remotely can reduce the amount of career growth conversations one has with their managers by 25% or more.[1]

But not all of the switch to more remote work has been negative. In many cases, employees actually quite like it. Employees have reported better work/life balance, better focus and productivity, and more happiness. Remote work also helps reduce commute time and lessens greenhouse gas emissions. Nearly 70% of Millennials would trade other employment benefits for having a flexible work schedule.[2]

There are certainly pros and cons that we've seen from the move to remote work. The flexible workspace model grows 13% per year,[3] and no conversation we have is going to stop that. But we can discuss ways to minimize the drawbacks and maximize the benefits. The move to remote work highlights some issues with the conventional ways we used to work by purposefully moving away from them, but without replacing ways to receive the benefits we may be off worse as a result.

## People Are Staying at Companies Shorter

These new types of employment options have led to an upheaval of American rootedness and culture. In addition to moving to flexible workspace models, we are also being encouraged to engage in more contractual and independent work, free from the constraints of structured full-time employment. 20% of American jobs are currently held by a worker with a contract, and NPR predicts that number could rise to 50% over the next ten years.[4]

The median tenure of employees at one company has increased since 2000, when it was 3.5 years. It is currently 4.2 years (in 2016 and 2018), but peaked at 4.6 years in 2012 and 2014.[5] At my job, I was encouraged by a senior-level software engineer to switch companies at least every five years. In the world of information technology specifically, the motivation for doing so is the desire to constantly be learning new skills, coding languages, and software development practices. This would be in addition to other benefits like increasing pay with job moves and increased networking opportunities. I was also told by a former manager that he "knew developers tend to get skittish about their careers every three years."

This is true for all other industries, not just IT. Over the entire economy, Forbes' Cameron Keng wrote in 2014: "Staying employed at the same company for over two years on average is going to make you earn less over your lifetime by about 50% or more." Keng argues that the US economy, post-2008 recession, is not ready to shell out 5% annual raises nor rapidly promote their best employees. Keng offers a solution that we see commonly today, instead of getting a 3% raise every year, employees should switch companies for a 10-20% raise every two years.[6]

Right here is the motivation for companies and business owners to get onboard with rethinking employment models to the benefit of their employees. Maximizing tenure is beneficial to these businesses as it decreases turnover costs, allows relationships to foster, increases organizational knowledge, and increases team performance.[7] So if employees are becoming keener to leave their jobs in search of better pay and benefits, it might be time for companies to self-reflect and think about offering those increases preemptively to their employees.

When an employee leaves a company, they are making a trade. They are choosing to give up trust, cohesion, and the relationships they've made with their team in search of better opportunities and better pay. There's a loss of culture that goes hand-in-hand with the national lowering lengths of employee tenure. We're due for a conversation about the ways we can utilize our desire for good-paying jobs, recognition in the workplace, and career opportunities in ways that aren't as destructive to our national culture.

## Freelancing

Freelancing is good for employers. Retirement, pensions, and 401k matching are all concepts that employers can forget to worry about when hiring contractors. Not even half of all contract workers receive benefits from the employer.[8] Employers can take their hand out of the bag, letting their contract employees manage their own money, insurance, and retirement.

Additionally, it allows employers to be flexible with their labor demands. If a technology company is building new software, it may need 200 programmers every day. 2 years later, after the product is launched, that demand might sink down to just 20 to maintain and improve the product. Google uses this model of employment in equal parts to their normal, full-time, salaried staff. Bloomberg claims that about half of Google's staff are contract workers.[9]

While the Google example is IT-specific, the rise of contracted work also impacts industries like manufacturing and law. In the manufacturing world, demand for workers can fluctuate based on market demand for products. Although lawyers were under contract or retainers before the digital economy, it is now easier for companies to scale up or down their legal workforce, based on demand, and use contractors.

Much like the move to working remotely, the move to freelancing has been beneficial to employees. Freelance employees have more flexibility to sleep in, less need to commute, and better work/life balance. Also, by being tied primarily to projects instead of companies, freelancers get exposed to many more work opportunities, types of industries, and ways to practice their skills. A freelance graphic designer who specializes in websites might get to try their hand in video game artwork for a few months, and from that exposure get to choose to do it more often or never return to that side of the industry again.

As was stated before, the move to freelancing is like the move to working remotely. It has a lot of benefits but also a lot of potential drawbacks. We need to examine who is benefitting from the move and what we can do to lessen the negative. I think it takes a highly individualistic person to thrive in those kinds of settings, and I think the majority of people just aren't prepared to lose the level of social interaction that a workplace provides. We'll need to find other ways to engage and socialize with each other if we're going to get rid of the common workplace.

## First and Second Wave of Automation Disruption

Advancements in artificial intelligence, trained by advanced analytics, big data, and machine learning, as well as the Internet of things and computational power, will lead to the further changing of the work we do. Before, computers were seen as efficient but stupid. They helped achieve productivity goals but still required a human to operate and do the mental heavy lifting. Computers now have the ability to perform highly analytical problem-solving tasks in place of humans. This automation will lead to more displacement of jobs.

Due to the growing closeness of computer power and human capability, more and more jobs appear to be at risk of being automated in the future. A 2013 study revealed that 47% of all US jobs are at high risk of being automated over the next two decades, with another 19% at medium risk. For the 33% of jobs at a low risk of automation, most involve a level of perception, manipulation, creativity, or social intelligence that a machine could not match—at least not yet.

The industries of retail, sales, transportation, production, construction, and farming were all at high risk of being automated. In the medium risk range were the services, installation, maintenance/repair, and office administration industries. Conversely, the industries which were considered low risk of automated replacement were management, business, healthcare, computers, engineering, education, legal, and community service. The study reported that the difference between the low and medium risk categories "could be interpreted as two waves of computerization, separated by a 'technological plateau.'"

Automated driving cars are being prototyped as we stand today. They will come very soon and will computerize and automate the transportation industry. Similarly, industrial robots are systematically taking over the manual jobs of manufacturing. Big data and analytics will make the logistics and planning of the office administration industry automated as well. These giant waves of industry disruption will come soon, and they will hurt.

The study describes a "technological plateau" in which automated machines will get marginally better at social intelligence and dexterity skills. This will take place after the initial wave, and will provide some buffer time before further high-risk industries are disrupted, such as sales, retail, and construction.

For retail workers and cashiers, the amount of interaction with clients and customers is high, but these interactions don't require a great deal of social intelligence. At least, not nearly to the level of a therapist or prosecutor. Companies like McDonald's have already started replacing cashiers with manual ordering machines, though these don't fully capture the job of a cashier as there is no back-and-forth interaction between the customer and the machine. These machines are more akin to self-checkout at the grocery store than truly automated machines doing the jobs of cashiers in their entirety. However, the first wave of socially intelligent machines will likely cause these industries to be automated completely.

The construction industry could also be automated easily, by reforming the industry to make pre-built parts. This would shift the human workload to be simple oversight of the operation, while the construction of individualized pieces would be done by machines. While this industry is possible to be automated, and is indeed in high risk of automation, there has not been a focus on automating it yet. This will cause it, most likely, to be part of the second wave.[10]

## Incomplete AI Can Punish Unevenly

Automation isn't necessarily a bad thing, and machines can even be made to be better than humans at certain tasks. Fraud detection has become a task completed entirely by computers, because computers are simply better at detecting fraud over data sets than humans. This is due to all the mentioned reasons: computers have more data, better algorithms, and more computational power to conduct analysis. From an ethical perspective, the computerized algorithms can even be better than humans, because it's possible to remove biases (though this is not always the case). However, even if computers have the ability to discover wrongdoing over data sets, we should be careful to examine which wrongdoings we would like to see stopped more than others.

In the world's most popular online video game, League of Legends, programmers have often had trouble detecting abuses and the breaking of their rules. Early on, the game grew past the point where human employees could investigate reports of rule-breaking behavior. Almost all of the rule-breaking detection is now done by computerized algorithms.

There are many ways to "break the rules" in League of Legends. Abusing bugs, verbally abusing other players, intentionally dying, account sharing, leaving active games, etc. are all bannable behavior. In analyzing the computerized algorithms' strengths and weaknesses, it is clear that the algorithms themselves have had a cultural impact on the game itself.

Because certain types of behavior are easier to detect through automation, those behaviors are punished more consistently. For example, verbally abusing another player is easy to detect—it simply requires an algorithm to parse a chat log for harmful language. The same goes for leaving active games, did the player leave the game before it ended? Did they attempt to rejoin? These questions are easily answered by a computer.

On the other hand, it has been incredibly hard for the creators of the game to make algorithms that detect intentionally losing. The questions become harder: Of the player's deaths, how many were on purpose? What does it mean to lose on purpose? Should the computer's algorithm analyze every losing situation to determine if the player had victory within their grasp? Even if they did have ways to win, could the computer prove that the player legitimately intended to lose or just made a simple mistake and lost?

The computers' detection algorithms, so far, have been unable to easily identify this information. Following that, a vast majority of player punishments are given for verbal toxicity and leaving games, and a low amount of punishments are given for intentionally losing. This has had a negative effect on the game, with the perception being that the game producers considered saying a "bad word" as worse than losing on purpose, despite the community thinking the opposite.

One of the game's most popular players, a YouTube video creator named Jason Gastrow, famously quit playing League of Legends and making videos about the game in 2015. In his video explaining his reasons for quitting, which has over 10 million views, he revealed that he was banned for verbally abusing a player that was intentionally losing the game. In his own words: "Now, there is so much wrong with this. First, why am I being banned for talking s**t in a video game? I can understand being banned for cheating, or going AFK a bunch of times, or [not playing the game conventionally], or [losing] on purpose, but talking s**t to some guy that is a total dumba**?"[11]

Advancements in technology have made detection of bad behaviors possible. However, when analyzing things more important than video games, such as crime detection, it will be important to ensure that the society's priorities remain aligned with the implemented analysis algorithms. Just because law enforcement is able to create autonomous detection mechanisms to catch every red-light runner doesn't mean they should. An implementation of this could lead to a criminal justice system that unfairly punishes traffic violators over more prevalent criminals, such as perpetrators of violent crime, if simply because automated detection of violent crime is harder to accomplish. This would be a bad result caused by the incompleteness of artificial intelligence.

I'm not saying we shouldn't use automated detection to catch petty crime, but surely it would be better to let hundreds of people run red lights if it could be traded for bringing a murderer to justice. Yes, running a red light is dangerous and can lead to accidents, but there are simply more important things for our justice system to spend its time on than prosecuting cases of red light-running. I have trust that our justice system prioritizes the prosecution of some crimes over others, and if automation is allowed to flood the system with detected petty crime, we have to ensure that prioritization remains intact. Even if the system retains its prioritization but loses public trust, that is still a negative and must be considered before forging forward.

## Automation Needs to Help the Lower Class

As a country, the United States cannot withstand losing half of its jobs to automation. The digital economy will need preemptive legislation to absorb the impact of half of Americans losing their jobs and their income. It is time to abandon any hope in trickle-down economics, and rewrite the tax code to benefit people over profits. The United States' economy is at a turning point, and its citizens will be faced with this dichotomy of direction.

A corporation creating an automated machine which removes the need for human capital can be positive or negative. Generally, I'd like to believe that it's positive, because of the less work required of humans is an indicator of humanity's progression. But we must tether ourselves to reality. If I asked a 50-year-old blue collar worker if they're happy about getting laid off because of manufacturing automation, the answer would be "no."

Work is supposed to be a mutually beneficial agreement for the employee and employer. Work drives profits and revenue for the employer, and for the employee a job leads to fulfillment and money to live and support themselves. In the event of a job loss to automation, the employee suffers immensely while the employer gains. Even if "humanity" is better off having created machines to empower our lives, in the case of losing employment, the individual is worse off. Of course the laid off worker will say "no," the tangible benefits to employment have been stripped from them.

The government relies on strong individual incomes for tax revenue to pay for its social services and public costs. With half the jobs going away to automation, we are going to have to find innovative ways to fund the government. Currently, 110 million Americans are on some form of government assistance,[12] while there are 157 million employed Americans.[13] There is some overlap of these individuals, for example, 37 million people enrolled in Medicaid live in households where at least one person works full time.[14]

This balance is important to have, as social safety nets are required to support the less fortunate, but require the income taxes of the working population to maintain. Income taxes and sales taxes make up 85% of the entire tax revenue the government receives.[15] For comparison, corporate income taxes make up only 7% of the US tax revenue. And that number is dropping, down from 9% in 2017, before President Trump's late 2017 tax cutting bill.[16]

The disruption of jobs caused by automation will throw this out of a proportionate balance. Without changing the current system, there is a risk that this will cause irreversible class disparity. Not only will the government lose the tax revenue from those who lose their incomes, those people will also be added to the other side, needing the social safety net. Meanwhile, we can't rely on the corporations themselves, whose profits will soar, to pick up the pace and help their countrymen.

Politicians will perpetually stay in power by promising more government aid, more welfare, and incremental shifts of power back to the citizens. Corporations and the wealthy elite will never allow true change to occur, they will never let go of their power, and they will fund the political system to keep it that way. Automation will allow them to control economic capital unimpeded. The public will have no power at all against them, since the supply and demand curve for human capital will be forever tilted towards the ruling class.

The current tax code and pro-corporation attitude in government will do us no favors when power is further consolidated to the wealthy. We simply must reverse course, as soon as possible. In the situation where the populace and the wealthy corporations have no need for the other, wouldn't we prefer the government be on the side of the people? At this point, everything about our legislative branch seems to imply that the opposite power dynamic will be at play.

There are a number of options that have been suggested as ways to recuperate the taxes lost by the incoming workforce displacement. One proposal that could work is the taxing of robots, where corporations who replace human workers with automated machines have to continue paying income taxes as if a human was still doing the job. This money could be used to fund a proposal like universal basic income, which would guarantee economic security for the vast segments of the population that are going to have to reeducate and retrain themselves to be successful in the modern economy.

We are going to have to get creative to figure out ways to make this upcoming economic revolution work in favor of the American worker. The people are relying on the government to ensure that they are prioritized over profits and corporate interests when the power starts to shift further to the wealthy, ruling class. The time will come when we can no longer rely on the lower and middle classes to support each other through taxes, and there is no excuse for the most affluent participants in our society not to pull their own weight. It is unsustainable.

## The Dangers of the First Wave

We need to do everything in our power to preempt the first wave of automation with legislative reform. It's important to understand just how great the impact of the first wave of automation will be. There is a potential that we will see 20 million US jobs automated away in the next ten years. For perspective, the 2008 to 2010 Great Recession saw the loss of 8.7 million jobs.[17] This wave of economic disruption would be over double the amount of jobs lost. Even worse, these jobs aren't being lost to economic downturn where they'll eventually come back—once these jobs are gone, they are essentially gone for good.

There are 12.8 million manufacturing workers in the United States.[18] That group of workers run a 92% risk of being automated when the first giant wave of automation comes. That's a potential loss of 11.8 million jobs. There are currently 3.5 million truck drivers.[19] That occupation has a 93% risk of being automated, which would lead to 3.25 million lost jobs.

2 million stock clerks[20] and 1.7 million bookkeeping and accounting clerks[21] with an 86% risk of automation. 3 million general office clerks[22] with a 61% risk of automation. 4 million secretaries and administrative assistants,[23] and another 1 million receptionists,[24] with a 53% chance of being replaced by automation. Calculated out, that's 7.6 million clerical, planning, and administrative jobs lost.

The first wave of automation replacement has the potential to disrupt 20 million workers in the United States. These three industries are being mentioned solely because we've already seen progress in their automation. Even more industries will become victims in the future, but it is paramount to get ahead of the first wave. 20 million jobless people, with neither the tax structure nor the social services required to sustain them, would be devastating. However, we have the chance to get in front of this challenge and use it to our advantage, if we have the willpower to fight for legislative change that will help the affected groups.

## Amazon's Abuse of Their Laborers

At the world's biggest online retail company, Amazon, warehouse and operations workers are working alongside automated machines right now. Amazon rose to the top of this industry by overworking and underpaying their employees. In an effort to remove the "underpaid" stigma of their workers, Amazon set a company-wide minimum wage to $15/hour.[25] At the time, this seemed like a play to save face from complaints about Amazon mistreating their workers.

This was a widespread, never-before-seen policy to be adopted by one of the world's biggest companies. However, it's likely that Amazon was only willing to make this move because they knew it would be temporary. Most of this overworked and underpaid labor force is entirely susceptible to being automated in the near future. The sheer amount of profit to be made from automating this workforce in the long term would be well worth paying these employees a little more in the short term and not further risking a negative public opinion.

In 2016, Amazon filed a patent for cages to put warehouse workers in as they worked alongside the automated machines. The purpose of this was to keep the workers safe from any harm the robots might accidentally cause, but how undignified does that sound? After the patent was reported on in 2018, Amazon dropped the idea. It's still an indication of Amazon's pro-robot and anti-human stance on the mixture of their workforce.[26]

In the same year, Amazon had to close an entire facility for a day and send 24 workers to the hospital because a robot punctured a can of bear spray inside a warehouse.[27] Clearly, Amazon has set the dignity, comfort, and safety of their employees aside in the pursuit of profits and workforce automation. Why not simply wait until the robots are actually safe before introducing them into a workplace with human laborers trying to do their jobs?

We are already seeing the negative effects of the first wave of labor automation on our country's workforce. Abuses like the ones Amazon has pushed onto their workers will become the norm in workforces prone to automation, simply because the workers become expendable to the employer. These are the workforce injustices of our time that we must firmly stand up to and fight. These workers are humans, worthy of more dignity and respect than what Amazon gives.

## The Dangers of Uncontrolled Technological Change

In 2010, the Australian metal band Parkway Drive wrote a single titled "Sleepwalker." The song follows a protagonist who was born into a world of vast technological expansion, but they begin to question the purpose of this progress. They understand the bleak result of progress describing their city as "lifeless catacombs, our tombs they have become." The protagonist sees the utopian technology as "an enemy that does not rest; who will never relent" and as something that's "strip[ped] away [their] humanity." Society is being encouraged to "sleepwalk our lives away" as they are "lost souls." At the end of the song, the protagonist declares: "not one more step in the name of progress, in the name of blind ambition."

If automation, technical progress, and innovation only serve to enslave the people and empower the ruling class, we must reject them. When companies and corporations make decisions that greatly affect the lives of their employees and the public, the public deserves a say. We need to be meticulous in our analysis of the costs to changing the structures of our economy and of technological advancement.

Companies like Google, which constantly make decisions "on the public's behalf" without consulting us, operate purely antithetically to this. Tech companies invade our privacy, both online and offline, and tell us that it's all worth it because those invasions help their algorithms, and their ad businesses. They are correct that the tradeoff is between the public's privacy and their algorithmic efficiency, but don't give the public the chance to make any decision that it's a beneficial tradeoff. In this way, tech companies deployed technologies are "in the name of progress," but to the public it is "blind ambition" — we are only told that the change is good, but we rarely see the benefits, and most importantly, we never get a choice.

Capitalism isn't the foundation of American principles, it's the means to that end. If unbridled capitalism starts oppressing and holding the people down more than it lifts and empowers, than it is our duty to reel it back in line. We should never give away our freedoms and happiness just to bow to an economic system. Capitalism is healthy and has worked for the United States for hundreds of years. Let's preserve capitalism as an institution, but in a way that acknowledges capitalisms' ability to cause injustice and seek to use political power to qualm those injustices.

Ability to work should always be promoted and idealized. Even repetitive jobs that could very easily be replaced by a computer, like basic bookkeeping, still give fulfillment and happiness to the job holder, as well as providing an income and therefore means to enjoy life. Due to their nature, though, I would be skeptical if an office bookkeeper would claim to be doing everything they wanted during their working time. The automation of this job should give that worker freedom to pursue education and more meaningful employment, not put them into the shackles of a poorly funded welfare system and be disregarded.

Technical progress, as a manifestation of capitalism, can be used to greatly benefit our country. I believe that we should continue to make technical progress, just as I believe we should continue to use capitalism. However, both of these systems are on track to do more harm than good if left unchecked and primed to do the ruling class's bidding. We need to do a better job of forcing cooperation with the technology industry's goals, so we can have debate and discourse about whether their proposals are positive to the public—before those proposals' implementation.

## Classic Resistance to Progress

The overarching idea that I'm espousing is that technological progress which replaces employees can be negative. This is not an uncommon ideology to carry and has been made as early as the 16th century. In 1589, the inventor William Lee created a knitting machine which would have replaced Britain's hand-knitting workforce. Lee got the opportunity to show his proposed invention before Queen Elizabeth I for approval, but was told to "consider thou what the invention could do to my poor subjects. It would assuredly bring to them ruin by depriving them of employment, thus making them beggars."

The 2013 Future of Employment study notes the Queen's opposition to Lee's invention came mostly from the hosiers' guilds who thought "the invention would make the skills of its artisan members obsolete." The Queen stood up for those guilds and denied Lee's invention: "The guilds' opposition was indeed so intense that William Lee had to leave Britain." In terms of technology that replaces workers by automation, "the decision whether to adopt an innovation is likely to be resisted by losers through non-market mechanism and political activism."

"Workers can thus be expected to resist new technologies, insofar that they make their skills obsolete and irreversibly reduce their expected earnings. The balance between job conservation and technological progress therefore, to a large extent, reflects the balance of power in society, and how gains from technological progress are being distributed," the study concludes. In this case, the guilds and their members had the societal power to resist this change. Their power is exemplified by the Queen's support of them.

430 years in the future, in 21st century America, who do you think would come out on top in this situation? Who would the American ruling class stand up for, the workers' wants and desires or the innovator looking to replace them and make money? Would that innovator be ran out of the country for proposing something so opposed by the public, or would they be safeguarded and allowed their way?

For 180 years, the British guilds used their power to resist workforce replacement by automation. It wasn't until legislation was passed in 1769 "making the destruction of machinery punishable by death" that the British government started taking the sides of the innovators over the wishes of the workers. This shift in power was due to the British worrying that delaying technological automation in their country would cause Britain to fall behind on the global economic scale. The British Parliament stated in 1779 that "destroying [the machines] in this country would only be the means of transferring them to another…to the detriment of the trade of Britain."[28]

This is true for the United States as well. Resisting automation does negatively impact our workforce: it means that we're delaying benefits such as increased efficiency and precision on tasks, and we're binding our workforce to working jobs when they could be retraining or working elsewhere. All of these things are technically bad for an economy, but there are other regulations we place on our economy that put it at a disadvantage.

We don't let companies poison lakes, even if it would increase factory output if they could. We don't let children work, even if adding them to the workforce would increase the GDP. We have all sorts of regulatory agencies and restrictions on our economy in this sense. It's about being conscious about who the winners and losers are of certain change, and resisting it if it doesn't benefit the people or poses threats to things like the environment.

Keep in mind, however, that I don't oppose automating jobs away. Quite the opposite, I think the reduction of humans doing menial and repetitive work would be hugely beneficial to progressing humanity. The caveat to my position is that the structure and social services have to be in place to absorb the downsides of the disruption, so people who get displaced have economic security to move on to better things and don't get despair from economic anxiety.

Concerns about economic disruption, fearing that the workers' ability to succeed would be compromised, are far from new. It is dangerous to paint resistors as anti-progressive, when the concern is not that technological advancement is bad, just that it benefits the wrong people. This quote is so perfect that it demands reiteration: "The balance between job conservation and technological progress ... reflects the balance of power in society." We are not concerned that technological progress is not positive. We are concerned about the power it will give to people who have not yet proven themselves worthy.

## The Great Divergence and the Neoliberal Lie

The division between the haves and the have-nots has never been greater in the United States. Put simply, the rich are getting richer, and the poor are getting poorer. This problem has become worse and worse since the "Great Divergence" of the 1970s, as economist Paul Krugman calls it.[29] My entire life has borne witness to this widening disparity.

In 1980, the top 1% of income earners owned 10% of the nation's wealth.[30] Today, they own nearly 40%.[31] For CEOs in the 1950s, the average pay was 20 times that of the average worker. In the early 2000s, their pay ratio became 361 times that of their average worker.[32]

The factors that caused this trend are all institutionalized. For example, one reason for America's income inequality is that the supply didn't keep up with demand for skilled, college-educated labor. Thus, Americans didn't obtain those high paying jobs. But, one of the reasons why Americans didn't get those educations (and continue not to) was because education has become astronomically more expensive—rising 1120% between 1978 and 2013.[33] So America's lower and middle class are told that their inability to become adequately educated is the cause of their income and wealth strife, however, the cost of that education proves that the blame doesn't fit the mold.

At the start of the Great Divergence, "nearly a third" of American workers were part of unions;[34] in 2013, just 11.3% were.[35] The ruling class tells Americans that they might have been more successful if they had stayed in their unions and used collective bargaining. This is completely contradictory to what the ruling class told workers during that time, when workers were told that unions were unnecessary hurdles to innovation and company flexibility.

In addition to other factors, "low skilled" (bottom ten percent) American workers' wages were further suppressed by the country's immigration policy, which brings in more "low skill" laborers. This caused wages to drop 7.4% for this class of American workers from 1980 to 2000,[36] a time period when foreign-born immigrants in the United States went from 6.2% to 11.1%.[37] These factors, however, were not at all the actual fault of American workers. These are government policies; their implementation is decided by the ruling class.

Similar to the rise of immigration, the world's economy also globalized during the time period of the Great Divergence. This allowed entire sections of companies' operations to be offshored and outsourced to other countries. While this didn't have an impact on suppressing the non-ruling class in America, it did allow companies to massively reduce their own labor costs. This contributed to income inequality simply by the gigantic wealth gains that the 1% was able to make. And again, there's nothing the average American could've done to stop this; these decisions came from the ruling class themselves in order to maximize their wealth generation.

Ronald Reagan sold America on the ideals of neoliberalism and a laissez-faire economy in the 1980s. Since then, it has been the prevailing economic thought among politicians. Neoliberal economic policy is generally thought of as a set of trickle-down and pro-globalization practices that promote the economic theory that a rising tide lifts all boats. Reagan's Presidency saw the top marginal tax rate (the tax rate on the highest income bracket) drop from 70% to 28%.[38]

"The rising tide lifting all boats" could not be further from the truth. From 1973 to 2017, productivity of workers increased 77%, while workers' wages only rose 12.4% (after adjusting for inflation).[39] This highlights the greed of corporations and the wealthy elite. They will keep what's theirs, they will not share, and the workers will live off scraps. Without regulation, capitalism ceases to live up to its reputation as the great equalizer, but rather acts as a perpetrator of inequality.

Amidst this rise in productivity, Americans are finding it more and more necessary to have dual-income households. In households with married couples with children under the age of 18, situations where both parents work has increased from 25% of the time to 60%, from 1960 to 2012, with most of those gains being made from 1960 to 1990.[40] No class of income earner seemed to make the gains that the upper class did during the Great Divergence.

1973 through 2017 was a bustling time for technological advancement. In the early 1970s, ATMs were just becoming popular and more utilized.[41] By 2011, more than half of all jobs required working with technology in some capacity.[42] Computers shaped our economy and helped improve its productivity. While the 1% has gained massively as a result of this, the common individual has not.

The wealthy ruling class' economic fortunes were not a product of luck or happenstance. Rather, the ruling class's goal was to create this level of disparity between the classes. Warren Buffett, a billionaire and fellow Nebraskan, admitted in 2011: "Actually, there's been class warfare going on for the last 20 years, and my class has won. We're the ones that have gotten our tax rates reduced dramatically. If you look at the 400 highest taxpayers in the United States in 1992, the first year for figures, they averaged about $40 million of [income] per person. In the most recent year, they were $227 million per person—five for one. During that period, their taxes went down from 29 percent to 21 percent of income. So, if there's class warfare, the rich class has won."[43]

This, frankly, is an unacceptable output of our Governing bodies. It is plain as day that, for the past 40 years, institutionalized economic favors have gone solely to one group of people. In the meantime, the rest of America, the 99% of us, have had to make sacrifices and adjustments to make ends meet. We get stuck with debt trying to get competitive advantages. The ruling class is willing to cancel our jobs in order to make just a little more money, and the government has been entirely complicit in these abuses. Between people and profits, the government has picked profits every time. It's time to change that.

Hindsight is 20/20. We can clearly see that neoliberal economics have only increased the disparity between the elites and the non-elites. We're on the cusp of being hit by yet another wave of technological progress, this time in automation that will end the labor viability of tens of millions of Americans. This time let's use the economic gains made possible by technology to increase the livelihood of everyone, instead of just the wealthy few.

## The Bottom Two-Thirds of the Country

With the future of the economy on our doorstep, we must speculate who will be the winners and losers. Clearly, low skilled and low educated workers will lose their jobs to automation. That's a loss for them. Eventually, the workers of slightly-more-complex industries will lose their employment too. All this will occur while power shifts upward, toward the elite and ruling class, leaving the lower classes out.

It's been stated that, if the country were divided into "haves" and "have-nots," the divide would be a staggering one-third to two-thirds. These metrics define who reaps the benefits of societal change and who misses out. "Whether the subject is out-of-wedlock births, fatherlessness, obesity rates, 'financial worry,' 'neighborhood trust' — name the metric — the same basic pattern holds: in each case, things are going relatively well for the top one-third, but heading into disastrous territory for everyone else."[44]

If we recall the amount of jobs at risk of automation, this split is along the same margins. 66% of the workforce is at a high (47%) or medium (19%) risk of losing their jobs to automation. That means that if the entire automation revolution were to happen today, only one-third of the country would be okay and even more successful in the new economy while the other two-thirds would become jobless and dependent on less fulfilling means to live. This would contribute to the same divide in inequality that we see for every other societal metric.

Those in the bottom two-thirds would initially scramble to find jobs in the maintenance and service industries, such as fixing automated cars or managing the phone lines of some giant corporation. Even those jobs, however, are still automatable, so getting into them would not be a permanent solution. In addition, the flood of workers attempting to get into these jobs would drive wages down to oppressive levels. There would still be other avenues that the bottom two-thirds might attempt to try, but would have smaller chances of success, like entertainment and sports.

The smartest (in my opinion) would go to school and try to get an education in technology, business, or healthcare: jobs in industries that would be hard for automation to eradicate. Even then, the demand for education will increase, and prices will rise even more than they already have in recent times. The high price of an education would make a barrier for entry in these incredibly sought career paths and industries, even more so than the one that exists today.

This will lead to major and negative changes to many people's lives. When the primary mode of fulfillment in a society, working, is no longer an option handed to a society's populace, drastic change will occur. We are starting to see the effects of this desperation today: the hopelessness, the drug use, the suicide rate, etc. I speculate that this is in no small part due to the lack of fulfilling options that we have as workers.

## Google's Monopoly on Uberization

In his book *Them*, US Senator Ben Sasse marvels at the wonders of what the new economy will bring us. Sasse writes optimistically about a future where an individual needs to use a drill for a building project, and instead of buying a drill, the person can rent one. Then, using an automated delivery device, the drill would be sent to the person. The same (or a different) delivery device would come back and retrieve the object once the individual is done. The end result is that the person has saved time and money from having to go buy a drill.[45] A $20 and a 45-minute round trip to Home Depot has been reduced to a rental cost of $2 and about 5 minutes total time.

This is the utopian dream of the "sharing" economy: An economy where people don't own things, they rent them. Owning is expensive, renting is not. Why? Because at the end of the day, not everyone can afford a hammer (or a more expensive tool), but nearly everyone can afford to rent a hammer. While the borrower gets a great deal on getting the tools they need to use, the renter gets a nice profit margin and requires almost no work of their own to achieve that.

But wait—that's not the entirety of the deal. It's not a hand-delivery of these tools, made by two people who know each other and agreed verbally. In fact, no part of the process even involves personal interaction: the borrower doesn't even get to know the person whose tool they'll use, and vice versa for the renter knowing who is using their tool.

Almost every part of the interaction is done by technology, except for the renter putting the tool up for rent and the borrower requesting a hammer. The application the trade is made on uses technology. The automated delivery machine uses technology, not just technology for knowing how to drive or fly itself, but also technology that tracks its location and gives it directions. That leads to more questions: who owns the technology? How much money are they making off this deal?

If location services are going to play a massive share in the "uberization" of our economy, shouldn't we consider who will be profiting from an economic shift that relies on location services? Too often ambitious dreamers like Sasse make these oversights. In their un-technically trained world, location services are a given. I can imagine what the thought process must be like: "Uber does it today, so it must be a replicable technology that every industry will use."

They're wrong, unfortunately. Location services are not a replicable technology, they are a monopolized technology. The top 5 most popular driving direction applications, based on market share, are Google Maps (66.5%), Waze (11%), Apple Maps (10%), Mapquest (9%), and Google Earth (2.2%). It should be noted that one company, Google, owns three of these services: Google Maps, Waze, and Google Earth, giving Google an effective market share of nearly 80%.[46]

By far the most routing and directions services are provided by Google Maps, including Uber's own routes and directions (note: the Uber iPhone application uses Apple Maps).[47] Every online service that gives some form of location-based service is reliant on some external technology (mainly Google Maps) in order to be functional. The alternative would require writing new location services software from scratch. If a company were to do that, they might as well just be a company that makes and sells location services software.

Google Maps is not a free or even cheap technology. It costs the application developers to use Google Maps' technologies. Asking for a simple set of directions one time costs $0.005 cents. Asking for that data to be fleshed out with traffic information makes it cost double. Similar pricing models exist for other location services data, such as distance and roads information. A request to know the speed limit of a single road is $0.02.

These costs seem small, but over time they add up. Uber completes 15 million rides a day,[48] and each one of those rides includes an unknown amount of map, distance, route, and road information requests to Google. Let's do a theoretical example on Google's profitability off Uber. Let's first be conservative and estimate that one-third of all Uber rides are done via iPhone and therefore Apple Maps, so 10 million daily rides are done with Google Maps.

Let's also assume that each ride requests information from Google 20 times, at a cost of $0.005 per request (requesting information can be done piecemeal, so knowing the speed limit of road A and the traffic on road B might be two requests). That means that for each of the 10 million daily Uber rides, Google would make 10 cents. For Google, that's a million dollars a day, just from one application!

It's also worth mentioning that Google Maps' prices for their services has gone up. A price increase in June 2018 effectively made each request cost ten times more than it previously did, although the direct comparisons from line item to line item was also changed. What used to cost $0.50 for every 1000 requests now costs $5. And to be clear, Google didn't make dramatic upgrades to any of these services that would merit the price increase; the change simply came after they monopolized the location services software market.

This is a critical infrastructure baseline for a shifting economy. We shouldn't be giddy about the uberization of the economy, yet. There needs to be more legislative and regulatory involvement. It's the job of agencies like the FTC is to protect against monopolized industries implementing abusive price hikes, yet there's no word from them on stopping these practices occurring on Internet technologies. The proof that the market is uncertain and unstable comes from Google Maps pushing a 1000% price increase on its customers who rely on it for their applications to work.

## Google Is the New Bad Landlord

The alluring vision of the sharing economy is worthy of destruction. As a country, we can't afford to let such grandiose and forward-thinking promises become reality if they have dirty, greedy, and abusive underworkings. While lawmakers like Sasse talk big about how great the new economy will be, they refuse to see how it adds even more power to the ruling class.

A more classic and familiar example of this problem might be renting an apartment versus buying a house. It is very easy to hype up renting—it's cheaper and renters are less obligated to look after the property. But to only speak about the greatness of renting and compare it solely to buying ignores the potentially harmful tools that renting needs to use.

In this example, the landlord provides the service. The landlord is necessary for the renting process to work, just as location services are necessary for the shared economy to work. Landlords aren't the ones who primarily benefit from renting, but more renting is good news for them. Based on the work they do, landlords have the capability to be good or bad.

In the past, landlords haven't always been great. Some aren't even great today. Because of abuses and mistreatments, lawmakers passed laws that protect renting tenants from the power of landlords; Important laws that give renters the ability to fight back against abuses of power, harassment, and discrimination. Now imagine watching a politician talk about how great renting is without mentioning how much power mass renting would give to landlords. It seems trivial to most, but it's important that those new powers have equal regulations in the law, in case of bad landlords.

In the case of location services, it's not just some services that are bad. Google has a market share of near 80%, and it's beyond bad—it's downright evil. We can learn our lessons from the past, we can write preemptive legislation that will limit Google's ability to flex its monopoly muscles on this necessary industry. Or we can take Google for an innocent bystander, let them increase their prices, and watch as the shifting economy hands more power over to the technology elite.

Once we base our entire society and lives around technologies made by a small set of companies, how much power do we have left to give? There's no indication that Google would cease being evil after getting an even larger and more dependent user base. Thus, it's important to recognize when people are going to run out of ways to fight back against these technology companies, and give them the protections they deserve.

## Cloud Computing Monopolies

Another example of power being slowly leaked out of the hands of the public and into a technology company's is Amazon's takeover of Internet infrastructure. In the beginning of the Internet, anybody or any company wishing to publish online needed to host their own server. From a technical point of view, a server is a physical piece of hardware. It's essentially a locked down computer with the purpose of hosting content, running programs, and receiving requests.

Having to physically own and operate a server was a barrier of entry to publishing websites and services. In addition, it was a pain for small but fast-growing companies who had expanding user bases and traffic. The time and monetary cost to set up servers was great in comparison to the company's technical team's size and financial options. Similar needs were found even by the average user, whose digital life began taking a heavy digital storage toll. Buying and installing easily accessible storage to hold all the games, photos, and videos of years past was tiresome.

Thus was born the "cloud" which provided a solution for needing physical computing machines and storage devices. It should be stated that "cloud" was an ingenious but entirely false misnomer— there is no invisible space in the air which holds the information, it's just more servers in a location so far away users needn't worry. Cloud computing offered companies the ability to run websites without needing to own a single server. Cloud storage offered users the ability to store all their photos without needing to own a hard drive bigger than their smartphones.

Of course, such convenience comes with a price. Not just a monetary one, but also the lingering questions of uncertainty: who controls our fate? If our fate is at stake, who protects it? If Amazon or Google or Microsoft is in charge of storing my data, who's to say they don't misuse that data? Who's to ensure they keep it secure?

Ideally, this would be a duty of the FCC, who has the job of regulating these kinds of transactions. The problem then comes back around to the people and the companies themselves. What's the price of convenience? Would we trust an unregulated, uncontrolled beast of an industry with questionable motives (read: surveillance capitalism) with our secrets?

Like almost everything in the world of technology, cloud computing services are heavily monopolized. Amazon Web Services (41.5%) and Microsoft Azure (29.4%) hold over 70% of the market share collectively.[49] If there was a genuine competitive market, I could understand why the need for regulation wouldn't exist: if a company misuses personal information or has unsafe practices, then switch to a competitor. As regulators have always known, though, this model doesn't apply in monopolized situations.

Private citizens and companies aren't the only people throwing money and business at the cloud computing industry. Even the government has become an avid client, securing on-demand server resources for its intelligence agencies through Amazon Web Services (AWS). The US government signed hundreds of millions of dollars in contracts to AWS in order to optimize how it shares data between agencies.[50] The Pentagon has also requested that cloud computing companies submit bids for a ten-billion-dollar contract.[51]

If we shouldn't be using the cloud, what's the alternative? For cloud storage, I think it's as simple as using external hard drives or other physical storage devices. For cloud computing and server hosting, however, I don't think there is a straight-forward great solution that everyone benefits from.

If we go back to the way we did things 20 years ago, we're going to have the same problems with the fatigue of physically owning and setting up servers. That exposes a lot of risk, since companies then have to be committed to the owning and maintenance of a set of servers. Those servers will need security patches and a tech team to ensure they are safe and operable. There's a reason why cloud web hosting became so popular, and it's because it took away a lot of those aspects.

The best solution is regulation. Perhaps the FCC or the FTC or a new regulatory agency could have a deep dive into how Amazon and Microsoft operate their cloud technologies and write rules and restrictions which would deny those companies the ability to do abusive practices. People deserve to know the inner workings of what happens with their data and information when it is stored on the cloud.

The same process flow as the location services problem applies here. Before we march forward, we should know what we're going to step on to get there. We're relying on cloud technologies as infrastructure for the new economy, but as a country, we can't afford any more individual privileges, protections, or rights be fed to the ravenous teeth of big technology companies. We must do a better job of assessing these risks, because if we keep forking over power to big technology companies, we're going to keep seeing the same results.

## Instacart and Erasing the Middle Class

Instacart is a company that, in many ways, piggybacks its business model from Uber. In their case, Instacart allows for their employees, called "shoppers," to pick up lists of groceries for Instacart's customers and deliver them, using the shoppers' personal vehicles, to the doorsteps of the customers. Instacart, a $7 billion company, had bought into the Uber business model, the company's primary service being a connection service in the grocery-shopping industry, connecting grocery shoppers with people who want their groceries shopped for them.

Like Uber, Instacart's workers are all contracted, and therefore receive no benefits or formal employment, but also receive more flexible schedules and convenience to their jobs. Workers received a base pay of $10 per order, increasing with order size. Once the order had been completed, the customer would be able to give the Instacart deliverer a tip. This money would be given to the worker in addition to the pay offered by Instacart.

In October 2018, the company changed its payment policy for the sole purpose of maximizing profits at the expense of its workers. Instacart instituted a policy which changed how tips would calculate into the worker's payout. Instead of being completely supplemental, tips received would add to the base pay offered by Instacart. A $10 tip would mean that Instacart paid their employee ten dollars less for that order.[52] Overall, their employees claimed that this substantially lowered their pay.

Ro Khanna is the US Congressional Representative of the district that includes Silicon Valley, where Instacart (and a plethora of other technology companies) are headquartered. At times, he appears to be one of the only members of Congress bringing up the struggles that many Americans will face in the new economy. In an early 2019 interview with Tucker Carlson, Khanna questioned Instacart's practices and accused the company of "wage theft, stealing the tips that should go to the employees to lower their base pay… it's a scam." Khanna said:

> The digital revolution is creating an extraordinary amount of wealth. They can afford to make sure there's a middle class…. If you [big technology companies] want to make sure that we have a unified country, then do some very basic things. First of all, make sure that everyone is participating in the benefits of technology, not that all the wealth is going to very very few individuals….We don't need to be outsourcing 200,000 tech jobs, why aren't we partnering with rural

communities to participate in the digital revolution?…If you want to prevent a populist backlash in this country, you need to be forward-looking.…We just had half the country vote against the coasts because they didn't see any economic opportunities in the new economy.…Henry Ford woke up in the early 1900s and he doubled wages.

Khanna ended his defense of the middle class by stating: "Another thing is, who's going to buy the Instacart groceries?"[53] Khanna is correct on this issue, but the solution needs to be more nuanced. In the future, the vast majority of the jobs we know today will be wiped out by automation, including those in the service industry like Instacart's shoppers. At that point in time, is Instacart going to be paying 10% in taxes while the social benefit fund runs dry and the unemployed with no economic opportunity live off the divided scraps? Or should Instacart pay taxes that sustain that fund so their former employees can still live dignified and fulfilling lives in the wake of permanent industry disruption?

In February 2019, Instacart announced that they'd be rolling back their changes to their employees. A mass organization of vocal opposition from the company's workers led to the company loosening its grip.[54] It's positive that these workers were able to use their employment as leverage for their economic opportunity, but all did not stay happy for long. Instacart workers continued to be at odds with their employer for making decisions that put them in second place. After the workers took to a 3-day strike in November 2019 to try to get the company to increase wages, Instacart removed potential bonus offerings for highly-rated shoppers. This move was seen by some as retaliatory.[55] How can we make it permanently clear to the companies of the gig economy that the middle class deserves to exist, and they are the ones responsible for its upkeep? How do we apply the "forward-looking" attitude from here?

## Educating the Future

All signs indicate that the best way to stay economically relevant during the next economic transition will be to obtain an education in technology, engineering, law, healthcare, or teaching, as well as creative and expressive forms of work like art, therapy, and people management. A majority of these industries require post-high school education. Therefore, I suggest evening the playing field and making education more encouraged and affordable in these studies.

Additionally, if the automation revolution occurs the way it's predicted, we're going to need to educate people in these exact areas anyway. This is a simple matter of giving people the future-proof economic opportunities they need to succeed. I would propose subsidizing these fields, or a more specific list of studies, that are both safe from being automated and necessary to be worked after the economy undergoes transition.

In speculating the negatives, I find it worrying that if the automation revolution happened today, so many members of the lower class would have so few opportunities. That is unjust and we should proactively look for ways to use economic transition periods as means to correct socially unjust paradigms. If my prediction of the economy doesn't pan out as I expected, then at worst we've educated the members of all classes equally in industries that are relevant anyway.

Even before college and university, we should do a better job of encouraging students to find their paths and explore industries like computer science, engineering, teaching, and healthcare. I found my love of computer science when I was fourteen and in my freshman year of high school, and I ended up making it my career. I realized my calling simply by being encouraged to try coding at an impressionable age.

The reason why we don't focus large portions of our time on progressing humanity isn't because there's no interest, it's because our economy is focused elsewhere and we don't have the levels of education to push those boundaries. Scientifically, we've only scratched the surface of topics like transhumanism and space travel. I say we take full advantage of this economic transition period as a means to uplift our education and reignite our societal interest in these fields.

# VIII

## Internet Service Providers

The United States should nationalize Internet service providers. Internet service providers (ISPs) are evil, corporatist organizations that consistently put profits over people. Their greed has led them to rob the American taxpayers of millions of dollars with lies and false promises. ISPs have been broken up by antitrust laws before to no effect. Local municipalities are already choosing to run their own as infrastructure.

### ISPs Have No Competition

Internet service providers thrive on non-existent competition. Fewer viable options means less competition, which means complacency in service quality, resulting in less value to consumers. For Internet service providers, operating in a monopoly is practically the norm. Over half of all Internet consumers in the US only have one choice for high-speed broadband.[1]

This is a phenomenon that is unique to ISPs. Building an ISP network is a gigantic infrastructure investment over a very large area. It's essentially laying wire and cables in the ground all over a city or region. There are high costs associated with the physical building of the infrastructure. 80% of an ISP's entire expenditures come from the initial installation costs of building the network, with the remaining 20% going to the support and upgrades of that network in the years that follow. Additionally, the bureaucracy and planning stages take a very long time to organize and get through. The bureaucratic procedures can be lengthened or even stopped entirely by a failure to reach an agreement with other private companies, as not all areas of the city are owned by a neutral or publicly-accountable party like the government.[2]

When Google Fiber was being added to the city of Austin, TX, Google determined that it needed to place cables along telephone poles owned by AT&T. AT&T, not willing to give their direct competitor any edge, simply denied their request. Part of the 2015 FCC's Open Internet Order was to abolish practices like this, which were anti-competition and therefore anti-consumers. While the 2015 order was passed, it was repealed in 2017. This critical case shows how ISPs, AT&T in this case, simply don't want any competition or to lose their monopoly-status, even if that competition would add value to consumers.[3]

Huge amounts of time and money are required to build viable alternatives to existing Internet infrastructure. Newcomers to the industry need to navigate deals with existing ISPs, who can treat them poorly simply for being competition. Time and effort must be spent on governmental paperwork and permit-gathering to start building. On top of it all, a serious amount of financial capital needs to be available to pay for the high costs of infrastructure implementation.

## Municipal ISPs Work

There are currently independently governed cities and areas in the United States where the cities themselves built their Internet's infrastructure and now run public ISPs as utilities. These government-run options are successful at being fast and competitive, which is causing more municipalities and cities to join in. In 2018, a government-run ISP in Longmont, CO took PC Magazine's title for the fastest broadband in the country.[4] That ISP has above 50% adoption rate among the city's population.[5]

Longmont wasn't the first city to have this idea. Starting in 2008, the city of Chattanooga, Tennessee started creating their own purely fiber optic Internet infrastructure called EPB. The network was completed in 2011 and covered 600 square miles. This infrastructure has been credited for getting a Volkswagen manufacturing plant and an Amazon facility to be built in the city. It currently costs the public $70 monthly. In the previously mentioned 2018 ISP rankings, EPB was the fourth fastest ISP in the country.[6]

Taking Longmont's example, the Colorado city of Fort Collins also passed a ballot measure to allow their city to build its own ISP. The city claimed that the business plan would require at least 28% of Fort Collins' ISP subscription to be effective.[7] Across the country, in a small Western Massachusetts city, voters chose to approve a $1.4 million expenditure to build a government-run ISP, in favor of a deal offered by Comcast which would have cost the city $1 million less.[8]

On the other coast, the city of Brentwood, California adopted a city code in 1999 that forced buildings to have a 4-inch conduit pipe, which would be owned by the city. The goal at the time was to pave the way for a second cable company to set up shop, though that never happened. So it ended up that the city owned 120 to 150 miles of conduit pipes reaching 8,000 buildings. When the city requested proposals for Internet service providers, the only response was from a regional ISP called Sonic. The existing infrastructure took out such a large investment chunk, of both money and time to deal with bureaucracy, that Sonic offered Internet to the city's schools for free. Today, Sonic in Brentwood offers gigabit speeds to the public at only $40 a month. In the aforementioned 2018 ISP speed rankings, Sonic came in third across the country.[9]

It's clear to see that publicly-accountable ISPs and government-run ISPs are viable and popular. The main hurdles in setting up new ISPs are getting funding and cutting red tape. Through the nature of voting and handing processes over to the government, which has the ability to tax and self-collaborate, government-run ISPs get over those hurdles. In addition, people are outright rejecting companies like

Comcast in favor of plans that cost millions more. The sentiment is clear: Americans are tired of dealing with ISPs and want better solutions.

## How ISPs Gained Control

Internet service providers as a whole have made massive promises to the public in regard to building infrastructure. To support these pledges (that were not kept), they have taken billions of dollars in government subsidies, which they claimed was to help build this infrastructure. The end result was massive profits for the companies, monopolization of the industry, and very little improvements made.

Bruce Kushnick is the author of *The Book Of Broken Promises*, which details the excessive lies that the telecom industry said to consumers. He's been following their misdeeds since 2010. Kushnick observes that since the initial deals from 1991 and 1992, the American taxpayer has paid over $500 billion in subsidies, tax breaks, and rate increases to build Internet infrastructure. Since then, at least one half of America has never been upgraded.

The origin of large-scale Internet service providers in the United States comes from the 1934 Communications Act. This act spelled the way forward for telecommunications, primarily for telephone, radio, and cable. It also created the Federal Communications Commission (FCC) to oversee and regulate the industry. The first section of the Communications Act includes the following: "For the purpose of regulating interstate and foreign commerce in communication by wire and radio so as to make available, so far as possible, to all the people of the United States a rapid, efficient, nationwide, and worldwide wire and radio communication service with adequate facilities at reasonable charges."

This directive from Congress while creating the FCC makes it clear that the industry should focus on creating wide-reaching infrastructure that gives as many Americans as possible access.

Additionally, the industry should make improvements in speed, quality, and efficiency of communications. Lastly, the charges to the public must be reasonable.

The Communications Act was effective at achieving these initiatives. 35 years after the Communications Act, most of America was connected by the telecom industry's infrastructure and could have a landline phone. This wasn't without consequence, as it led to monopolization across the industry. Also, each state's infrastructure was owned privately, meaning that the states themselves owned little in telecom infrastructure. The company which held the monopoly over the telecom industry was called Bell Telephone Systems.

It wasn't until 1984 that Bell Telephone Systems was broken up using antitrust laws. These new companies were called "baby bells," and were divided along state lines (as a general rule). The baby bells were given ownership of the telecom infrastructure. These private, small, state-bound companies are referred to as "state utilities" by Kushnick. At this point, most of the telecom infrastructure was made of copper wires which spanned vast networks and led directly to houses.

Starting in the early 1990s, the world became fascinated with the prospect of the Internet. Internet connectivity quickly became as high a priority as cable and landline telephone connections. As such, it naturally fell under the FCC's umbrella of regulations.

In the early days of the Internet, there was only one way to connect. Using dial-up Internet, a user's existing telephone wire could be utilized to gain an Internet connection. Commercial technology for this was first sold in 1992. However, dial-up Internet was rather slow. There was a lot of demand for fast Internet, which would become known as broadband.

The term broadband simply means "fast" or "faster than dial-up." In the United States, broadband was and continues to be primarily achieved by creating dedicated Internet connections on copper wire.

However, great improvements to speed can be made by using fiber optic cables. This was known even in 1983 when Newsweek proposed creating an "information superhighway" out of fiber optic cables in a 776-mile stretch along the East Coast.

In 1991, vice presidential candidate Al Gore announced that he would hope to create a national fiber optic network. This plan would have replaced the copper cable networks, which in some cases were nearing 100 years old (such as in New York City), with the fastest available connection infrastructure. It also would have used the model of National Research and Education Networks, which was a not-for-profit utility ISP used to connect Universities and schools to aid in the technological advancement of education practices. If this network had been made, we could very well have had a government-run and publicly accountable Internet infrastructure made entirely out of fiber optics.

However, this was a major threat to the telecom companies, which were now also Internet service providers. They used this ambition to secure government subsidies, driving the discussion away from government-run Internet and toward privately-run Internet with government money.[10]

## State Utility Lies for Funding

State-by-state the pitch was made: with government-funding and support, we can replace the old copper wires with fiber optic connections. Kushnick has retroactively dubbed this the "era of say anything." Here are some of the claims that the state utilities made, in Kushnick's words:

> California (AT&T) claimed it would spend $16 billion and have 5.5 million households completed with fiber by 2000. SNET, which controlled Connecticut, (then owned by AT&T) was to have the entire state done by

2007 and spend $4.5 billion. Verizon's entire East Coast (from then Maine through Virginia) was supposed to have 12 million homes done by 2000 and the company would spend $11 billion.

Under the guise of infrastructure improvement, the telecom companies lobbied the state governments to lower taxes and remove regulations. They claimed that absent those changes, replacing the copper wires with fiber optics wouldn't be profitable. Thus, taxes were slashed, subsidies and funding were given, and tax deductions were granted. Meanwhile, the telecom industry's profits went from 12-14% on average to 30%.

The atrocities committed by the state utilities seemed uncountable. Verizon Massachusetts promised in 1995 to have "all colleges and universities," "all psychiatric, chronic, and critical care hospitals," "all industrial office parks," and "330,000 residences and businesses" connected with fully fiber-optic networks by 1998. 1998!

Verizon Pennsylvania promised to have broadband deployed to 20% of rural, urban and suburban areas by 1998, 50% by 2004, and 100% by 2015. Instead of doing any infrastructure, they simply claimed that the existing copper wire connection speeds counted as broadband. Using their own logic, they met their 2015 end goal before they even started.

AT&T Kansas raised rates to cover fiber optic infrastructure improvements to rural areas that no one ever saw. This pattern of rate increases to fund infrastructure replacements, followed by no upgrades to the infrastructure, was all too common during this time frame. The state utilities completely lied and defrauded their customers.

The American people were duped out of being a fiber optic country by corporatist greed. All of these promises were not kept. Admittedly, in some cases the goals were a little bit far-fetched, like in the Massachusetts case. The fact is that the goal of even having the FCC was to oversee these companies and hold them accountable, and to keep rates reasonable for the public. None of these cases of outright lies and broken promises were investigated or regulated by the FCC.[11]

## Cross Subsidization of Fiber Optics

It was revealed by a New York Attorney General investigation that Verizon New York was using their network for multiple purposes, reclassifying expenses at the detriment to the customer. This would involve using a wire meant for telephone lines to host an Internet connection, or vice versa. In 2005, Verizon New York lied and claimed that the installation of fiber optic infrastructure was for the enhancement of their telephone network. For the record, no telephone network has ever needed the speed of fiber optic cables.

Verizon New York still classified it as such. By mixing service offerings, Verizon New York expensed all of its fiber optic Internet infrastructure as telephone network upgrades. Verizon New York then said that those expenses weren't profitable and reported losses, followed by requesting regulators for permission to increase rates on customers to pay for those losses. Verizon New York was able to get the New York Public Service Commission to sign off on that rate increase in 2009, and customers paying for telephone services received a rate increase for the installation of fiber optic cables.

Take this strategy and multiply it over many states. Essentially, Verizon uses its state-level companies to increase rates on their customers. The stated purpose is to maintain, enhance, and repair those states' telephone infrastructure. These enhancements in actuality pay for Internet infrastructure upgrades. So upgrades to the interstate connections, the Internet connections, which should be done by Verizon itself (not its state utility companies), are being financed at the local level. "It is a massive financial and accounting shell game that makes local service lose money while these other services garner obscene profits," Kushnick says.

Another important point is that there are no such thing as "wireless" Internet connections. I would speculate at least 99% of the distance that Internet data travels on a "wireless" connection is done on a wire. The remaining 1% is the device talking to a router or cell phone tower. Wireless connections are one way that ISPs gamed the system to claim they got more people onto fiber optic infrastructure. Those ISPs didn't actually install fiber optics into the home, they just installed fiber optics around the cell phone tower, so the entire wired portion of the "wireless" request's trip is done on fiber optics. This is used to inflate numbers about fiber optic connectivity and misrepresent progress.

Verizon is using its state-level utilities, which were created by Verizon being broken up by antitrust laws, as shell companies to maximize profits. Kushnick called this practice "cross-subsidization," where Verizon is getting subsidized twice by the taxpayers to build fiber optics. The first subsidization comes from the initial deals with the government to get subsidies to build fiber optics. Then, Verizon doesn't expense those subsidies correctly, so they introduce rate increases on the taxpayers to further subsidize them.[12]

## The Monopoly Revival

In addition to telling lies about the infrastructure upgrades they'd be doing, telecom companies/Internet service providers also reformed themselves back into a monopoly. Even though the Bell Telephone Systems monopoly was broken up in 1984, the 1990s led to the reformation of that monopoly. By making deals and lying about their capabilities, the broken-up companies merged back together. That's why today we still only have a handful of companies with real ownership of the telecom infrastructure.

There was a merger on the table to merge the companies SBC and Ameritech in 2000. In order for the FCC to sign off, they promised to compete in 30 cities in 30 months, which had a $1.9 billion-dollar penalty if it wasn't met. The companies also agreed to spend $6 billion in fiber optic upgrades across the new, combined network, and reach 77 million customers. This initiative to make the merger beneficial for all parties was called "Project Pronto."

The merger was approved; however, they never spent the $6 billion. In order to not pay the $1.9 billion penalty, they did have to be competitive in 30 markets. At the time, the competition requirement only required having three customers to count as being competitive. The new company never advertised or actually tried to be competitive in those markets, but it did get 3 customers in each. This apparently satisfied the FCC, and no penalty was paid.

In a similar situation, when SBC merged with BellSouth to create AT&T, the new company promised to bring 100% broadband to 22 states. This was supposed to be completed by 2007, and AT&T said it was done, but inconsistencies have come up against the claim. For example, Alabama was one of the states that AT&T had claimed was 100% broadband-covered. However, alternate court documents from 2015 and 2016 allege that 4% of Alabama does not have access to broadband Internet.[13]

Continuously, the FCC let companies across the industry make promises in order to let them merge back into the very dangerous monopolies that they broke up in the first place. Following that, the FCC didn't hold them accountable to those promises. The whole time the FCC has been failing its core duties of ensuring that the public benefits from industry moves, mergers, and business decisions made by the telecom industry. It's a true outrage.

## FCC's 25-Year ISP Complacency

The FCC was useless at holding telecom companies responsible for their promises made for Internet infrastructure improvement. They let every single one of those deals be a complete farce, and never punished a soul. In addition, they let different services offered by the same company cross streams, and they let a number of horrible mergers go through which did nothing but consolidate telecom corporate power and didn't benefit the citizens at all. The FCC should be disbanded from regulating ISPs after failing to do its job for the past 25 years.

For years, the FCC was tricked into thinking that it wasn't the fault of the telecom companies that they weren't making good on their promises and deals. The private companies effectively told the FCC not to butt in, because regulation would hurt profits, and if profits weren't big then there'd be no money for the infrastructure improvements the FCC wanted them to make. The telecom industry painted the issue as a catch-22, when in reality, they were just lying.

Because fulfilling agreements wasn't an option, the Internet service providers did the absolute bare minimum. AT&T even created a "new" type of wire which was nearly entirely copper but had some sections of fiber optics. They called this "U-verse" and claimed that it counted as fiber optic wire if there existed a fiber optic section every half-mile. Verizon-owned infrastructure was upgraded with fiber optic cables until 2011, when the upgrades stopped. At this point, more than half of Verizon territories remain unimproved.

In the past 25 years, half the United States' Internet infrastructure has not been updated and still has its original copper cables. Customers have experienced multiple rate hikes to pay for infrastructure that never came. Many agreements were signed to get fiber optic Internet infrastructure to Universities and hospitals which were not fulfilled. Taxpayer money has funded government subsidies which have gone to these same improvements. Collectively, the average American household is out $4000 to $7000 (varies state to state) for a total of over $500 billion.[14]

Remember the section from the 1934 Communications Act that promised to ensure reasonable rates? It's the job of the FCC to make sure rates aren't raised without good cause. If the FCC had investigated these instances where rates were increased, they would have found that there was no benefit given to the customers. If private analysts like Kushnick can find this out, surely it would be a slam dunk case for the FCC.

Internet service providers clearly defrauded consumers, but will face no punishment for it. The FCC is so ineffective at creating and enforcing regulations for ISPs that local law enforcement is taking matters into its own hands. As one example, Verizon New York is being sued by the City of New York for failing to fulfill its promise of 100% fiber optic connections to residential consumers.[15] But this shouldn't be the job of local law enforcement. This requires local New York investigators and prosecutors to become deeply knowledgeable about Internet infrastructure agreements, metrics, and enforcement. We already have the FCC to do that, or so we're told.

## ICANN Loses Sole US Oversight

The Internet Corporation for Assigned Names and Numbers (ICANN) is a non-profit organization that maintains the global databases which link website domain names to IP addresses. Essentially, when Domain Name Systems (DNS) servers generate a list of known destinations for domain names, they reference the databases of ICANN. This gives ICANN a lot of power, as the organization holds the effective power to decide who does and doesn't get to host their websites on the Internet.

Think of ICANN's role like a phone book. Imagine if there were $2^{128}$ possible phone numbers that one could dial (for reference that's 340,282,366,920,938,463,463,374,607,431,768,211,456 phone numbers). Additionally, when that person wants to call someone else, the expectation is not to know that person's number, but just to know their name. So, my phone number might be 555-402-1234, and my name is Brian Wolatz. If someone were to go into a phonebook and look for "Brian Wolatz," there must exist some lookup database which would link my name to my phone number. The power of the database, therefore, would be to simply refuse to acknowledge that request, stating they don't know who Brian Wolatz is. Well, they might know, but refuse to tell the requestor what my phone number is.

In ICANN's case, it's not a person's name, it's a company's website. And it's not a phone number, it's an IP address. ICANN holds this power over the entire Internet. If ICANN wanted to, they could make google.com disappear, simply by refusing to tell the entire world's traffic how to get there. Naturally, this means that heavy oversight is required into how ICANN operates and the decisions it makes. For eighteen years exactly, from September 30, 1998 to September 30, 2016, ICANN did their job under the exclusive supervision of the United States, specifically, the US Department of Commerce.

This solution was not perfect. As stated earlier, ICANN has the power to kill communications across nearly the entire Internet, and this power was solely held accountable by the United States' Department of Commerce, which is in turn run by the Secretary of Commerce, which again is appointed by the United States' President. This could have led to a totalitarian takeover of the Internet where an unhappy, angered President might forcibly start removing websites from the Internet. The power structure was in place to do so, but luckily that has never happened.

It can't be overstated how great of a job ICANN does. ICANN truly honors what it means to be a facilitator of the world's greatest connector, and is very honorable in their approach to ensuring a free and open Internet. In a world where so many facilitators opt for being players instead of referees, ICANN has chosen to not even be a referee, hardly ever abusing its power to remove or block domain names from being addressed.

On October 1, 2016, ICANN's oversight switched from strictly being overseen by the United States' executive branch to a board of oversight with hundreds of representatives from over a hundred countries. This move was two years in the making as Internet users from around the globe worried about the control a country had over the reins of the Internet. Seemingly, the move was a step forward for democracy and representation. The Internet is indeed the world's tool, not just the United States'.[16]

Although on paper I agree with the move to more democratic oversight, it does remove power from the United States. According to a 2016 Pew Research poll of 38 countries, the United States' population holds the #4 spot in valuing Internet freedom, with 91% stating that Internet freedom is important. That 91% is matched by Spain, and is only beaten by Argentina (92%) and Venezuela (93%).[17]

In terms of picking a good country to represent Internet freedom, I'm puzzled by the questioning of the United States' ability. Further, if the United States is in the very upper echelons of countries polled, then certainly we are higher than the average country of the 110+ that are represented in ICANN's new oversight board. While making the organization answer to more democratic oversight, ICANN effectively lost support of their values for Internet freedom.

Generally, ICANN tends to stay away from the spotlight. Their decisions and record don't get pulled into the court of public opinion often at all, at least not like their for-profit industry peers at Google, Facebook, and Amazon. This is a positive thing for a non-profit organization seeking merely to facilitate the good faith use of the Internet. That doesn't mean that ICANN hasn't made controversial decisions.

In July 2018, it was reported that ICANN had been secretly refusing to register domain names that ended with .islam or .halal, even though its own panel had agreed it would be okay to register them. The original requests from 2012 for .islam and .halal domain names came from Turkey, a Muslim country, but those requests were told to not be honored by other Muslim countries in 2014. Following that request, ICANN placed that status of the Turkish-requested domains "on hold."

"The organization was fiercely criticized for creating an 'on hold' status out of thin air—effectively creating a new policy to suit its own political ends, ignoring years of policymaking," wrote Kieren McCarthy of The Register. "ICANN was also criticized for holding a series of secret meetings with government representatives over the issue, and refusing to tell the applicant—Asia Green IT (AGIT)—what it had discussed. It refused to provide documentation about those meetings or any subsequent discussions by ICANN's staff or board, claiming they were confidential."

After years of battles and repeatedly being told that ICANN had no authority to deny registering the domain names, ICANN still has not registered the domains. The issue has been investigated by its own internal review teams and all had reached the same conclusion: ICANN was breaking its own bylaws and rules by denying the domains. Even despite threats of lawsuits from the Turkish applicant, AGIT, ICANN still claims that it can do "whatever it wanted whenever it wanted."[18]

The delay in fulfilling AGIT's request has continued through the US's sole regulation to the multinational model. While it wasn't ideal that the request wasn't fulfilled during US oversight, it also hasn't gotten better. Perhaps once it is returned to US oversight ICANN could be regulated by an agency that would be dedicated to Internet freedom, such as the one we should put in place to facilitate the national ISP network.

## 2015 Net Neutrality Laws

Net Neutrality is the moniker of the argument that ISPs must remain neutral parties in the flow of information, that their job is simply to relay information between two connected parties, and no preference or censorship must occur. These behaviors could occur in the outright refusal to connect users to certain sections on the Internet, or in more subversive ways, by intentionally slowing down or "throttling" connection speeds to those services and websites while intentionally giving other traffic bound to "preferred" (read: paid for) services priority treatment with blazing fast speeds. Net Neutrality means that ISPs must treat all data equally.

Laws enforcing Net Neutrality are perhaps the only regulation that the FCC has attempted to place onto ISPs. In spring 2015, while the FCC was under Obama Administration-appointed leadership, the United States passed its first set of Net Neutrality laws. The final vote for the rules was 3 to 2.

The laws reclassified Internet services as forms of telecommunications, like radio, telephones, and cable. Like the providers of these other services, ISPs would have to engage in non-discriminatory practices for the content they transmitted. This would ensure that the information sent across the Internet wouldn't be blocked, prioritized, or restricted in any way.

People feared that unregulated ISPs would sell "Internet fast-lanes" to corporations. This traffic would have been given priority over other traffic, creating a paywall to accessing the Internet at fast speeds. Of course, it would have been massively profitable for ISPs.

As it currently stands, paying for Internet access means paying for access to the whole Internet. Another common fear was that ISPs would block traffic to and from certain websites, and sell that access for a premium. In these nightmare scenarios, ISPs would be able to sell access to otherwise free sites. So even if Facebook is a free service, meaning it doesn't charge users to have accounts, it's free to download the application, etc., access to Facebook could still be restricted based on whether the ISP was blocking that traffic.

The passing of these rules was a huge win for the people; the decision was a manifestation of people-over-profits legislation. The policies, correctly, promoted the idea that the Internet was opt-in, and that individuals had the freedom to choose which content they wanted to see and engage with, and vice versa for content they didn't want. As then FCC Chairman Tom Wheeler wrote: "no one—whether government or corporate—should control free open access to the Internet."

One of the dissenting commissioners, Ajit Pai, argued that the FCC was over-regulating Internet service providers. Pai had been a lawyer for Verizon before he was recommended to join the FCC by Republican Senator Mitch McConnell. Pai argued that the FCC was making mountains out of molehills, and that there wasn't just cause to implement rules over practices that had yet to be committed.

Ajit Pai was arguing from a stance that people associate with the Republican party's economics. The stance that regulation is inherently a detriment to corporate productivity. I agree that economic freedoms are essential to a free market, but I think Pai is missing the mark. It's not regulating to say that a corporation can't start to engage in practices that limit individual freedoms. As Tom Wheeler pointed out: "This is no more a plan to regulate the Internet than the First Amendment is a plan to regulate free speech. They both stand for the same concept."

In 2017, the Republican Party took over the presidency of the United States. For the FCC, this led to Wheeler's ousting and Pai becoming the new chairman. Pai spent 2017 focusing his work on repealing the 2015 rules that he had opposed. Due to the now-Republican majority on the commission, he was successful.

## The Vanishing Case for the Repeal

Pai argued that the 2015 Net Neutrality rules had decreased the amount that ISPs were willing to spend on infrastructure investments. His data to support this claim came from a $1 billion difference between 2014 and 2015 infrastructure spending. Further evidence revealed that year-over-year swings in infrastructure spending were very common over the past 20 years, and this led to Pai being accused of "cherry-picking data to make his case." In dissent of the repeal, a fellow commissioner stated that they had yet to see evidence that the 2015 rules themselves caused the drop.

If Pai argued that the Net Neutrality rules had caused a lack of infrastructure investment from ISPs, then surely repealing those rules would increase that investment. We have the benefit now, a year later, to analyze the results of that repeal. Three big ISPs, Comcast, Charter, and Verizon had less infrastructure investment in 2018 than in 2017. This trend continued for 2019.

For the companies that own the nation's wire infrastructure, AT&T and Verizon, wireline investments are set to fall from 2018 to 2019. Wireless investments, on the other hand, are predicted to rise in 2019. This is not due to the FCC's removal of any regulations; however, it is entirely explained by the rise of 5G wireless networks which require investments.

An FCC lawyer who helped write the original Net Neutrality rules, Gigi Sohn, said, "The cornerstone of Ajit Pai's net neutrality repeal order has quickly crumbled … The broadband industry's reduction in investment and [capital expenditures] in the wake of Ajit Pai's repeal of the net neutrality rules proves what advocates for Internet openness have known all along—neither the rules nor Title II authority had any effect on broadband investment."[19]

## FCC Comments Section

In an attempt to rile support for Net Neutrality, late night television host John Oliver encouraged his viewers to make official comments on the FCC's website against the proposed repeals. This was broadcast on May 7, 2017. On May 8, the next day, the FCC's comments website crashed and became unavailable. Also on May 8, the Chief Information Officer (CIO) of the FCC claimed that the site was attacked. The next month, in June, Chairman Pai would echo these claims in a letter to the US Senate.

The attack, the CIO claimed, was done by a "designated denial of service," or DDoS. DDoS attacks attempt to overwhelm a server with requests, to make the server generate a gigantic backlog of pending processes in order to bypass security. DDoS attacks are common and fairly simple, but they are criminal hacking attacks and can be prosecuted. Additionally, because requests are logged by the server, DDoS investigations have a starting place: they know where the attack came from.

However, it became increasingly clear that there was no intent to crash the servers or website by any hacker. External factors, like Oliver's television segment, could have caused the site to become overwhelmed and crash. From a technologist's perspective, a server at capacity is not necessarily a server under attack. I worked on a scheduling system which enabled users to select shifts they wanted to work as those shifts became available. If a server went down as a shift-opening time was nearing, the logical reaction wouldn't be that we were under a DDoS attack—we would first look at the sensible external factors.

The FCC's Office of the Inspector General (OIG), an internal auditor and regulator, investigated the attack and would eventually conclude that there was no foul play or malicious intentions. Yes, a 3100% increase in comment traffic took place between May 7 and May 8, 2017, but there was no evidence to conclude that this was caused by anything other than the television segment.

The OIG also investigated the statements made by the CIO and Pai to determine if any false information was spread. This investigation revealed that the CIO had been told before issuing his claim of a DDoS attack that the television segment was probably the cause of the increased traffic. The OIG said that "At best, the published reports were the result of a rush to judgment and the failure to conduct analyses." Pai's letter to the US Senators "made several specific statements that [the OIG] believe[s] misrepresent facts about the event or provide misleading information."

In addition to making false claims to the public about the downtime that their website had received, the FCC also used fake comments made as a basis for claiming that the public was in support of the Net Neutrality repeal. Pew Research indicates that 57% of the comments made on the FCC website were from "temporary or duplicate email addresses." "Seven popular comments accounted for 38% of all submissions," although that may be partially driven by Oliver's push having pre-filled out forms, not just fake comments. It was also revealed by Chairman Pai himself that half a million, of the 22 million total comments, were made from Russian email addresses.

It's hard to determine why anyone, including a hostile foreign state, would create and publish the fake comments. By "fake comments," I'm referring to the comments that were duplicated or from unverifiable sources. The fake comments might have been politically charged to throw confusion into the ring, perhaps in an attempt to invalidate the system. Regardless of the reason why they were made, the FCC refused to improve its comments process to clear out fake comments or to make the section more meaningful. This has been characterized as "turning a blind eye to fraud." Because we can't rely on the fake comments to show any meaningful data, let's take them out of the discussion.

After filtering out the fake comments, an investigation revealed that 800,000 of the 22 million had been real and unique (unique meaning that the comment was not duplicated elsewhere in the comments). Of these 800,000 comments, 99.7% of them were written in favor of keeping the Net Neutrality rules.[20] If 99.7% of all commenters being in favor of Net Neutrality isn't hard enough evidence, a 2017 University of Maryland poll indicated that 83% of voters support it. That 83% includes 75% of Republican voters and 89% of Democratic voters.[21]

These levels of public support for any issue is almost unheard of. In a divided and tribalistic America, it may be one of the only issues where both parties have the same consensus. As it turns out, individual rights being sacrificed for the economic gain of corporations just doesn't sit well with America.

## Proposing a New Commission

The 1934 Communications Act, the act that created the FCC, laid out a very clear plan for the future of technological infrastructure: rapid speeds, efficient processes, empowerment to the people, available at reasonable costs. The FCC has been given enormous power to goad telecommunications companies and ISPs into behaving in ways that achieve those goals.

But in regard to the Internet, the FCC has failed.

In the process of attempting to achieve these goals, the FCC has let promises go broken and infrastructure be neglected. The only meaningful ruleset imposed on ISPs was only in place for two years before it was repealed. The FCC let rates be increased for infrastructure upgrades that never came. The public has spent $500 billion of its taxpayer money on subsidizing these companies' Internet ventures.

The FCC has lied to the public about being attacked, when it was the public itself barraging their servers with requests for them to do their job. The FCC let fraudulent requests be treated as equal among the real desires of the public. The FCC refuses to consider the wills of the people, which overwhelmingly support regulations and rules that the FCC actively works to remove. The FCC cherry-picks data to match their claims, which is the exact opposite of how policy-making should work. The head of the FCC is himself a former Verizon lawyer. Essentially, an unrepentant bank robber runs the bank and lets other robbers off the hook, hiding behind the veil of Republican economic policy that Republican voters don't even support.

In 2017, after Donald Trump took the office of the presidency, the FCC changed leadership from Democrat to Republican. In April of that year, one of their first moves was to lift a restriction on ISPs from selling data generated by their customers' Internet traffic.[22] The rule had only passed five months prior. It serves as another astonishing move to shift power away from the people and to the corporations.

This would effectively allow ISPs to become more of a monopolistic cash cow. Not only would the public be expected to pay them monthly fees for access, as well as subsidize their infrastructure, now ISPs have the option to generate and sell customer data for more profit. With products like Google and Facebook, it's slightly understandable why they should be able to sell some of our data. We use their services for free, and the data we give them is a product that they can sell. While I don't think the current tradeoff of services-to-information is worth it, nevertheless it is better than a services-to-information-and-money agreement.

It was reported in January 2019 by Vice that AT&T, along with Sprint and T-Mobile, were selling the location data of their users to massive third party "location aggregators," which are then accessed by people like bounty hunters in order to locate people.[23] If ISPs start selling user data, then this muddies the waters between telecommunications regulation and consumer protections from businesses. The former is the sole responsibility of the FCC, while the latter is more generally seen as the Federal Trade Commission's (FTC) job. But this situation points to a broader problem, where the FCC has traditionally been seen as the regulatory power of the Internet, but has barely laid a finger on Internet companies outside of ISPs. The FCC shouldn't simultaneously be in charge of regulating the Internet and actively be trying to shed that responsibility.

I propose removing the FCC's capabilities to regulate ISPs. Since the services offered by ISPs are a necessary part of Internet freedom, like the services provided by social media websites and applications, I would propose making a commission solely for the purpose of regulating the Internet in all its aspects. The FCC has proven to be useless in creating regulations that reflect the will of the people.

In 2019, nearly 30 years after the Internet became a mainstream product used by the public, we should not be having a conversation about who is in control of its regulation. These questions should be answered by now. If the responsibility of controlling the Internet is constantly being neglected, it's time to create this new commission or agency with the sole responsibility and domain over the Internet.

This is especially important if companies like ISPs are going to start blurring the lines between the classic telecom business models and the digital age Internet service business models. Back in time, in the 1930s, I can't imagine any telecommunications company being able to sell their customer's phone data without the FCC getting involved, or public outcry. Nowadays, it's just par for the course on the Internet. We expect everything to be saved, monitored, and recorded, even if it doesn't have to be that way, or wouldn't be that way if any regulation existed.

For too long the offerings of technology and the Internet have been unchecked. The scope of the Internet that needs regulation, from social media to ISPs to ICANN, is clearly exceeding what the FCC and FTC are meant to regulate. Not just the scope, but the speed of innovation and improvement on the Internet is also outpacing them. This has led to a number of cases where ethics has taken a back seat to profits, and the people have felt the backlash of poor decisions made by all powerful and unaccountable technology corporations.

We didn't elect representatives to elect representatives. We elected representatives to represent us. And among us, there is a demand for more oversight and regulation. The public massively disagrees with the practices of technology companies all over: for example, the 80%+ of Americans that believe Net Neutrality should be enforced for ISPs or the 75% of Americans that want the ability to navigate the web without being tracked. Digital rights and Internet advocacy groups can be found in every corner of the web. If a vast majority of the population is no longer represented, the system needs this massive overhaul. I say we give the people what they deserve.

## Nationalize ISPs

State utilities may have to be the way forward for traditional telecom companies. It seems to work for them. The infrastructure is in place, the technology is determined. For the Internet, however, it would be best to simply switch to a nationalized model. In fact, the model that Al Gore proposed in 1991 might have been a vision for what the future of the Internet would be: fully fiber optic, government-created and ran, and fully accountable to the public.

It's hard to deny the benefits of a more efficient and functional electric, water, road, or gas system, and improvements to the Internet are no different. Upgraded Internet benefits every single individual and business, from the technology firm running a data warehouse to a retail store processing credit card transactions. A fully nationalized Internet would be conducive of more information shared and more people connected.

Internet service providers cannot be trusted to upgrade their speeds and infrastructure unless competition exists. This would be a good argument in favor of increasing competition, however, efforts to do this haven't actually created more opportunities. There were some specific but helpful rules that were passed with the 2015 Net Neutrality rules, but those have subsequently been repealed. Over half of Americans still deal with the burden of only one choice of ISP, an ISP that will never be prompted to increase performance nor decrease prices.

With the investments we the public has made into Internet infrastructure, it's a slap in the face for ISPs to treat us as a lesser priority than their profits. Many municipalities have taken initiative against these practices and are giving ISPs the boot entirely, building their own fast and efficient infrastructures. The time has come for these initiatives to take off on a national level. Let's make sure we clear bureaucracy and ready our buildings for fiber optic deployment, and begin building Internet infrastructure where service to the people is the priority.

# IX

## Security

If technology companies are to continue to build new technologies, user safety and protection are an absolute concern. An unthinkable amount of private user data exists on the web, and the security around the apparatus is very loose. High-volume breaches of sensitive user data happen at a high rate that points to delinquency on the part of the technology industry. This lack of attention and prioritization towards security constitutes a need for regulation.

### What Software Developers Can Do

As a software engineer, I am appalled at the carefree attitude towards data security in the industry. The public as a whole, the average Internet user, has put a large amount of faith into our work to be secure. They want to and expect to be able to use our technologies without worrying about their private information's safety. However, we developers have picked up a bad reputation for having a laissez-faire attitude toward the security of our products.

To this day, many web applications still have SQL Injection vulnerabilities, and many web forms don't sanitize input. A 2018 study done by Imperva, an IT Security company, found that 19% of vulnerabilities are injection-based.[1] For the sake of brevity, I won't dive into what SQL injection and input sanitation are, but they have been known risks for decades and still developers ignore their potential harm. It is a failure on the entire technology industry that these vulnerabilities still exist on the open Internet.

No reasonable person would expect software developers to make 100% secure and bug proof software. We're humans, we're flawed, and the things we create are flawed too. But when we've identified risks and warned about them for decades, at some point not checking for the vulnerability must be our responsibility.

It's important that we take more ownership of the flaws that only we can see. If a program or application has a functionality flaw, such as a button not working, it is very likely to get caught by Quality Assurance Testing (QA) or Product Ownership (PM) as unacceptable. The end user won't see the final product until its feature set is locked down and bug proof. Developers need to go the extra mile and look out for the missing pieces that QA or PM won't see. We need to diligently check our products' security and vulnerabilities, because we're the only ones who know to look for those potential problems.

Common vulnerabilities of new code should be discussed frequently. The industry, through some means, should assemble and approve of software development techniques that have a zero-tolerance policy for this kind of code. It would be universally beneficial to create these standards that prevent known vulnerabilities from continuously rearing their ugly heads. In the modern age of web application development, we shouldn't see any new software that allows for the same kind of hacks experienced during the early 2000s dotcom bubble.

We must pay our own dividends of attention to security flaws, simply because no one else will. Unless a company has a hacker QA team, no one besides the development team is even looking out for those security risks. It's not necessary to be dramatic and perform test hacks, however, it is sufficient to be mindful of security risks while examining the code. By increasing our security threat assessment during code review, we can take some of the responsibility of the application's security and protect users' interests.

In this way, we can become more responsible for ensuring that we're developing in a secure, industry-approved manner. Currently, no party takes a brunt of the responsibility for security risks that make it to the end user. It simply must be our responsibility. This must change if users are to feel important and protected while using our applications.

## Online Communities' Role in Picking Presidents

The 2016 presidential election could be the most technologically evaluated event of all time. Data has been shared which shows which candidates were receiving which kinds of attention on which platforms on a day-by-day, hour-by-hour level. It is truly remarkable to look back and analyze how public opinion changed on social media in parallel to the roller coaster of events that took place.

My personal favorite example is to watch a timeline of Reddit's "neutral" political hub over the months of July and August 2016. It's fascinating to watch the conversation move from pro-Bernie Sanders/anti-Hillary Clinton, to anti-Donald Trump, and finally to anti-Donald Trump/pro-Hillary Clinton. Meanwhile, the rest of Reddit, unbound from the tethers of promised neutrality, ran abuzz with many pages such as SandersForPresident, HillaryClinton, and The_Donald all receiving massive amounts of popularity throughout the entire election cycle.

Allegations of election rigging, from both sides of the political aisle, prompted investigations into the technological methods used to campaign and promote candidates. Many Donald Trump supporters accused Hillary Clinton's campaign of "astroturfing" online content (astroturfing being a phrase used to describe fake grassroots political movement). Many Hillary Clinton supporters, after Donald Trump's victory, accused Donald Trump's campaign of having used subversive Russian influence online to secure victory.

Pretending to be a real, volunteering, engaged Hillary Clinton supporter online when a user is actually a paid campaigner is not illegal. Working with a hostile foreign government to win a presidential campaign to become the leader of the free world is treasonous. So when Donald Trump surprisingly won the election, the allegations became very serious.

The election's result, and the circumstances surrounding it, was shocking. Unfortunately in America, politics are treated and covered like sports, and presidential elections are essentially the Superbowl of politics. The winner of the presidency and Electoral College was Donald Trump; however, he lost the popular vote by nearly three million votes. This caused an intense and somewhat circus-like debate about the use of the Electoral College. Statisticians figured out that if Hillary Clinton had switched just 107,000 votes in specific states, she would have won the Electoral College and thus the presidency.

## Cambridge Analytica

Under normal premises, this would have just been another statistic in explaining close losses. But there were other factors that caused this statistic to be twisted and picked apart in determining how Donald Trump won. What if, the investigative journalists asked, instead of Hillary Clinton needing to have switched those 107,000 votes, it was Donald Trump who had successfully flipped them himself using influence provided by the Russians?

This narrative was repeated for over a year without any substantiating evidence. In 2018, it was revealed that Cambridge Analytica, a British political consulting firm, had scraped Facebook's data and gained access to the personal information of millions of users. According to the investigation, Cambridge Analytica had then used their political science-driven algorithms, in combination with the users' data, to target on-the-fence Facebook users with political advertisements to sway them.[2]

Cambridge Analytica was hired by Donald Trump's presidential campaign in 2016. Could this have been how Trump flipped his 107,000 voters that he required to win the election: by using a British political consulting firm's algorithms in combination with scraped user data used specifically to target advertisements?

To be fair to President Trump, there are a couple of points that need to be clear. First, there is no indication that he himself nor his campaign knew about Cambridge Analytica's intense methodology. Despite having hired them, consulting firms tend to leave their methods and algorithms private. Additionally, what actually happened in 2016 differed greatly from the original allegation: Instead of the Russian government working with the Trump campaign under the table, it was actually a British private company working with the Trump campaign with complete legality.

## Facebook's Response to Cambridge Analytica

In response to the investigations into Cambridge Analytica and their methods, Mark Zuckerberg testified before Congress. As the CEO and creator of Facebook, Zuckerberg was uniquely poised to describe which parts of Facebook were used by the firm to help the Trump campaign. Zuckerberg explained the process to Congress: Advanced political profiles were made for these targeted users, created in part by Facebook and in part by Cambridge Analytica's own methodologies. Cambridge Analytica made extremely complex algorithms to determine swing voters, then used the individualized data given to them by Facebook to find out who those voters were. Once those users were identified, Cambridge Analytica displayed pro-Trump advertisements to them on Facebook. Some of the advertisements displayed were provocative in content and, under Facebook's discretion, qualified as hate speech.

Multiple times, Zuckerberg stated his deep sorrow that his platform had been used in this kind of political targeting, foreign interference, and hate speech. But if not for political targeting, why does Facebook include information about their users' politics in the first place? For what other reason, other than political targeting, could that information be used? Zuckerberg also explained that he understood it was his personal responsibility as the company's leader to do better about staying within the boundaries of what the public expects the company to do. In response to the Cambridge Analytica incident, Facebook gave users helpful notifications about how they can limit the data shared with third party applications and websites using Facebook-provided tools.[3]

As a leader in technology, Facebook needs to do a better job of understanding what kinds of data they have on their users and do a better job of protecting it from getting into the hands of harmful people. Putting the onus of monitoring with which companies a user's data is shared on the user is bad practice. More thorough vetting should be required on Facebook's end to even allow sharing data with that website to begin. And, although he takes personal responsibility, it doesn't just fall on Zuckerberg. It falls on all of Facebook, the industry at large, and all of the industry's employees.

Cambridge Analytica, which has ceased operations since the extent of their operation was revealed, is not the first nor the last consulting firm with a million-dollar algorithm or method. These companies are going to be more and more common, and it will become more common to ask the technology industry to supply their algorithms with all the data they can think of. So long as data scientists and political consultants exist, the threat of using big data for political targeting exists.

The technology industry needs a better action plan to understand what these algorithms do and what kind of information they reveal. The industry needs to stand up to these kinds of use cases.

If the end result is harmful, discriminatory, or doesn't help humanity as a whole, then the technology industry needs to be the one to determine it's not worth it. If the industry cannot, then we must use regulation on how data is shared and used.

We have our own ethics and moral guidelines, and we have a right to say we won't enter into a partnership that will use subversive methods or harm people's lives. This is our duty as ethical people. This is our duty as Americans who wish to improve the lives of our fellow countrymen and –women, and who don't want to watch their lives be manipulated behind the curtain by someone with an interesting algorithm and an abundant amount of data.

## Voting Machine Security Threats

Voting machines present a hacking threat that is vital to our nation's function. We must secure our voting machines from being attacked or hacked in order to ensure our democratic integrity. As reinforcement of this belief, the United States Department of Homeland Security classified the US Election Systems as "critical infrastructure" in January 2017.[4]

To this day, our electronic voting machines are capable of being hacked. Voting machine hacking has been demonstrated as recently as September 2018 by J. Alex Halderman, a University of Michigan Computer Science professor. He showed that a specific voting machine used in 18 states and exclusively in the state of Georgia was vulnerable in multiple places. His demonstrated hack was done by executing malicious software on a pre-programmed chip inserted into the machine with election information.

Halderman notes that every single voting machine in the United States "suffers vulnerabilities that would enable vote-stealing attacks," and that "most of the country uses machines that are at least ten years old." However, to steal an election at a national level, an attacker would have three challenges to surpass.

First, the voting results are separated by county, district, and state levels. There is no "master database" with all the results from every state centralized in one location. But, hacking at this level might not be a requirement. Because presidential elections nearly always boil down to key districts in key states, a little bit of research can go a long way. An attacker doesn't necessarily have to deal with the extremely Democrat California or the extremely Republican Utah, just the 107,000 votes in the rust belt that won Donald Trump the 2016 election.

Second, the voting machines are not connected to the Internet. This would mean that attackers would have to physically go to each machine. Halderman says that that's not the case, and that for most machines getting malicious code onto the pre-programmed chips which hold the election information is enough to "hack all the machines." Since the computers that make those chips are, at times, connected to the Internet or other electronic devices, a hacker could steal an election remotely.[5]

The threat of remote hacking may be more pressing than Halderman leads on. In July 2018, the country's top voting machine maker, Election Systems and Software (ES&S), admitted to Congress that it had installed remote-access software on machines that were sold to states. The time period of these installations took place was from 2000 to 2006. Given that most of the voting machines used in the US are at least ten years old, this raises concerns about which ones still have the remote-access software installed. In response to the admittance, US Senator Ron Wyden said that installing remote-access software and modems on election equipment "is the worst decision for security short of leaving ballot boxes on a Moscow street corner."[6]

Finally, over 70% of US election voting is done on paper. This "physical failsafe," as Halderman describes, is not a sufficient defense. Even though the votes themselves are done on paper, they are scanned by an electronic machine. This electronic machine, just like the other mentioned electronic machines, can be hacked. The fact that there's a paper trail gives a false sense of security, and Halderman claims "most states do not do any kind of rigorous audit of the paper."

Securing our nation's elections is vital to our ensuring our great democracy lives on. In the wake of the most foreign-influenced presidential campaign ever in 2016, finding ways to protect against cyber interference is crucial. Halderman recommends that states fully switch to paper voting, implement auditing of the paper trail, and apply cybersecurity best practices. Changes like this are necessary as the stakes of our election integrity is too high to ignore.[7]

## Social Security Numbers and Credit Reporting

Credit reporting companies in the United States are a major security threat. Credit reporting companies gather information from an extensive list of various lenders about people's outstanding debt. This gathered data is stored by individual, and the end result of all the collected data is a "report" which indicates the riskiness of lending to that individual. The credit reporting industry hinges on being able to reliably identify any individual's credit score in a quick manner to help lenders.

Because names alone are not always uniquely identifiable, to accurately identify a person's credit report from another's, credit reporting companies need to use a cross section of data to ensure that the "right" credit report is issued or altered. For example, there are 31,000 "James Smiths" in the United States.[8] This means that when any James Smith's credit report is requested, more information must be given to identify "which" James Smith. The extra information could potentially come from a large number of resources like addresses, phone numbers, or other personally identifiable information. In the United States, however, credit reporting companies use an individual's Social Security number (SSN) for identification.

There is a tradeoff to using SSNs. One pro of using SSNs is that they are truly unique. A US Citizen is given one at birth and likely knows it off the top of their head. This means that the information can quickly be verified, and reduces the knowledge burden on the individual. Instead of having to remember every address they've ever lived and those homes' phone numbers, individuals need only remember a small amount of information to accurately identify themselves. Another benefit of using SSNs is that the population is supposed to keep them secret. The SSN is to never be shared or published publicly in any way. This decreases the likelihood that someone would commit fraud in order to obtain a loan, since knowing secret information like an SSN is harder than knowing public information like addresses and phone numbers.

The SSN's primary intent is to uniquely identify individuals for the government, for the purpose of social benefit enrollment. By that use case, individuals are incentivized to keep the number secret, lest someone else assume their identity and sign up for government assistance or social programs in their name. This means that the government itself is responsible for managing SSNs and their disputes. If there is an issue with a compromised SSN, then it is the government's prerogative to resolve it.

These are the pros as to why private, non-governmental credit reporting companies would want to use individual's SSNs for identification, but by and large these benefits are nothing more than covers for laziness. The credit reporting industry could have taken on the task of creating their own set of parameters for secret identifiers to uniquely identify their users. Like always, though, technology and data collection companies get a pass to do whatever they want without repercussion or the public getting a say.

The obvious flaw in the whole plan to use Social Security numbers to identify people for a non-governmental business model is that the information is specifically for the government to use. Additionally, the population is told to keep that government-issued information a secret, so the entire industry's success is hinged on people being willing to defy that directive. It is pure laziness for private companies to simply expect citizens to use information they are supposed to keep between them and the government as identifiers for their business models.

## Equifax Security Breach

In 2017, perhaps the worst data breach in recent years happened to Equifax, one of the largest credit reporting companies. Hackers breached Equifax's data centers and stole personally identifying information, including Social Security numbers, of 147.9 million Americans. For perspective, only 325 million people currently live in the United States. That means that half of Americans had their personal information and Social Security numbers stolen as a result of Equifax's greed. By Equifax using and storing private information, and subsequently from their laziness in securing it, the credit reporting giant cost the country a great deal.[9]

Equifax's response was laughable. The company offered free credit report monitoring for a year: this means if a new account or loan was opened with an individual's identity, that person would be notified.[10] That's it—that's all they offered in terms of retribution to people who had their secret government information stolen. Equifax, after the intrusion, hired a cybersecurity firm to conduct forensic analysis and lock down the data to prevent future hacking.

Equifax also received criticism for the timeline of events. The attack occurred in May 2017, but wasn't discovered until July 2017. The intrusion wasn't reported to the public until September 2017, and the announcement came after many Equifax executives had the opportunity to sell stock. At least two Equifax executives were found guilty of insider trading, they were fined and sentenced.[11]

In July 2019, the Federal Trade Commission announced that Equifax agreed to a $575 million-dollar settlement in response to the event. The money would be used to pay off penalty fines to states and the Consumer Financial Protection Bureau totaling $275 million, as well as $300 million for compensation for the 147 million affected Americans to receive credit monitoring services. If the $300 million is not enough to compensate for the affected people's use of the services, Equifax will have to supply another $125 million.[12]

While the fines and compensation are large, they don't solve the issues that led to the situation in the first place. The FTC focuses blame on Equifax's security negligence rather than the process which allowed a private company to store the private, secret, identifying information of 147 million Americans. Data security is hugely important, but it's also important to evaluate what data companies have and if they should have it.

As an American, one whose data was stolen in this attack, I have to be frustrated with this kind of response. A year's worth of protection of information that will be permanently compromised for the victim is not adequate in the slightest. One would think that the theft of half the population's governmental, secret, and personally identifying information would've prompted national outrage and sweeping changes. There needs to be an incentive to securing private and personal data, and if the government refuses to hold those responsible accountable, then businesses will continue to forego security costs in favor of a prettier bottom line.

Here's some ideas of how the government could have punished Equifax, in ways that prevent a similar situation from happening in the future:

- Force Equifax to fully reimburse the government for the issue of new Social Security numbers to all affected people.
- Jail Equifax leadership for endangering the population of the United States and for aiding and abetting the theft of their identities.

- Ban any and all private companies from requesting, storing, and using Social Security numbers in any fashion.

The public not only has to scrutinize Equifax for their mishandling of information, but must also look to their governments and representatives for answers as to why Equifax got off with just financial restitution. Do our members of Congress understand the impact of these security lapses on the public? These aren't bank robberies or burglaries that affect small, localized areas and whose effects fade away. These are national emergencies that affect roughly half of the population—hundreds of millions of Americans—and we'll always feel these effects since our Social Security numbers are now compromised without replacement.

## House Committee Report on Equifax

The House Oversight and Government Reform Committee did investigate the Equifax data breach and determined that the problems were caused by systemic flaws in Equifax's security policies. In essence, the Committee concluded that the data breach was "entirely preventable." It was the company's negligence of security, not any individual engineer or technician (as Equifax tried to claim), that caused the vulnerabilities exploited in the attack.[13]

Specifically, the Committee's report claimed that the company lacked "clear lines of authority" in the structure of its IT department to report incidents. Equifax's "complex and outdated" security systems didn't keep up with the growth of the company. Basic security missteps were taken. The program dedicated to monitor network traffic, which would have caught an external actor downloading 147 million people's records, had been deactivated for 19 months due to a certificate expiring without renewal. That specific certificate was one of 300 expired security certificates across Equifax's IT system.

The Committee's recommendations, which came over a year after the attack, include similar suggestions to what I made. The recommendations include greater transparency on data collection and security risks, a replacement of Equifax's outdated IT system, a reduction in private industries using Social Security numbers, and a review of how federal contractors are held accountable for introducing security risks.

Additionally, the Committee suggested evaluating whether the FTC, which oversees consumer protection in the United States, had enough power and oversight into dealing with massive, national-level data breaches (It should be noted that this report came out before the FTC's fines were announced). Unfortunately, most of the recommendations put forth by the Committee haven't ripened into policy or bills. While Congress twiddles its thumbs, Americans become even more victimized by greedy technology companies refusing to pay for adequate security on personal information. In terms of data protection, the system isn't working for many Americans.

## Private Companies With Government Information

There becomes a huge problem when a private institution is responsible for the data security of government information. What happens in case of a data breach? If the government's data centers were breached, there would be no doubt that the investigation would be restless and the hackers brought justice. However, the lines are not so clear if a private institution holding government data gets breached. Whose job is it to rectify the situation?

This applies to more than just Social Security numbers collected by credit reporting agencies. In 2018, it was announced that the US military (the Pentagon) would be spending $10 billion investing in private technology companies to host its data in the cloud, rather than on government-owned servers. This follows a $600 million contract given to Amazon Web Services (Amazon's cloud storage service) by the Central Intelligence Agency in 2013.[14]

The benefits of having government data saved on the cloud will make it easier for branches of the military to share intelligence and information. Additionally, it reduces the need for the military to own and operate its own technology infrastructure. These same benefits existed for the CIA's contract. There are currently 17 mostly independent intelligence agencies in the United States' Intelligence Community, so the ability to share data with ease is appealing.

This brings more than just the population's personal identifications into the conversations. Now, we are willing to save our national secrets and intelligence on private property. Of course, benefits exist to this decision, but the risks exist as well. Should Amazon suffer the same level of breach as Equifax did, the risks would be higher than identity theft. I personally see this as a far lesser chance of happening, but risk is measured by likelihood multiplied by impact, so the risk might be higher.

The American people want their data to be secured. Private industry wants to save on money and boost their bottom lines, and an easy way for this to be accomplished is by not spending on IT security. The current system allows corporations to have their cake and eat it, too. They get to collect, record, and save endless amounts of personal information about private individuals, then, they don't even have to be burdened by securing it. In a philosophical battle of people or profits, we should favor the people. Do lawmakers share this sentiment?

## Amazon's Big Data Security Problems

Smart speakers are equally dangerous as they are popular. This is a phenomenon considering how intrusive they are, compared to the little benefit they provide to making life better. Smart speakers can record anything that's said around them, and those recordings are sent to big data warehouses, analyzed by the algorithms, and then forever stored away. One would hope that storage would be secure, but there may be reason to doubt that.

In 2016, the European Union passed the most comprehensive individual privacy law yet. The General Data Protection Regulation (GDPR) allowed users to have knowledge about which companies had stored their data, allowed those users to request that data be sent to them, and in some cases allowed the users to request the data be erased. The GDPR also put restrictions on data-storing companies, such as ensuring that personally identifiable information was kept separate from behavioral data and limiting the periods of time between data breaches happening and being reported. In May 2018, the law went into effect.[15]

The same year, in December, a German man requested his personal data be sent to him, using the newly enacted provisions. He did not own an Amazon Alexa smart speaker, so he was surprised when Amazon sent him his files which included 1,700 Alexa voice recordings. After failing to get in touch with Amazon, the man went to a German media outlet. That company was able to use the recordings to determine the other person's identity, and contact him about the situation. As it would turn out, he too had asked for his data be sent to him under the GDPR, and Amazon had made a mistake and sent the wrong data to the wrong people.[16]

Imagine if the 1,700 recordings included saved evidence of premeditated crime or scandalous behavior. Imagine if the user who was erroneously sent the data was a bad actor, and hadn't immediately made it his responsibility to solve the problem. To be completely fair, it wasn't his problem to solve. The responsibility falls solely on Amazon and they didn't even respond when he reached out.

Transparency also needs to be a priority for security lapses. The public deserves to know the scale and impact. About a month before the Alexa recordings incident, Amazon sent out cryptic messages in November 2018 informing some users that their names and emails had been exposed due to a "technical error." No further information was given about how many users were affected or what the error was.[17] This shows how little companies regard personal contact information as well as the need to wear their shame and explain situations of this nature.

If our data is not going to be kept secure, we can't trust companies with it. Modern technology companies have flooded their big data storages with every savable aspect of our information; information that could be used to damage, blackmail, or target us. It was their prerogative to save it and store it, it must be their prerogative to keep it secure as long as they keep it. The world's biggest online retailer has no excuse for incidents like these to happen with such spectacularly disappointing responses.

## FBI Hacking of Child Porn Sharers

Those seeking to undermine our digital security and hack us aren't always stereotypical hackers. They don't always seek to do harm, hold people for ransom, or gain access to secrets. In 2015, the FBI hacked a private service on Tor (an anonymous sharing and communication network) disgustingly called "Playpen," which was used to share and distribute child pornography. The FBI hacked into the network traffic of the service and thousands of computers. It discovered 1,300 IP addresses of the service's users.

"This is a scary new frontier of surveillance, and we should not be heading in this direction without public debate, and without Congress carefully evaluating whether these kind of techniques should be used by law enforcement," said Christopher Soghoian of the American Civil Liberties Union (ACLU). This case was years ago, but it never made it to Congress having a discussion on the ethics of the operation.

Even though the case never made it to the national stage of debate, like it should have, organizations like the ACLU and the

Electronic Frontier Foundation (EFF) have been outspoken about the dangers it poses to Internet privacy. The users who were identified via IP address were all searched because of their activity on the server hosting Playpen. Typically, one would expect each one would have their own case and be given an individual search warrant before their computers could be hacked by law enforcement. However, in this case, just one search warrant was used to gain access to all of their computers.[18]

In one of the cases challenging law enforcement on these practices, a federal judge ruled in 2016 that even the one search warrant was more than what was required, and the hacking could have been done by law enforcement without any judicial approval. This is a pretty clear diversion from the Fourth Amendment, which guarantees protections against unreasonable searches. The judge wrote: "The court finds that any such subjective expectation of privacy—if one even existed in this case—is not objectively reasonable."[19]

Of course, neither me nor the vast majority of the public will be rushing to these people's defense. They tried anonymously sharing child pornography, some of which "contained some of the most extreme child abuse imagery one could imagine," as described by the FBI. The EFF eloquently phrased the problem: "the decision underscores a broader trend in these cases: courts across the country, faced with unfamiliar technology and unsympathetic defendants, are issuing decisions that threaten everyone's rights."[20]

We have a right not to be hacked, by law enforcement and bad actors alike. If courts rule that any computer connected to the Internet should not be expected to have any privacy, then we must change laws and regulations to counter those rulings. The Fourth Amendment wasn't written to protect child pornography distributors, and each one of these cases could very well have had legal search warrants issued before the hacking occured—it was simply a matter of circumventing legal process for convenience.

The Fourth Amendment was written for the very reason of protecting us from unreasonable searches, and this disregard for the rule of law by law enforcement does set a dangerous precedent. I won't stand idly by while my own and others protections are robbed from them in favor of governmental conveniences. And if we won't fight for others, why should others fight for us? "Those who deny freedom to others deserve it not for themselves"—Abraham Lincoln, 1859.[21]

## The Five Layer Model

When discussing security online, it's important to look at all the potential areas in which vulnerabilities can occur. In order to understand what is meant by certain aspects and topics, it will be necessary to discuss in a basic sense the levels of technology which make the Internet work. Essentially, a framework called the TCP/IP Model describes Internet networking and activity as accomplished by five distinct layers.

The first layer, the one that I would expect people to know the most about, is called the "Application layer." This layer is composed of the applications that people use to do various activities on the Internet. An online video game is an application. Snapchat and Messenger are applications. Web browsers are a type of application. These can all be interacted with directly with the user, and are the most well-known touch points with the Internet.

The second layer in our model is the operating system. You might know what an operating system is, or at least know that Windows 10, Windows 7, and Mac OSX are all operating systems. The main goal of an operating system is to interpret the inputs and commands of the applications and convert those commands into what the actual hardware needs to do. For this reason, certain applications may or may not be compatible with multiple operating systems. This is because this interfacing can be difficult, and applications that are built to interface with one operating system may be hard to get working on another. In a definition true to its name, the operating system is the system that takes commands and operates the machinery.

The third layer is the hardware. This is the layer of the physical processor, the physical memory stick, the Ethernet port, the graphics card, etc. At some point, commands need to stop being commands and become work that needs to be completed, and this is the layer that accomplishes that. Taking commands from the operating system, the hardware moves the bytes (computer-readable information), generates new bytes, and runs calculations on existing bytes. For example, the hardware layer is what takes a set of bytes that create an image and sends a signal to the screen to display those colors.

The fourth layer is the router-level network layer. Using some method, a WiFi transmitter or an Ethernet port, the hardware sends signals out to the router. The router is another computer, with its own hardware, operating system, and applications, but its primary purpose is to move network commands around. Most home Internet networks have only one router, and this router is connected to the rest of the Internet using an address book of websites, called a DNS server. Requests for information (which are now just blocks of bytes called packets), get sent to the router, to do its natural task of routing those requests to the correct entity.

The router's connections are supplied and maintained by what is called an Internet service provider (ISP). ISPs are the fifth layer of our model. ISPs control the physical wires plugging into the router, and control the physicality of that wire connection up until the request is completed or it is handed off to another ISP, in which case it will wait for updates on the request/packet. There are generally considered to be three tiers of ISPs:

- Tier 3 ISPs will connect to user's networks and other high-tier ISPs. They do not have the connections to send requests across the country or world without "peering" with other ISPs. A local municipality in charge of their own Internet would probably be a Tier 3 ISP, not having the reach or physical network to connect to a Tier 1 ISP.

- Tier 2 ISPs are the ones that most people are probably most familiar with. These are generally larger, more national ISPs that connect to other ISPs of all tiers. They connect to everyone. Cox, Comcast, Verizon, and Century Link are all Tier 2 ISPs.
- Tier 1 ISPs are the companies that laid the cross-continental Internet wires. These are the companies that own and maintain the Internet connections that span across oceans and the wires that run from Los Angeles to New York. These are the "backbone" of Internet connectivity.

From the Tier 3 ISP, where the packet is originally placed, the entire process works in reverse. The packet is sent through Tier 2 and 1 ISPs to the destination network's router. The router sends the information to the correct computer on the Network which will take the request, this computer's hardware interprets the packet's bytes, and the receiving computer's operating system and running applications interpret the request for processing.

There's a lot of concepts and information that are glossed over here, such as the sheer amount of technical protocols followed at these levels. While important to how the Internet works, it is not important to discuss these for the purpose of these arguments. However, if anything written here has piqued an interest, just know that I'm hardly the architect of any of this, and all of it can be independently researched and dove into.

All these different layers and processes can be attacked and maliciously surveilled. Thus, each aspect of the technology poses a security threat to the user's system and privacy. Technology companies need to take these concerns seriously and ensure that users are safe online. In the coming sections, we'll get a closer look at how each layer can be targeted and the steps to be taken to secure them.

## End Users Are Their Own Risk

The first hacking risk, and what some have characterized as the most dangerous, is the user themselves. Users have the ability to be swayed into making unwise, uninformed, and insecure decisions about how they handle their safety and privacy online. These types of attacks include hacks that attempt to have users give away their passwords, commonly referred to as "phishing," and hacks that attempt to get users to willfully download malicious software, such as viruses, Trojan Horses, and worms.

There are measures that technology companies can use to increase user awareness to these kinds of exploits, but ultimately the responsibility falls into the user's hands to be cautious, safe, and secure online. Some companies have put helpful reminders into chat boxes, reminding users not to give away personal information or passwords. In 2018, Google's email platform Gmail was updated to include substantive anti-phishing warnings and features.[22] Other technologies, like modern day web browsers, can keep users safe by vetting downloaded packages to ensure their legitimacy.

A March 2019 report by BetterCloud surveyed 500 IT professionals and found that "62 percent believe that the biggest threat they face comes from the well-meaning, yet negligent end user." The report reads that negligent end users "mean well, but they can be careless and unintentionally expose sensitive information. They are particularly dangerous because they have access to critical assets, but lack the training or knowledge to keep sensitive information safe as they do their jobs."[23]

As stated earlier, not every evil actor can be contained, and the reality is that users simply need to learn safe practices online to protect themselves. Professional workers that handle a lot of IT resources but are not IT-trained, such as human resources, customer service, and public relations workers, are a particularly high threat and should take extra steps to ensure the information they receive digitally is secure.

## Application Layer Risks

The next layer of technology, the applications, have a large amount of security risks as well. Applications, most notably websites, can have many exploitable features often hidden from public view. Websites can hide sensitive information in source code, send superfluous sensitive information from the database to the user interface, save too many cookies that can be breached, and have unsecured entry points for accessing the underlying database.[24]

All of these security holes can be exploited by vigilant hackers. The effects of such an attack can be small, for example an online game might be hacked into giving away in-game content for free, or an online retail store could have fraudulent orders placed. However, in the case that the database is breached through the application layer, the consequences can be massive: millions of records of data with personal information can be deleted or stolen by the attackers.

Especially for websites, there are a large amount of third-party automated security systems that can check for these vulnerabilities. These include automated code scans, which work over popular coding languages like Java and Python. They can also be full system scans which find exposed access points and database vulnerabilities. Applications need to be locked down to only have the ability to give authenticated users access to small pieces of information.

One of the many ways in which businesses have used the Internet to their advantage has been by "going green," replacing traditional paper documents with online versions. However, if a company is going to save information online, that information must be secured. There are no shortcuts when it comes to user privacy.

In 2019, it was revealed that 24 million mortgage documents had been exposed on an unsecured database. This exposed files from CitiGroup, Capital One, Wells Fargo, and the federal government which included sensitive information such as "names, addresses, birth dates, Social Security numbers and bank and checking account numbers," as well as loan information about amounts owed, balances, and rates. The documents had dates from 2008, and perhaps further back.[25]

This is just a single example of companies attempting to reap the rewards of the Internet's innovation without taking the precautions to ensure user security. Knowing the potential effects of poor security decisions, and failing to maintain effective preemptive security, should be met with harsher punishments. The American people and their privacy deserve better than to be neglected by companies seeking to increase their profit margins. Even if companies were just trying to "go green," the benefits of that decision are outweighed by the negative consequences and privacy violations that were incurred.

## OS Security Risks

The operating system takes control of the machine's hardware and manages everything about the system. Operating system risks are a huge risk, and the biggest operating system developers (Windows, Linux, Apple, Google) need to be extra cautious that there are no exploits in their systems. Operating system vulnerabilities accounted for 61.5% of all vulnerabilities in 2017: 43.8% on desktop operating system and 17.7% on mobile operating systems. Compare that to 31.3% and 7.3% of all vulnerabilities being found in applications and web browsers, respectively.[26]

Operating system vulnerabilities can mean that users can get into areas of the machine without proper access. It can mean compromised applications can gain access to sensitive and personal information by exploiting security holes and privileges. A security hole in the operating system may not even necessarily be the fault of the developer, it may have been a security feature disabled by the user and never turned back on.

In May 2017, a Windows operating system hack called "WannaCry" was launched. WannaCry exploited a security hole in the way Windows implemented the Secure Message Block Protocol. Once it gained access to the system, WannaCry began encrypting files, leaving them locked away from the user. WannaCry was "ransomware," malicious software that asks for money to be sent in order for the attack to cease. In this case, WannaCry asked for $300 to be delivered for the user's files to be decrypted, to be paid in Bitcoin.

What's interesting about WannaCry's story is that the fix was already created before the attack began. The first people to notice to exploit in the operating system was actually the NSA in the United States. However, instead of working with Microsoft and telling them about their vulnerability, the NSA simply developed code to exploit it and planned to use that code to hack Windows machines. The code to exploit the bug was stolen from the NSA, and Microsoft gained knowledge of the vulnerability in April. A month later, when the WannaCry attack began, many vulnerable machines had already been patched.[27]

Entire industries, however, were brought to a standstill due to the hack. Any industry that runs Windows computers but doesn't upgrade them frequently was probably caught in the attack. Britain's National Health Service (NHS), and many healthcare organizations in the United States, have very locked down machines that do not receive automated updates. In the case of the NHS, Britain's countrywide healthcare system, most of the machines were still running Windows XP, an operating system that had ceased receiving patches and updates since 2014.

Trust me to know how slow healthcare organizations can be to adopt new technologies: For my job, I had a task to write code to support Internet Explorer 6 in 2017. For reference, Internet Explorer 6 received its last update in 2008. If there was any good thing about WannaCry, perhaps it reminded some industries how fast technology grows, and how security updates shouldn't be seen as bothersome but as essential.

The WannaCry attack showcased how dangerous operating system exploits can be. I think most of the blame should go to the NSA, who knew about the exploit and wanted to take it for their own power. Microsoft did a good job of proactively fixing the problem once they learned about it and pushing a fix, whether users got that fix is a different set of problems. Operating systems are the most powerful software that runs on the system, and they should be secured accordingly. Dangerous, industry-threatening attacks can come from the power of a successful operating system hack. WannaCry could very easily have stolen all of the affected users' information and files, but instead chose to encrypt them and hold them for ransom instead.

Operating systems certainly pose risks, but there's a lot of trust that users just have to have in the developers to make the product secure. The amount of technology companies building operating systems is a lot lower than the amount of companies building websites and applications. Operating system developers have a lot of responsibility in the regard of security, and while they do a good job of staying on top of threats and patches, there can be tense moments where it slips. For users, staying on top of operating system updates and patches is best practice and will keep you secure.

## Hardware Level Risks

From operating system-level hacks, hardware attacks become less common but also very dangerous. In order for a hardware hack to occur, the physical pieces of the computer must be compromised, not just the software that runs them. As a result of this, hardware-level attacks are hard to notice, as the software itself can't be relied on to detect a difference in the way the physical components of the computer are acting. It also means that hardware is extremely difficult to hack, since an attacker must gain access to the pieces they wish to compromise, usually before the computer is put together.

In 2018, Bloomberg reported a heavily rebutted accusation which alleged China had built chips that could spy on computer activity and implanted them into the targeted computers' motherboards. The original allegation came after Amazon was evaluating the hardware used to build its Amazon Web Services (AWS) infrastructure, which today hosts over 40% of all cloud computing servers. A discrepancy between the servers' motherboards and their designs showed that an additional chip, no bigger than a grain of rice, had been added. The article says:

> During the ensuing top-secret probe, which remains open more than three years later, investigators determined that the chips allowed the attackers to create a stealth doorway into any network that included the altered machines. Multiple people familiar with the matter say investigators found that the chips had been inserted at factories run by manufacturing subcontractors in China.

> This attack was something graver than the software-based incidents the world has grown accustomed to seeing. Hardware hacks are more difficult to pull off and potentially more devastating, promising the kind of long-term, stealth access that spy agencies are willing to invest millions of dollars and many years to get.

The article stated that, in addition to having affected the entire AWS infrastructure, nearly 30 total companies in the United States had been victims of "the Big Hack." The article stated the great lengths at which China would have had to gone to get this operation working: "developing a deep understanding of a product's design, manipulating components at the factory, and ensuring that the doctored devices made it through the global logistics chain to the desired location."

Because of the difficulty in pulling off a hardware hack, scrutiny is usually limited. "Hardware is just so far off the radar, it's almost treated like black magic." China is responsible for making 75% of the world's phones and 90% of the world's computers, so they weren't at all limited in access. "But that's just what US investigators found: The chips had been inserted during the manufacturing process, two officials say, by operatives from a unit of the People's Liberation Army."[28]

It was noted earlier and it should be noted again that this report has been disputed by the alleged victims and China itself. Amazon stated "We've found no evidence to support claims of malicious chips or hardware modifications." Apple stated that "[We have] never found malicious chips, 'hardware manipulations' or vulnerabilities purposely planted in any server." The Chinese Ministry of Foreign Affairs also responded stating innocence and dedicating their commitment to "supply chain safety in cyberspace" and "tackling cybersecurity threats." Bloomberg has stood by their reporting.[29]

I have no opinion on whether the story is true or false. I do believe in the danger of hardware-level security threats, and that all parts should be verified in ways that ensure user privacy and are regulated to ensure neutrality in processing. If the allegation is true, if over 40% of all the United States' cloud computing servers including ones used by US intelligence agencies are compromised, then it is time for a country-wide conversation about supply-chain security and the dangers of compromised hardware.

In addition to being massively powerful, hardware-level attacks are hard to remedy; this is because the compromised piece can be hard to identify (it may be smaller than a grain of rice). The piece could be a critical part of the system that cannot be replaced. On top of all this, new, fixed physical components must be created, shipped, and installed on affected computers. Unlike a software patch, this cannot be sped up by a quick Internet download and installation.

While the alleged Chinese hardware hack is in contention, there are other examples of hardware-level security being compromised. In 2013, Edward Snowden stole and leaked documents created by the NSA. In these documents was proof that the NSA, specifically their Tailored Access Operations team, had been intercepting hardware and installing/replacing components with parts equipped for surveillance. The intercepted devices were being shipped internal to the United States and internationally, in hopes of creating a vast spying network.[30]

Among the affected devices were routers, USB plugs, and motherboards. Intercepted routers were equipped with beacons which act as backdoor surveillance tools on network traffic. Altered motherboards have their BIOS software updated, which is the software that runs the decision making and control of the computer's physical components. This new software surveils the entire computer and sends the data to the NSA. When the changed USB cords are plugged into a computer they act as surveillance tool that transmits data through radio, not through the computer's Ethernet port or Wi-Fi transmitter, which makes them virtually undetectable.[31]

The NSA has a huge problem with unconstitutional privacy violation, but the focus here is on their hardware modifications for the sake of global-scale undetectable surveillance. Hardware hacks are very hard to detect, but also hard to accomplish. The NSA had to set up a way to intercept the hardware packages and deliver them to a secret laboratory in order to be outfitted with the surveillance mechanisms. The documents claim that these operations were done "with the support of Intelligence Community partners and the technical wizards in TAO."[32]

Hardware-level attacks can hand over a lot of information and give an extreme amount of access in a very unnoticeable way. This requires extreme care for the parts and components used in our computers. Vetting and security needs to be the outright number one priority of selecting trusted manufacturers of hardware components. If possible, the technology industry should look for ways to create auditing tools that monitor a system's hardware to ensure no activity is occurring under the table, out of sight from the operating system.

## Router Level Risks

If the user's command is Internet-bound, then it must go to their network's router. The purpose of the router is to know the locations of the rest of the Internet and to manage traffic for users on the network. This means that the routers handle a significant amount of information about the kinds of content and Internet traffic belonging to all users on the network. Compromising a router therefore gives a greater amount of Internet traffic information than compromising a single computer or device, and securing routers is integral to securing Internet privacy.

Similar to hardware attacks, router-level attacks can be hard to detect as the end users' devices are not notified. Users themselves, most of which are generally oblivious to these topics, are required to maintain the security of their networks. This means giving the duty of vigilant monitoring and preemptive action on the user, which is a recipe for negligence.

On the other hand, assigning culpability to actors besides the user can be difficult. Should the router's manufacturer be blamed? Not in all cases, because a manufacturer isn't solely responsible for any hardware or software bugs that could be exploited within the router. Should the ISP be required to monitor the router's behavior for irregularities? Probably not, since it would be easy for the router to appear uncompromised.

In 2015, a report by Incapsula revealed that as many as 40,000 personal (not corporate-owned) network routers had been compromised and made part of a "botnet," which uses compromised computers to launch attacks on other Internet locations. The initial belief was that the exploit was based on a hardware or operating system bug of the router, but "further inspection revealed that all units are remotely accessible via HTTP and SSH on their default ports. On top of that, nearly all are configured with vendor-provided default login credentials."

This means that access was gained on the routers based on user negligence. The owners of the routers had never taken the time to change the login passwords or to assign different network ports in order to connect to the router. The router manufacturer tried to shift blame in this direction, stating that their products must come unlocked and insecure because their target customer is not a layman home user but rather ISPs and technically savvy users. The manufacturer recommends "any ISP deploying our products should definitely change default credentials, as well as block unnecessary management access."

But this shift of responsibility is unhelpful. Can't the ISP just simply make the same claim, that their level of control is limited so as to not step on the toes of their technically-inclined users? That's why Incapsula researcher Igal Zeifman argues that manufacturers should make their products more secure by default, stating "[d]istributors, resellers and users all share responsibility for their routers' safety...vendors should share that responsibility as well....I don't think that router devices should only be produced with the sole purpose of 'making the lives of a competent network admin easier'...Our message here is that of shared responsibility."[33]

Router-level attacks are becoming widespread and common. In 2018, it was reported by Talos, the vulnerability intelligence and assessment division of the Cisco router manufacturer, that 500,000 home network routers had been compromised by a malware called "VPNFilter." The malware has the power to "steal personal information, redirect web traffic, infect other devices and even 'brick' infected devices to make them unusable."[34;35]

Luckily, the attack was software-based and could mostly be resolved by resetting the router to factory settings. The scariest part about router hacks is that the users are generally unaware. Not even the affected network's connected devices would have any idea that the router was compromised. For most people, it takes a press release stating the danger and threat to their technical security to encourage safety precautions, vigilance, and best security practices.

In order for routers to know where to send traffic, they rely on "Domain Name Servers" (DNS). DNS acts as a sort of address book that can translate a domain name like "google.com" into a server's IP address, which is much more friendly to Internet traffic. DNS has been attacked and taken offline in the past, meaning that Internet users had no way of getting to otherwise online sites. In October 2016, the United States and Western Europe were taken offline for a day when Dyn, a DNS company, was attacked and made unreachable.[36]

Router security breaches give a dangerous amount of access to the attacker. Left undetected, compromised routers can silently leak data and personal information for years. Routers must be made and distributed with the intent that the average user will not perform regular health checks and maintenance. The responsibility for router security breaches cannot land on the unaware user, it must be given to a more vigilant party, like the manufacturer that makes the routers and the ISP that installs them. To be clear, this does not mean that the ISP and router manufacturer should control or have dominion over the router after it is installed, just that the default and preinstallation settings of the router need to be less generic and focused on user security for laymen, and that the ISP should be more culpable for inauthentic traffic on its network, even if it is stemming from a user-owned router.

## ISP Wire Attacks and Network Stack Vulnerabilities on the Receiving End

After the router hands off the user's request to the Internet service provider, the request will travel across physical wires to get to the destination. Along the way, the request may stop at multiple other routers just to "get directions" to the next location in order to fulfill the request. For simplicity, re-explaining the dangers of a compromised router is not required. Although it is possible that the ISP or its wires could be hacked, as in the wires themselves were modified and outfitted with something that could alter or log the traffic, this has not been majorly demonstrated in the contemporary digital age.

While it wasn't due to being hacked, there have been instances where ISPs have been taken offline by their wires being cut. In 2018, the entire country of Mauritania lost its Internet access due to an underwater cable being severed.[37] In 2011, Armenia lost Internet access when a 75-year-old woman in Georgia accidentally cut through the underground wire.[38] But these outages have happened as coincidences, because the locations of these inter-continental wires are not well documented. It's not that attacking an ISP's physical network is not feasible, but the attacker would have to somehow get access to the wires (which are buried and hidden) and then set up a surveillance apparatus without being detected.

Once the request gets to the destination, the entire process on the receiving end must be secured. This means that the destination's router, hardware, operating system, and application layers must not be compromised to ensure the data privacy and security for the end user. A user with an entirely secure network stack could be sending Facebook messages to someone whose operating system has been hacked. This would compromise that conversation's security for both parties, even though the first user has no issues on their end.

Securing all aspects of one's network stack is a large feat, and expecting it of everyone else on the Internet would be foolish. However, laws against hacking are actually quite strong, and so long as the culprit is an individualized or rogue group of actors prosecution from law enforcement like the FBI is likely. It's important that as many people as possible understand all the different layers and avenues of attack that hackers can take, as knowledge is a way to combat their tactics. It is especially important that regulators and legislators understand these intricacies for our society that is becoming more and more reliant on and integrated with technology.

## Corporations Compromising Information Makes Security Seem Silly

As stated previously, it is not only the hackers and attackers seeking to capitalize on technology vulnerabilities that must be checked. Businesses, the ones in charge of handling the secured information, must also be held accountable. If Facebook secures its application and no one else can see the user's activity, but Facebook itself is recording that activity, then what have we really solved?

The users' expectation isn't that evil hackers don't acquire and abuse their private and personal data, it's that no one will acquire and abuse that data. Because at the end of the day the people responsible for the technology industry recording one's Internet activity, the government surveilling one's Internet activity, and the hackers trying to steal one's Internet activity all have something in common: They are all corrupt, greedy humans who should never have that kind of power over another individual's information and life.

No matter how hard the technology industry and government try to sell it another way, the belief that another individual can appropriately be given access and control over another person's life is wrong. No amount of technical security will fix these core problems of data monitoring and individual rights. Thus, we must seek to address the villains in the room. Hackers must be fought with security, powerful corporations must be fought with regulation, and governments must be fought with oversight and accountability.

# X

## Encryption

Encryption is a tricky issue to regulate. Typically, technologists and technology journalists will complain that a certain law or regulation will "break encryption." Ultimately, encryption is a vocabulary word describing the way that data can be scrambled, only able to be unscrambled by a verified key or password holder. Encryption is used as a failsafe in case data is intercepted or obtained outside the "normal" ways a user might use it.

Encrypted data is very commonplace, and some data is required by law to be encrypted whenever possible. For example, the Health Insurance Portability and Accountability Act (HIPAA) was passed in 1996, and is used to ensure the security and privacy of patient data in the healthcare industry. HIPAA regards sensitive healthcare and medical records of patients as Protected Health Information (PHI), and specifically states that technology which facilitates healthcare should "implement a mechanism to encrypt PHI whenever deemed appropriate."[1] Millions of records saved in databases in every industry are obfuscated for encryption purposes, to secure the data from being deciphered by unauthorized parties without the correct credentials.

Encryption is how websites save sensitive data like passwords. To the end user, the website just accepts a password input of a simple string (Like "password321"). Before the password gets saved into the database, it gets encrypted by the website so in the database, the password does not appear as "password321," but rather as encrypted, scrambled data. If a hacker were to access the database, they would not be able to read the password and access user accounts. Instead, the only software that can read the passwords remains the website, which has the decryption key. This is how data encryption works.

There's also end-to-end encryption, which describes the encryption of data before transmission across the Internet. Essentially, before sending a message to a receiver's phone, my phone would encrypt the data so that only that receiver's phone could read it. This would prevent someone from simply reading Internet traffic and reading our conversation plainly. Instead, they would see packets and data flowing between the two phones, but would not be able to make sense of the data without the decryption keys.

Most of the time, when laws and regulations are accused of "breaking encryption." they are referring to the former. The government and investigators want access to the physical, stored data on the device. Thus, the government writes laws that require the encryption technology to "allow backdoors," that is, decrypting the data without the decryption key. This is acceptable practice as long as the legal routes are taken: obtaining warrants, issuing subpoenas, and fairly protecting their individual's right to privacy.

## End-to-End Encryption Breaking

More and more often, governments are asking technology providers to give them access to continuous monitoring of Internet traffic to track Internet crime in real time. This has been met with valid criticism over the rights of people to not be surveilled and that governments are undereducated to write meaningful laws that deal with encryption. Some countries have decided to hand off continuous monitoring as the duty of technology providers themselves.

In July 2015, France passed what has been called the "French Patriot Act," which placed monitors on every web server, meaning that all traffic is recorded and saved. This allows the French to engage in real-time Internet monitoring, all packets and data are examined for key phrases or topics. If a user sends or receives a message with a key phrase, then the user is flagged. Only then will the actual saving of data occur, until then, all their data is just passing through for processing.

However, the Act does not require the real-time decryption of data. Only flagged users have their encrypted data saved, and it is then decrypted at a later date. The French do have the legal ability to decrypt data, as of November 2001, and technology providers that fail to provide decryption keys can be fined or given jail time. Because of this combination, there is no need to decrypt encrypted data as it passes through the server's algorithm, and end-to-end encryption can remain intact. The weakness is that if data is encrypted, it cannot possibly be flagged as it is unreadable, and that data passes through the monitors without being caught, even if it would normally be flagged.[2]

In late 2016, the United Kingdom passed a law that requires ISPs to save all of a user's traffic for up to a year. The same bill also provisioned that ISPs need to disable any end-to-end encryption they're doing at the requests of the government. This is an interesting case, since ISPs are not the keepers of encryption. I'm not even certain how ISPs would tackle encryption on their end, because as soon as the packet goes to another ISP's network, the new ISP has no way to decrypt the data. The entire encryption/decryption algorithm and process happens at the application level, once the data has completed transmission (and completed its use with the ISP). An ISP would not have access to the decryption key, only the application would.[3]

Popular communication applications like FaceTime, iMessage, and WhatsApp use end-to-end encryption. Their owners, Apple and Facebook, took adamant stances against the bill. Their claim was two-part. First, end-to-end encryption is incredibly important to securing communications from eavesdroppers. Secondly, making end-to-end encryption optional would require an extensive rewrite of their applications and of encryption technology as a whole. Other critics, like famous whistleblower Edward Snowden, spoke out against the law for making encryption seem like a nice-to-have feature, rather than an essential one. Nevertheless, the U.K.'s 2016 Investigatory Powers Bill passed.

## Responsibility to the Internet Service Providers

The Investigatory Powers Bill compels ISPs to be ready to undo any encryption that the ISP themselves put on the data. This is a clear indication of a lack of understanding of the process. Data is encrypted before and after it is given to the ISP; the ISP plays no role with encryption. But the Bill further compels ISPs to aid the U.K.'s spying on its citizens by forcing ISPs to keep "Internet Connection Records" on their customers for twelve months. Internet Connection Records log what time a user accessed websites, but not every page that was visited within the domain.

It is possible for any government agency to request and access these records without a judge or a warrant. That means that law enforcement can access what websites any person in the country visited, without any oversight. This is basically compulsory spying by U.K. ISPs on U.K. citizens, which is accompanied by an effective gag order which silences ISPs or ISP workers from acknowledging that data has been requested.

The U.K. isn't the only country where this kind of unaccountable data requesting occurs. The United States basically has the same power—the Federal Bureau of Investigation (FBI) can use National Security Letters (NSLs) to gain access to any service usage records that an ISP has for an individual. As some examples, an individual's use of banking, telephone, or (most importantly for us) Internet services could be requested by an NSL.

Using NSLs does not require the oversight of a judge. Just like with the Investigatory Powers Bill, the ISP is only required to give "non-content"—instead of detailing what was transmitted or received, the ISPs need only report that a transmission happened. And also similar to the Investigatory Powers Bill is that using NSLs gags ISPs from speaking about the data that's requested of them.

One difference between the two programs is that NSLs can only be written by members of the FBI's leadership, whereas requesting information from ISPs in the U.K. could be done by any law enforcement member. Despite this limitation, the FBI has issued approximately 30,000 per year since 2006. The increase in use comes from the 2006 PATRIOT Act which loosened the requirements for them to be issued.

Across the globe we are seeing countries ask more from their ISPs to aid in surveilling the population. From an encryption perspective, the ISP is not being forced to decrypt all the data that comes across its network. This is a correct agreement, as ISPs are not the ones doing the encryption. But increasing the demands on ISPs is unsustainable, because ISPs are not the only piece of the industry that needs to be compelled to spill its guts by law enforcement in investigations.

We need to rethink how we write regulations about how ISPs interact with law enforcement. I agree that companies with information should give it over if it is relevant to investigations or prosecutions, but that determination should be made by a judge or at least something accountable. We need insight into how our justice system is using the tools we give it, and that is impossible if the people and companies interacting with it are silenced.

## How Should the US Government Approach Encryption Problems?

It is perplexing that in an era where we know that technology giants track everything we do online, the government feels the need to gather data from Internet service providers. In the world of technology, an Internet service provider is only going to have a small understanding of the online interactions a user has, not the content of those interactions. Wouldn't it be a much more lucrative endeavor to ask the actual applications what kind of interactions took place?

An Internet service provider can tell an investigator that a user was logged into Facebook for 20 minutes on December 18, 2018. On the other hand, Facebook could tell that same investigator that the user was online for 20 minutes, messaged 3 people, and give the entire message logs (this may require backdoor decryption). I'm not necessarily advocating for that kind of intrusion, but clearly querying the latter would be much more helpful than the former.

I am for the lawful decryption of stored data on a device or server, if the data may be material evidence for use in a criminal proceeding. This means that the warrant or subpoena issued to gather the evidence would have to be upheld by a judge. The United States government should create laws which make it clear that there is a time and a place in which individuals may be compelled to decrypt files and data.

A common counter argument to this is that it violates the Fifth Amendment rights of the individual not to be compelled to testify against himself. But, giving a password or decrypting a file is not necessarily a testimony. It's a discovery of evidence, evidence that could exonerate the individual just as much as it could be used in their prosecution.

Creating backdoors in encryption algorithms is a maybe. I don't think it would be a good idea to force technology companies to redesign encryption to work with the government. Still, there are cases in which it's necessary to open encrypted files and data, with no means of gaining the decryption key. If I were to support this, the technical design would have to be approved by a variety of technicians and technology companies to ensure the security of encryption and to safeguard against government abuse.

However, it was concluded by a 2015 MIT study that no such tool or design exists. This is the first paragraph of the report's executive summary: "Political and law enforcement leaders in the United States and the United Kingdom have called for Internet systems to be redesigned to ensure government access to information—even encrypted information. They argue that the growing use of encryption will neutralize their investigative capabilities. They propose that data storage and communications systems must be designed for exceptional access by law enforcement agencies. These proposals are unworkable in practice, raise enormous legal and ethical questions, and would undo progress on security at a time when Internet vulnerabilities are causing extreme economic harm."[4]

Think of an encrypted file as a piece of paper in a safe. Ultimately, due to a criminal case, law enforcement needs access to that piece of paper. Lawfully compelled decryption would be forcing the owner of the safe to open the safe. This would require a number of judicial proceedings, oversight, and transparency before it would be allowed.

Backdoor decryption would essentially be giving the government a saw to get through the safe's walls. Or perhaps, a second combination lock to which only the government knew the combination. This solution would be appropriate only if the combination lock or saw were effective, but not so effective that safes everywhere suddenly became vulnerable. Currently, no designs exist that don't carry these risks.

Encryption is much more than a nice-to-have feature in the current day and age. Communicating by means which are eavesdropper-proof makes living with technology easier for everyone. Storing data with password protection from intruders is necessary when there are more hackers than ever. The public takes advantage of encryption, and I'm happy they do. Law enforcement agencies have the right idea in mind in wanting to expand their ability to conduct investigations. I have faith in them not to abuse their power, but they should pursue investigation powers that can be overseen and regulated by the public.

## Attempts to Solve the Encryption Problem

A 2016 US Chamber of Commerce statement declared its "[opposition for] government mandates, whether regulatory or technical. Top-down requirements would likely limit collective gains in information security while making American enterprises less competitive in global markets. Any legal requirements need to be reasonable and technology neutral."

The government shouldn't have a stake in which encryption technologies users use. The statement cited that the US doesn't dominate markets on encryption, that only 1/3rd of encryption products worldwide are made in the US. This means that even if the US forced its technology companies to alter encryption and install backdoors, it would only be on a third of all devices. The regulations would, in effect, simply weaken the US's encryption products on the global market.[5]

A Homeland Security Committee report, also from 2016, laid out the reasons why encryption is a complicated matter and described the conversation as "security vs. security" rather than "privacy vs. security": "Encryption protects critical infrastructure, trade secrets, financial transactions, and personal communications and information. Yet encryption also limits law enforcement's ability to track criminals, collect evidence, prevent attacks, and ensure public safety." The committee concluded that "there is no silver bullet regarding encryption" and "we did not discover any simple solutions."[6]

This supports the position that any form of regulation or legislation on encryption would have to be extremely careful to even be considered. Federal regulators—that is, Congress—needs to learn more about the problem in order to make educated decisions. After the Homeland Security Committee's report was released, a bipartisan bill was submitted to create a National Commission on Security and

Technology Challenges. This "Digital Security Commission" would be a team of expert stakeholders from law enforcement and technology, combined with advocates for civil liberties, with the end purpose of informing Congress with suggestions for regulating and legislating for encryption. However, the bill was never passed and the commission was never created.

Just like the Homeland Security Committee states, there is no silver bullet. Moving forward on tackling the encryption problem, the Digital Security Commission should be created. There are a lot of stakeholders, technology companies responsible with making the products, law enforcement responsible with investigating and prosecuting, human and digital rights advocates, regulators, etc. Every one of those groups has valid use cases and it will take collaboration to reach any sort of solution, so getting that group of people together is the next best step.

# XI

## The Difficulty of Regulatory Change

### Limited Government Leads to Limited Change

Our constitution, written primarily by James Madison (our 4th President), wrote the foundation of a government that in itself had so much red tape, checks, and balances that it would be difficult to make sweeping change in a short amount of time. The reasoning has lasted the lifetime of the document: People are flawed. They will see problems and, in their hastiness to solve them, use the government's power without necessarily caring for the long-term consequences on the people or the country.

James Madison's government is still in working order today. When Donald Trump took office, he enacted an executive order which blocked travel to America from countries in the Middle East. Before the executive order was enacted, however, it was challenged and blocked by a federal judge named Derrick Watson on its legality.[1] Trump supporters, outraged that a judge in Hawaii was "impeding" Trump's agenda, failed to realize that this action was entirely permissible under the Constitution. In fact, it's proof that the process works: A person wasn't able to hastily use the power of the government to solve a problem, at least not without having to have its legality confirmed and some time to reflect on its potential effects.

Perhaps true to his ideals of not wanting people to use government power to solve their problems, James Madison's Constitution does not give or restrict any power to or from private companies, nor give rights to the people to be free from them. This is true when examining an issue like the freedom of speech. Just because the freedom of speech limits the government's ability to punish people based on the words they speak doesn't mean that private corporations cannot. But the limited powers of the government also hurt us in that infringements on our rights (like our right to privacy) are not squashed, for the reason that it is private companies doing the infringing.

James Madison was absolutely correct to want to limit the effects of a reaction-based government, and the Constitution he fathered is effective in this regard. The weakness of the US Constitution is that it fails to be reactive in solving societal problems as they arise. Right now, there are 1,200 applications we Americans could have on our phones which will send our precise location data to private companies in real time.[2] This is a problem in society that people should absolutely have a say in whether or not they agree with or condemn those functions. However, due to our slow-moving government, we haven't even begun to put our hands around the idea of legislating these issues.

## Politicians as Celebrities and the Abandonment of Reaching Out to the Other Side

We've become so tribalistic that we've stopped having serious discourse. We stopped looking for nuance in the issues. We constantly adjust our demeanor, word choice, and attitude to better position ourselves to be in the right. Our politicians became so afraid of giving too much credit to the other side that they stopped giving credit at all.

We live in a world where lawmakers and policymakers have more data than ever before to influence their decisions, but confirmation bias and tribalism prevent anyone from changing their minds. Instead, having the most accessible and greatest amount of data in any point in human history to create influenced and varied policy, we use it to pick outliers that support positions we already held. In

2016, Oxford named "post-truth" to be the word of the year.[3] Nothing could describe our current political climate better.

The American population needs to return to a mentality of seeing lawmakers as leeches, not gods. Politicians need not be revered, but treated as humans. Their holding of power ought to be seen as temporary, as it was when George Washington and James Madison founded this country. We should make greater use of our votes to oust those who make no meaningful impact in Congress from their positions, even those who "do the job" of toeing their party line. If their tether to reality comes loose, they should be removed. We absolutely must regularly remind our lawmakers that their job is to represent their constituents in policy decisions, and nothing more.

I'd imagine, for the run-of-the-mill politician, that the post-truth political climate has been quite the blessing. Emotions are easy to convey and repeat. Humans can read emotions from tone, facial expression, volume, and a number of other cues. On the other hand, there's very few ways to convey one's ability to understand facts and data. In a political climate where simply sharing the emotional outrage over one event can convey which "side" one is on, instead of having to dig into any issue and demonstrate understanding, the career politician thrives.

A Democrat can demonstrate their position on foreign policy and prison reform by being outraged about Brett Kavanaugh's nomination to the United States Supreme Court amidst sexual misconduct allegations. A Republican can represent his views on the economy and immigration by having an emotional reaction to Hillary Clinton's email and data security violations. Not because these stances and news stories have any correlation, but because sharing an emotional response and feeling with a voter is so much more important than taking a layered and nuanced approach to multiple issues and arriving at the same conclusions as them.

One of the blessings of the digital age is that breaking news can reach billions of people in a matter of hours. One of the curses is that that level of outreach is profitable, and we live under the constant stress of the 24-hour news cycle. To a news site, cable network, or YouTube channel, all news is good news. Unfortunately, this perspective is not too different from a politician's.

As a politician, it's valuable to stay relevant in the public's eye, just like for celebrities and news organizations. The best way for politicians to reach out to their constituency isn't to hold a town hall or public meeting, it's to make a post on social media. It's fast to deliver, easy to consume, and in all likelihood, reaches the most amount of people. Politicians, however, can get trapped into the same feedback loop as everyone else in the public eye.

Politicians will oftentimes not wait for the details of an event to fully be released before posting. This is dangerous because it de-prioritizes facts and certainties in our political decisions. It rewards confirmation bias. Especially in the case of a tweet, in which the amount one can write is limited, these posts abandon nuance and understanding for divisiveness and tribalism. When the hottest take gets the hottest attention, that behavior is incentivized.

We need to examine how we reward politicians for behaving in these kinds of reactive behavior. My ideal representative doesn't spend their days in an office on Twitter or scheduling appearances on cable news to gain political clout discussing the latest outrage. We should reward the representatives that spend their days with their peers, using science and data to discuss and debate the best ways in which the government can help solve problems facing Americans and working to implement solutions.

## Americans Need Youth in Government

We need youth. Throughout America's Gilded Age, the time period after The American Civil War and before the First World War, the average age of a congressman was just under 50 years old. Today, that number is just under 60. The people in our current Congress lived their entire pre-political lives without modern technology. How can they be qualified to talk about technology to a nation that desperately needs guidance? How can they be expected to regulate it? Big tech thrives on the fact that our government will do nothing to stop them, for reasons of complacency or incompetence.

In 2018, many of the biggest technology companies were brought in front of lawmakers to answer questions about their companies' practices. The CEO's of Facebook, Twitter, and Google were all rounded up. It was frustrating to watch America's non-tech savvy representative body try to question the big technology CEOs about the intricacies of their companies' creations—it felt like they didn't even know what questions to ask. At one point, a congressman asked Google's CEO Sundar Pichai a question about his iPhone, which Pichai calmly answered, "we don't make iPhones."[4]

For this reason, among others, the United States needs term limits. The United States isn't meant to have rulers, and those who stay in office gaining political power for too long should take note of George Washington, who gave up power a number of times, all while knowing he could have been king himself. We need a House of Representatives that is *representative*. People who are out of touch, and people who don't understand modern technology, don't have the capabilities of leading our nation through the turbulent winds of economic transition. Those who haven't worked a day since the early 2000s have no experience to talk about or regulate the mobile economy.

America has always been young. The youth have always found ways to massively influence the culture, to influence the economy, and to influence politics. We're headed into another major economic transition of American history and unlike the older generations, young people in America don't need to write somber speeches about how those changes will affect their grandchildren, because they'll affect us the same.

It's also important to discuss how simply dangerous some of these people can be with technology. Perhaps it was out of pure naivety, as law enforcement has decided; perhaps it was for other reasons. The reasons why don't change the fact that, as Secretary of State not even 10 years ago, Hillary Clinton sent over 100 classified emails to an unsecured, private server,[5] and at least one foreign intelligence power gained access to that information.[6]

These issues are not siloed to one person or party. To this day, members of the Trump administration use unsecured personal devices and accounts to conduct official state business.[7] Our governing body isn't just technologically illiterate, its technical deficiencies are dangerous to this country.

A study published in January 2019 revealed that people over the age of 65 were seven times more likely to share fake news that adults 29 and younger. The study was conducted by looking at Facebook sharing of news over the 2016 presidential election cycle. The authors found that just age, not sex, race, education, or income, was the sole determinant in the likelihood of a person to share fake news. Now, this isn't a slam on the current Congress. Only 8.5% of American Facebook users shared fake news article even one time.[8] It's unlikely that, in that 8.5%, was a sitting member of Congress. This study only shows that young people have technology more figured out, and that the age group most prone to sharing fake news is just five years older than the average age of a member of Congress.

The American Intelligence Community is moving forward with new technologies as ways to streamline information sharing and enhance its operations. This is evidenced by the CIA getting a contract with AWS and the Pentagon starting contract bidding for a cloud services provider. But we are putting these tools in the hands of the wrong people, which means we are faced with a choice of slowing down the digitization of American intelligence operations or hiring people with better understanding of the new technologies.

There is clearly danger in trusting people who don't understand technology with technology that has highly classified information. We've already seen careless mistakes lead to classified information ending up in the wrong hands. The people who have access to that level of information need to understand data security and data handling practices, or else we are doomed to make more mistakes that undermine our intelligence operations and national security. We need to put the trust into the hands of the people who don't share fake news and have grown up, studied, and worked with technology every day of their lives.

## Disconnectedness Is the Enemy

This is not about bias against people of old age. As a young person, it is clear to me when wisdom and experience are necessary tools to guide through a problem. The problem, I think, comes from entrenchment that leads to disconnectedness. I want to believe that a congressman who spends 50% of the year outside of their congressional district can maintain a pulse of what their constituents are going through. Over small periods of time it's understandable that the tie between Representative and Community would remain unbroken, but the reality just seems so different.

Not a single member of the US Congress should feel comfortable with the uncertainty that many Americans are facing about the future. But what we see is the exact opposite: complacency and partisan bickering have become the cornerstones of congressional behavior. It baffles me that some of these issues are even considered partisan at all: Would a Republican be against a limit on Google's ability to manipulate search results behind the scenes, because they believe too strongly in free market Capitalism (even though there are plenty of similar laws in other industries)? Would a Democrat oppose the same law because it just so happens that those search result skews tend to be favorable to their party (even though in 10 years the exact opposite could be true)?

There's really no excuse for our current Congress's behavior and their failings to help the American people. Sweeping change will be necessary to get younger, technology-literate citizens into our most important governing bodies. But the effort has to be there, for a Congress that perpetually sets these problems on the backburner to deal with the latest media frenzy is ineffective, divisive, and directionless.

We are headed into an era of the American economy which will give unprecedented levels of access to services, entertainment, information, and comfort. At the same time, American hopelessness is rising. Suicide rates and drug overdoses continue to drag down American life expectancy. At a time when unprecedented technological advancement should be bringing optimism, many Americans have lost faith in America's institutions and government.

This is because of our ineffective and weak legislative body not acting to address our concerns and our issues. It is time to bring to Congress minds and spirits who are sick of the status quo, who want to fight for the everyday American, and create laws that will shape the economy in ways that truly benefit the people. How great would it be for the country to see real change in the way we fight back against the powers that be?

## Taxpayers Subsidize Billionaires

Our Congress is pathetic at creating laws and regulations on businesses that put people before profits, and big technology companies are perhaps the best example of this behavior. For a number of reasons, such as lack of lobbying regulation or gridlocked political processes, Congress is directly responsible. However, Congress's inaction does not absolve big technology companies of their involvement in the machine.

Throughout 2018, Amazon utilized a search committee to determine the location of their next headquarters. This search committee went from city to city in the United States, and in each metropolis they heard what that city would "offer" them to locate there. These offers would include laundry lists of tax benefits, promises of non-interference, and everything else that a private interest could possibly want.

In return, Amazon offered the cities the boom of enterprise. The new headquarters was planned to bring in 50,000 high-quality jobs in technology and business, with an average salary of $150,000 per position. Amazon also promised to educate, train, and hire local talent to help fill the openings. Even with initial tax deductions, the increased industry would generate enough money to increase tax revenue in the long term.[9]

It's deserving of outrage how effective the committee was. The committee got so many great offers they ended up splitting the headquarters and taking two. Our government—in this case our local governments—failed to resist the urge to offer tax breaks. Those cities offered to take tax revenue out of the hands of those in need and hand it to the biggest online shopping company in the world.

This was caused, undoubtedly, by the growing disconnect between the government, the private sector, and the populace. I'd imagine that few members of the public would be okay paying taxes which subsidize a company the size of Amazon. Whether you're on the political left and believe in taxes in the 50% range or a libertarian who would like to see 0%, everyone can agree that Amazon does not need our tax money.

When Amazon's search committee had narrowed it down to the final 20 cities, the public grew increasingly nervous about the effects that 50,000 new jobs would have on any city's transportation network and housing market as many (if not most) of those positions were filled by people who moved there for the job. Despite these rising levels of distrust, the cities' governments got so competitive on cutting Amazon a deal that they had to draw up a non-aggression pact to make sure that the deals didn't get too good for the company. It is absurd to consider the lengths in which the cities bent over backwards to give Amazon the best deal.

The final two cities were announced in November 2018. The first location was Long Island City, a neighborhood of New York City. It was offering Amazon $1.525 billion in tax breaks and benefits. The second city, Arlington, Virginia, promised Amazon $573 million.[10] By February 2019, just three months later, local activists and politicians protested the New York location to the point that Amazon backed out of that deal.[11]

This exact problem happens outside the world of technology, and has been a problem for decades. In the world of sports, it is very common for new stadiums or teams to not establish themselves in a certain city until the city puts up benefits and money. This leads to the government acting like another player in the game, rather than a referee. It also leads to billionaires gaining more wealth on less risky investments, since a $1.3 billion stadium can be taken down by $325 million in taxpayer subsidies, as was the case in 2009 when the Dallas Cowboys built a new football stadium.[12]

Employment in an industry used to be reasonably tied to the cities and local communities that the industry would affect. Now, the two are not so tied. Instead of working in a circular fashion, where spending money in a localized industry directly adds to the success of the regional business and positively impacts a community (both by profits to the business and taxes to the public), spending money on a national or international company may have no positive effect on one's community at all. A team of Amazon workers working in New York could pay a million dollars in income taxes to New York, but what about the communities that Amazon serves that have no Amazon workers?

We need to look at spreading the effects of taxations and benefits when industries cast enormously wide nets for gaining revenue. Perhaps it would be possible to set up systems where communities that spend money in industries are entitled to portions of the taxes those industries produce, including income taxes and property taxes which would typically just help the community lucky enough to be where the headquarters building is. And perhaps this spreading of the rewards would de-incentive local governments and cities from handing out massive tax breaks to these companies on the basis that their own benefit will be so large.

These institutions, from the private sector in technology to the private sector in Sports to government, are laughably incapable of self-regulation. Now more than ever, the public needs a champion government to set the rules, to examine the playbook, and throw the whole thing out if need be. This status quo is not working—The most powerful companies in the world should not be receiving tax breaks, and the result of sitting on our hands has been the public's suffering. The public loses its fighter when the government acts like a helpless beggar to private interests. It's time to change the government's approach.

# XII

## Regulating Big Tech

### Using Regulation to Create Culture

I worked at a Little Caesar's for over six years. In the food service industry, there are a lot of rules and regulations to follow. For reasons of worker safety, customer health, and company culture, it's necessary to enforce those rules every day. As a manager, ensuring that the rules are being followed is required to save the company from legal trouble and the loss of sales.

The rules and regulations come from a variety of sources. There might have been a rule about not handling food with unwashed hands. This rule probably would have come from the Food And Drug Administration (FDA) and was probably not Little Caesar's-specific, and would be expected at any restaurant. There were rules about not having cash variances in your register at the end of the shift. These rules might have come from the Little Caesar's legal or finance team which would want to minimize cash differences for accounting and responsibility purposes.

Regardless of a rule's source, supervisors and managers are the parties responsible for enforcing them on a day-to-day basis. This requires those managers to be fully bought into the culture created by the regulation. For example, a rule about not operating machinery without checking for hazards might be a federal regulation, but it is the manager's enforcement of the rule that leads to the store having a culture of safety and a work environment where safety is valued. A company policy about serving every customer with a smile will lead to a culture where customer service is valued, but only if the leadership is on board and supporting that policy.

At Little Caesar's, we had such company rules. We had a policy on how to answer the phone. We had step-by-step instructions on how to deal with complaints. We had a uniform policy. And perhaps above all else, we had a leader who genuinely understood the benefit of these policies and actively enforced them. These, individually and collectively, created a culture in the workplace that reflected in the customer's experience.

After I had been with the company for four and a half years, the store manager who had hired me quit. The new leader was and is a well-liked and well-respected employee, and I consider him a good friend of mine. However, he is not a hard-ass. He doesn't find value in the meticulously laid rulesets that were previously enforced as the store's religion. This was a hard U-turn on what employees had come to expect, as the former manager, and myself being molded by it, were very much drinking the proverbial Kool-Aid.

The degradation of the store's culture and sales after my old boss left was not immediate. It took time for old employees to shuffle out, and for new employees to come into their roles. And time ate away at tradition. Little by little, the policies of the store went to the wayside. It might have started with traditional greetings to customers being replaced by half-assed welcomes. It might have started with the once-rigid uniform policy slowly being tested. But everyone knows how it ended, with unrepentant gossip, constant bickering and bullying, unashamed insubordination, and plummeting sales, with zero motivation for improvement of both the store and self.

Work culture is incredibly hard to attain. It requires a vigilant attention and unwavering resolve to upkeep it, for the consequences of losing culture will always be the effects on the customer. In my former store's case, the customers did notice—sales dropped over 35% since the leadership change. This was accompanied by the departure of all the lower-tiered supervisors within one year of the change, them all feeling lost at a changed workplace without the leadership support they were used to.

The food service and technology industries are not fully comparable. When a pizza store loses its customers' trust, the impact will be brutal but localized. The customers will go to another store for pizza. For reference, there were five other places to get pizza within two miles of the store I worked at. It's also possible to stop supporting the store but getting the same product, by going to another location of the same franchise. Tech companies don't really have those options, their mass availability and united front gives customers fewer options to voice their opinions on the market.

I think that if the big tech companies had mainstream competitors for customers to go to, that their sales and users would drop too. Because they do have a culture problem. When people's rights and freedoms are consistently violated by these companies, and no one wants to steer the ship in a different direction, something needs to change internally. There needs to be a culture of valuing and respecting privacy and giving people the platforms to speak without being silenced.

## Dangers of Tech Not Having Rules at Work

I said previously that the rules which drive culture can come from a variety of sources. In the food services industry, there's organizations like the FDA, which write rules dictating the acceptable and unacceptable ways to prepare and serve food. In the technology industry, these rules are largely absent, and there's no agency even trying to make those rules. If 100 people who searched a phrase on Google get sick the next day, there is no regulator to make sure that the search results were prepared in a healthy way, as there would be if those 100 people had all dined at the same restaurant.

I mentioned how important it is to have strong leadership enforcing rules and ideals when trying to create a workplace culture. But in the technology workplace, it seems as though the roles are reversed, and the employees have the largest amounts of power instead of the managers. *Forbes*'s 2018 article titled "13 Reasons Why Google Deserves Its Best Company Culture Award" claims that Google's priority is to give all its employees "true flexibility" and "the freedom to be creative."[1]

In my opinion, this is a bad priority that has led to very bad results. Google's software engineers should not have absolute authority to be as creative as they want. These are not graphic designers with a blank canvas trying to create a new marketing campaign, these people have access to the most powerful technology on the planet and have the ability to use it against ordinary people. When we examine some of the dangerous and intrusive technologies that Google has pushed on us, it's clear that someone somewhere along the way should have told them to stop.

In the aforementioned Forbes article, list item #11 was "a dedicated focus on employee happiness." It seems as though the entire culture at Google is built on an inverted employee-to-employer relationship. How can managers push back on an employee's behavior and be expected to be taken seriously when the manager's contribution to the company's culture is to make their employees happy? It seems paradoxical.

We wouldn't expect a software developer working on missile software for the Department of Defense (DoD) to get unlimited access to the military's missile data because the DoD wanted to give them "the freedom to be creative." We would expect oversight and accountability into their work, and laws to exist regarding the acceptable use of the limited resources they are given for their focused work. I understand that the average Google employee probably doesn't have as much power as the hypothetical DoD employee, but the point is that by characterizing the power that technologists could potentially have we can understand the danger and need to regulate it.

It is so important that companies define rules that inspire meaningful and ethical cultures. However, it seems like Silicon Valley has no intention of doing this. In fact, it looks like their vision of the future is to give more power to the employees and less power to any code of conduct, human oversight, or set of rules. This is a dangerous recipe, as the decisions made by these employees can have massive impacts on the ways of life of many people.

To go back to our food services analogy: what would the government do if all restaurants showed no interest in making their employees wash their hands before preparing food? It might interview restaurants managers and owners to find out why these very simple and ethical practices are being ignored. What if the owners/managers said "we're powerless to the employees, we can't enforce it," or "we don't see the value in it, we won't enforce it," or "making employees wash their hands hinders their creativity"?

The government would make a law, I would hope, or appoint an agency (like the FDA), to write regulations for those restaurants. When an industry cannot, for whatever reason, self-regulate itself and continues to abuse its customers, then regulatory intervention is required. And if those laws don't work, if the agencies aren't effective, then they must be rewritten and reappointed by proxy of the people who have representation in Congress. We have the tools to combat the big tech companies—we just need to use it.

## Making Decisions as a Monolith

In addition to all the big tech companies acting the same way and creating all the same products, they also go further and at times conspire with each other. When discussing how to move forward on certain issues, the big tech companies meet as one unit to reach conclusions they will enact. This is evidenced by the previously discussed leaked emails which detail these secret meetings conducted to move as a monolith on the issue of combating election interference. This conformity makes it hard for new players with different ideologies to find partners in the industry and gain strong footholds.

A good comparison to draw would be the existence of organic food versus non-organic food. One could draw up a list of pros and cons for each: non-organic is probably cheaper, organic is probably healthier. Now, again without being an expert, I'd like to claim that we have a functioning free market in the food industry. This means that when businesses saw a rising interest among consumers for organic food, aspiring and competitive businesses filled that gap by producing and selling that organic food.

This is a great example of how capitalism allowed Business 1's shortcomings to cause the upswing in Business 2, if not the creation itself of Business 2. Then, 15 years later, say another ethical crisis emerges in the food industry. Maybe the way that the corn is grown is found to be unhealthy, but the alternate method of growing it costs twice as much for the farmers. Now Businesses 1 and 2 have another choice to make, do they tap into the market to please consumers? Or do they fold on the opportunity, saying that it costs too much or there isn't enough interest?

To relate this to the world of technology, imagine that at one point a similar free market existed. People would feel the shortcomings of one service, and simply move to another. Not every single person, that is, but just like the people who switched to buying food from Business 1 to Business 2. In the present day, however, big tech companies have ensured that new companies would never gain this kind of competitive edge over another. They conspire as one conglomerate to decide the right and wrong answers to the subjective problems posed by the Internet.

Just to clarify my position on this: I don't necessarily believe that this alone constitutes the need for regulation. I believe that, in a self-regulating system, companies whose practices foster negative opinions should feel the strain of competitors promising to be different. However, due to the nature of the technology world, and the fact that the free market is clearly not doing its job in the technology market, that regulation is in fact necessary. In the food example, it'd be the equivalent of a new company selling organic food not being able to find a shipping company to distribute their products or a grocery store to stock them.

## The Decreasing Fluidity of the Tech Landscape

In the 2000s, even into the early 2010s, the free market of technology seemed vibrant and alive. In late 2010, a lot of the popular internet streamers were on Own3d.tv. By early 2013, just two years later, the dominant streaming platform was Twitch.tv, and Own3d folded in their fight. Twitch offered better subscription, chat, and recording options, and at times, better quality. A similarly volatile market was seen on social media, where the pioneer Myspace took off in popularity between 2005 and 2007 but fell as quickly as they rose, being beaten by Facebook by 2008.

But from the late 2000s/early 2010s to present, there's been almost zero new companies burst into the technical scene—despite there being an incredibly high demand for more honest, free, and transparent companies in the modern technology marketplace. The top 10 websites in 2013 were:

1. Google (search engine/internet services, founded 1998)
2. Facebook (social media, founded 2004)
3. Youtube (video sharing, founded 2005, bought by Google 2006)
4. Yahoo (search engine, founded 1995)
5. Baidu (Chinese search engine, founded 2000)
6. Wikipedia (encyclopedia, founded 2001)
7. Blogger (social media, founded 1999, bought by Google 2003)

8. Windows Live (software products, launched 2005 by Microsoft)
9. Twitter (founded 2006)
10. Tencent QQ (Chinese social media, founded 1999)

Compare this list of top websites at the end of 2018:

1. Google (search engine/internet services, founded 1998)
2. Youtube (video sharing, founded 2005, bought by Google 2006)
3. Facebook (social media, founded 2004)
4. Baidu (Chinese search engine, founded 2000)
5. Wikipedia (encyclopedia, founded 2001)
6. Reddit (social media, founded 2005)
7. Yahoo (search engine, founded 1995)
8. Tencent QQ (Chinese social media, founded 1999)
9. Taobao (Chinese online shopping, founded 2003)
10. Amazon (online shopping, founded 1994) *

What trends do you see here? The top six websites remain in the top seven websites after five years. The bottom changed out a little bit, with Reddit and Amazon gaining massive amounts of popularity, as Reddit became a popular news aggregator over the Internet and Amazon becoming the number one online shopping company.

Overall, it's very sad, in a way, to see the old guard still around. With all the strife that Internet users have had with these companies, it is unsatisfying to see them continue to retain and amass power. One way that this is accomplished, certainly, is by simply refusing to give users a different option. When ethical problems arise, a functioning market would at least expect change from the top dogs. However, even this behavior is rare, much less often does a new tech company come up to offer an opposing stance.

* The number 10 website is actually Google's India domain name, but since the general purpose/American domain was already listed, Google India was omitted in favor of listing Amazon

## Balancing Freedom and Control

Based on the leaked internal Google slide deck "The Good Censor" from earlier, it's clear that there isn't an ounce of self-control or sense of restraint in Google. The report quotes Jason Poutin (an author on big technology topics) on the discrepancy between right wing and left wing personalities: "[Richard] Spencer doesn't get to be a verified speaker; Milo [Yiannopoulos] gets kicked off, but I know plenty of pretty abusive feminist users or left wing users, expressing themselves in exactly the same way that the right is being penalized for, who are permitted to perform certain kinds of speech."[2] If Google and the rest understand the gaping holes in their censorship practices, why not stop, fix the issues, and move on? Why continue down this destructive path?

This requires further pressing of the questions around the purveyors of truth. Ideally in discourse there would be no false information and no hateful or biased rhetoric, but we know that these are the classic fallacies of man. Humanity has long pondered the question "Who has the authority to determine what is true?"

230 years ago, our Founding Fathers drafted the Constitution of our country. While drafting it, they examined the rights of humans and the fallacies humans fell victim to. James Madison was staunchly under the impression that all humans were corrupt, greedy, and undeserving of such great powers. This country is founded on the principle that no one will ever have the authority of truth. In this way, not only is it un-American for the technology industry to shift away from the rights of individuals, it is also un-American that the technology industry is declaring itself to be reasonable, rational, and uncorrupted enough to determine truth in this age.

The technology industry is faced with a problem in which they can confer with our Founding Fathers for advice. Certainly, these companies must not believe themselves to be the first faced with this same problem. The medium changes, but the philosophy is identical. Will they listen to that advice? Is it arrogant not to? On the basis that Google can already present evidence that the technology firms of today have already failed to adequately apply their controls, I think the answer is clear: Don't reinvent the wheel. Promote freedom.

## Hidden Risks of Big Tech Remaining Unregulated

Companies in the technology industry are generally unregulated and free to run their businesses as they please. This, however, has led to certain processes being ignored that would typically require much more oversight if the companies were accountable to the public. Certain regulations that ensure fairness in presenting Google search results have come from these oversights and lapses in judgement.

Another example that comes to mind is Amazon's ability to donate to non-profit organizations through its Amazon Smile program. This program allows Amazon customers to donate some of Amazon's money on qualifying Amazon purchases to nonprofits and charities, specifically, Amazon will donate 0.5% of the purchase price to the charity chosen by the customer. It's meant to be something that users can configure once and continuously give to as they shop over time. However, due to Amazon's general size and status as the largest online retail company in the world, the size and power of Amazon Smile is relatively large as well. Amazon has made serious miscalculations about how small oversights in this program have led to large-scale consequences.

Amazon revealed in 2018 that it receives its list of approved nonprofits from the Southern Poverty Law Center (SPLC). This information was released after conservative nonprofits were taken off the Amazon Smile platform, such as the Alliance Defending Freedom (ADF), which is a Christian fundamentalist advocate group. The SPLC, a nonprofit organization much more on the ideological left than the

ADF, had decided unilaterally to label the ADF a "hate group" and took them off the approved list for Amazon Smile.[3]

This was a political attack, plain and simple. While the SPLC and the ADF are entitled to their differences in ideology, and it's healthy that those differences exist, the SPLC should not be using its power to make executive decisions that limit funding and donations for another nonprofit. That's an abuse of power, and it's a glaring oversight on Amazon's part to not understand the vast amounts of power that they handed over to a biased and vengeful organization.

Big technology companies simply need to be more responsible. Seeing as that continuously fails to happen, they at least need to be more regulated and more transparent. The fact is, the public had no idea that the approving of nonprofits for Amazon Smile was coming from a deeply biased organization until after that organization abused that power. That's unacceptable, and a direct result of a lack of oversight and transparency for Amazon's end.

As the public, it's time to stop assuming that these programs have ethical, fair, and unbiased processes working in the background. The bias of the technology industry still pokes its head out of the curtain, just enough to remind us that at the end of the day, these programs and algorithms and systems are designed by flawed humans. Traditionally, flawed humans receive supervision and systems of control to hold them accountable, but the tech industry fails to enforce those systems.

Petty abuses of power, like in the case of SPLC's banning groups from participating in Amazon Smile, could be happening very often, unbeknownst to us. Due to the lack of regulation and control the technology industry has, it seems likely that they are. Using power to silence political opponents and starve their finances on the basis they are conservative is anti-Free Speech. We should defend those who continue to speak out against mainstream ideologies as they receive unrepentant and brazen attacks from the powers that be, even if we don't implicitly agree with the message. "If liberty means anything at all, it means the right to tell people what they do not want to hear" — George Orwell, 1953.

## Forcing Big Tech to Protect Free Speech

In 1945, a woman from Alabama named Grace Marsh attempted to distribute religious text in the town of Chickasaw, Alabama. At that point in time, the entire town was owned privately by a shipbuilding corporation, and was growing due to a need for ships to fight World War II. Despite doing the distribution on a sidewalk outside of a post office, which are typically seen as publicly-owned and acceptable places of protests, Marsh was arrested for trespassing, on the grounds that the city was under private ownership.

Marsh's court battles went all the way to the Supreme Court. The debate was centered around determining if civil liberties were protected in the case when the entire infrastructure is privately owned. In the end, the court sided with Marsh—"While the town was owned by a private entity, it was open for use by the public, who are entitled to the freedoms of speech and religion....The Court stressed that conflicts between property rights and constitutional rights should typically be resolved in favor of the latter."[4]

Despite being a case from 75 years ago, Marsh v. Alabama sets a pretty clear precedent for how gigantic corporations owning platforms open to the public should be treated in regard to censorship and civil rights. We know that almost all of the United States' Internet infrastructure is owned by AT&T and Verizon. We know that a vast majority of online social media activity takes place on a very small number of platforms, and those platforms have problems with conducting transparent and unbiased political censorship.

We should apply the decision from 1945 into a mentality for bringing the technology industry in line. In this case, the town of Chickasaw only had a population of 4,920 from the 1950 census data. Marsh had a constitutional right to distribute religious texts to fewer than 5,000 people, compare that to the 2.1 billion people on Facebook that Americans are denied the right to reach because Facebook is privately owned. The individual's right to freedom of speech is more important that a corporation's right to evict and censor content, and we have a Supreme Court case that establishes precedent.

We need to stop these egregious violations of our right to public space, even if "public space" is private space open to the public, which these technology companies definitely are. If the powers given to individuals by the Constitution are not adequate to protect against industries and giant, monopolizing corporations, then the powers must be increased. This battle is worth new laws, new constitutional amendments, or any other legal measures. The individual's rights are too important to sacrifice, and we must find the desire to fight within us. As American abolitionist and liberal activist Wendell Phillips said in 1852, "Eternal vigilance is the price of liberty; power is ever stealing from the many to the few." Together, we must recognize the few's attempts to take the many's power and fight back accordingly.

This doesn't necessarily have to be without compromise. If we are to force that the technology industry, Internet platforms, ISPs, and Internet services are to act in neutral and unbiased ways, then we should affirm that they are free from responsibility to the content they host and the people they serve. The CDA gave them this privilege but also allowed them to abuse their discretion at the same time. If users are going to be given unchecked access to use the means and tools made by the technology industry, then the users must be the ones held responsible for the content, not the industry itself. This is a measure of fairness absolutely worth supporting.

## Explicit Opt-In Messages

The Internet and its services need to be reduced in their invasiveness. To accomplish this, the general philosophies regarding Internet tracking and user behavior modeling need to be refocused from opt-out to opt-in. With the current trend of making users opt-out in order to secure their privacy, users can unintentionally be giving away private and personal data that they wouldn't necessarily like being recorded.

If the intrusion of digital tracking is a must, then users need better visibility into when certain data is requested, and they should be prompted more frequently to give consent into letting that information be used and monitored. Users should know what the information is being used for, as not knowing can drive ill-advised decisions in the tradeoff of personal data for the benefits of technology.

For example, if Facebook requests access to my phone's contact list in order to synchronize my phone's contacts with my Facebook friends list, Facebook should be able to give a very clear message in order to get my consent. It could look something like: "Facebook would like access to this device's contact list for 30 minutes in order to complete a synchronization with Facebook's friends list. Accept or Deny?" Sure, it's not the most concise message ever written, but it gets the point across. The user is informed that Facebook will use certain data and what Facebook will use it for.

In the same example, Facebook might also ask for user consent to gain access to the device's camera and microphone in order to do a video chat. In that case, before making the call, Facebook would show a similar message asking for permission to have specific access, a specific length of time, and the purpose of the access. Instead of doing opt-in access with this level of granularity, however, Facebook shows a consent message only once when the application is first installed. This opt-in message grants unlimited and unchecked access for Facebook to use the camera, microphone, and contact list at any time until the entire breadth of access is revoked.

This wouldn't be entirely to Facebook's detriment. The fact that their complete and unchecked access of multiple features of a device has caused people to launch allegations against them for misusing that access. If Facebook was clearer about the times in which it used its access, as I've proposed, then it would be harder for people to make allegations that Facebook is permanently watching and listening to their users even when the application isn't open.

With the additional information, users would have better control over when an application is using its access rights. The department store Target has an application which, once downloaded, asks the user for permission to know the device's location. Presumably, this would be for a basic and simple functions such as finding the closest store. In reality, the Target application uses location data more insidiously: it actually changes the price of items depending on if the user is in the store or outside the store.[5] This is a complete subversion of user expectations and trust, but is completely enabled by the totality of access given to the application by the user. If more specific requests for access were given, the user might be more privy to the effect on the store's prices.

This behavior isn't uncommon. Another example is the Weather Channel application, which was sued in 2019 by the city of Los Angeles for selling the location data it gained on its unwitting users. As the prosecutor claimed, "the operator of the Weather Channel mobile app misled users who agreed to share their location information in exchange for personalized forecasts and alerts, and they instead unwittingly surrendered personal privacy when the company sold their data to third parties" and "its owners used it to track their every step and profit off that information."[6]

It'd be hard for the average user to speculate how useful location data could be to applications, but in fact there are currently 1,200 mobile applications that request permanent, unrestricted access to a phone's moment-to-moment precise location. If a company like Target can find an easy way to manipulate a user's data like that, then I'd bet most other applications can find a way, too. If a company like the Weather Channel can just track and save the data, have no use for it, and then sell it for profit, that's going to seem like a decent business model to other companies.

This feeds into the general problem that we are giving away and endless stream of personalized and private data, to a countless amount of consuming entities. The very few amounts of laws that protect users from these violations encourages it. While a company might believe themselves to be a department store, technology allows them to be a department store that also knows their customers' every move since they ignorantly downloaded the application. That kind of empowerment that blatantly takes power from the consumer and hands it to the corporation ought to be restricted. Our fundamental rights are at stake.

## Protecting Cross-Platform Data

In February 2019, German regulators wrote orders that told Facebook to stop combining user data over multiple sources. Facebook (the company) owns a number of social media platforms, such as Facebook, Instagram, and WhatsApp. This regulation would prevent Facebook from building out behavior models for each individual user based on their activity on all of Facebook's platforms. At least, not without their explicit, opt-in consent.[7]

At plain sight, this law simply states that, should a user suddenly start following guitar pages on Instagram, that cannot lead to that user being shown guitar advertisements on WhatsApp. Under the surface, however, this is a massive blow to Facebook's ability to participate in surveillance capitalism. By doing this, users would essentially be safeguarded if they were to portray separate personas on different platforms. This gives a lot of power to the user to control the data that gets recorded about them.

In addition to giving power to Facebook's cross-platform user base, this also increases data control for individuals who are not on Facebook. Facebook is known to build out these "shadow profiles" to centralize data on individuals who have not explicitly signed up for a Facebook product. This is enabled by external websites that embed Facebook tracking software (such as the extensive Facebook Pixel), as well as Facebook technologies which can identify faces of people who have never registered an account.

While Germany's effort is truly admirable, it hasn't phased Facebook one bit. Facebook will continue on a plan announced in January 2019 to allow its Facebook Messenger, WhatsApp, and Instagram users to message each other, consolidating the services' platforms and combining that data irreversibly. Even in the face of a distrusting public that wants more control over how their data is collected, stored, and used, Facebook will continue on its war path.[8]

These types of regulations only scratch the surface of the remedy we will need to take back our Internet freedom. These regulations are for Germany, but they serve as a good example of what America and other countries need to prioritize. Facebook was targeted because of their monopoly on social media services, where they have a considerable hold on the social media market share. But social media is only a single layer of the many on which we are tracked. Practically every technology on the Internet has a method of tracking and surveilling its users.

Simply put, the regulations need to be in place on more companies in more countries. The regulations need to be aimed at more markets than just social media. Monopolization is a genuine concern, but social media can't be the only focus. There are much higher and concerning market shares held by other companies, such as Google's hold on web browser, web search, and location services, or Amazon's market share in cloud computing. All of these monopolies need to be looked at and regulated for the best interest of the user.

## Functionality Fake Outs — Location Services and Do Not Track

While my suggestion is to change opt-out data tracking to opt-in data tracking, the technology industry doesn't even do a good job of honoring opt-out. It's a manifestation of this holier-than-thou mentality where giant corporations know what's best for you and make decisions based on that perception. And for some reason, no one has stepped up to the plate on a lawmaker's level to tell the industry that they need to stop lying to their customers.

Google location services on Android phones famously does not stop tracking users when location services are disabled, it merely prevents other applications from using the location detection. In a statement to The Verge, Google claimed "We make sure Location History users know that when they disable the product, we continue to use location to improve the Google experience when they do things like perform a Google search or use Google for driving directions."[9]

Google is essentially claiming that it wasn't using GPS to find out the user's location, but using the IP address from their online Internet activity. This follows a similar story from 2017 where Google was accused of the same: not actually turning off location monitoring when the location services were disabled. Back then, however, it was revealed that Google had been using the device's location by its proximity to cell towers instead of its IP address in this case.[10]

Essentially, Google has three or more options to determine a user's location, and turning off Location Services only disables one of them.

Similarly, most modern web browsers have a misnomer feature that leads users to believe they are opting out of being tracked online called "Do Not Track." This feature seemingly would stop websites visited from storing any information about the user or monitoring their activity. In actuality, the only function of Do Not Track is to send a request to the visited website to not track the user. It in no way prevents tracking nor compels the website to not track the user, it is just a request.

Privacy-centric Internet search engine DuckDuckGo conducted a study in late 2018 around the awareness of the Do Not Track feature. They found that between 20 and 25% of American Internet users are using Do Not Track features. 44.4% of users familiar with Do Not Track were not aware that it was completely voluntarily for companies to respect and follow the request. Among those who have Do Not Track enabled, a massive 41.4% didn't know that it wasn't a requirement to honor the request.

The study goes on to say, "most major tech companies, including Google, Facebook, and Twitter, do not respect the Do Not Track setting when you visit and use their sites – a fact of which 77.3% (±3.6) of US adults overall weren't aware." 75.5% of US adults think it's important that those big technology companies respect the request.

"There is simply a huge discrepancy between the name of the setting and what it actually does. It's inherently misleading.... So, in shocking news, when people say they don't want to be tracked, they really don't want to be tracked." When "people seek the most readily available (though often, unfortunately, ineffective) methods to protect their privacy," the technology we use is not living up to our expectations and is not improving, but rather damaging, our lives.[11]

A feature like Do Not Track's entire functionality depends on being honored and respected. So when it gets ignored and disrespected, it truly just becomes an ineffective mind trick used to trick users into believing they have control. As evidenced by their insistence that data tracking be opt out instead of opt-in, big technologies truly don't care about what the users want. Even when voiced with explicit requests to not track them, the companies say no. In a move that might be the nail in Do Not Track's coffin, Apple announced in early 2019 that their web browser Safari would be removing the option.[12]

When consumers do not trust technology to respect their privacy, but understand that they cannot live in the modern world without that technology, they act. They turn off location services thinking that'll stop their location from being tracked. They turn on Do Not Track thinking that will let them browse the Internet without being surveilled. When these solutions don't change a thing, not only does the consumer further lose trust in technology, but also in the system that's supposed to protect them.

The technology industry needs to do a better job of being transparent on a number of levels, and these are just some examples. Regulators will need to look at the ways that the tech industry writes feature descriptions to ensure that customers aren't being lied to. If companies offer features that they have no intention of honoring, they should be forced to rework or remove those features. In this case, there could be a rule that says if Google will not honor Do Not Track on its websites, then it should be forced to remove it as an option on its browser.

## We Never Got to Debate Having Our Phone Locations Monitored for Traffic

Tackling these issues in a timely manner is important, and of course, it's important to hear out both sides. The fear that I have, which comes from what I have witnessed, is that when issues aren't brought into the public's view, they tend to become the norms before we've even decided whether they're healthy to our society. We grow accustomed to the behavior, and question it less and less every day. Slowly, we learn to accept it as a reality of our life, without once vetting out the pros and cons as members of the public, as the group of affected people.

As Americans, we've become accustomed to the luxury of real-time path finding. GPS, which tracks our movement on every street, along with real-time traffic data to keep our route clear, quickly became a powerful duo that every American wanted. Over 77% of American smartphone owners use these navigation applications regularly, and 87% of the use cases are for driving directions.[13]

However, despite the technology being relatively old, we still see the anomalies and false positives from time to time. For example, we've probably all experienced a case when driving late at night with Google Maps running, and it paints the upcoming intersection a bright red, indicating traffic congestion. But we drive through that intersection without even slowing down, seeing no cars being delayed at all. It's times like these that remind me that it's an algorithm, an automated program that is generating all these results. There's no person standing at every street corner informing Google and Waze whether there's congestion and/or whether it's clear.

The realization that follows is that if any one of us was to be stuck at an intersection late at night for more than 5 minutes, there's a good chance they would turn that intersection bright red on Google Maps themselves. This isn't interesting or fun to me, it's unnerving. When did I decide that the benefits of accurate traffic predictions were worth the cost of the privacy of my location? Or more realistically, when was it ever put to a vote in Congress, where my congressman could have represented my interests to not be spied on?

These issues don't see the exposure of debate before they become normalized as part of our lives. In the digital world, the problem is especially persistent, as local and community-level governments don't have the power or reach to have a meaningful impact on these multi-billion-dollar international companies. In some cases it might even be useless to try, as local governments can be limited by interstate commerce laws into imposing regulation. It simply must be solved on a Federal level.

One of the fortunate side effects of a problem like the navigation application issue is that we still have time to regulate it. We can always pass a bill that bans the constant monitoring of phone location for the purpose of predicting and reporting traffic. It may seem like a bit of a retrofit, but that speaks more to the pace at which we get accustomed to these technologies than it acts as a criticism of the intention. This side effect, however, is not present in the case of other issues that technology has brought to us.

## Intrusive Technologies Never Stop Being Intrusive

My parents weren't yet born when the first satellite went into space in 1958. However, due to the rapid progressions in technology, it was hardly 40 years before private companies had made commercial use of them. I vaguely remember the rise of Google Earth in the early 2000s. Using satellite images (from NASA satellites) and 3D modeling, Google was able to map the world for all to see, including every building in every country. It also showed every secret, such as the location and layout of above-ground military facilities.

Much of the world was not happy; in fact, requests to blur out certain areas came from nearly every country's government. Some even ban the product entirely. Under the immense pressure from all the world's governments, Google caved in. Google blurred out areas of the world, omitting information from their once futuristic and utopian product. But, had the damage already been done?

It's reasonable to assume that the United States government/military did not gain any new information from what was reported through Google Earth, considering that the Satellites themselves belonged to the government. What about a third-world country that didn't already have satellites in space? Could they have gained valuable information about the US military, which they wouldn't have without Google Earth? And if they did, what ramifications did Google Earth face? Aside from a couple lawsuits — some from citizens and one or two from foreign governments — none.

Five years later, Street View caused the same exact nuisances and problems. Google sent cars driving down the street, taking pictures of all of our houses, and sometimes even us. Google Street View allows for all the public to view these pictures, with only opt-out removal.

In an episode of *The Office*, the character Dwight nervously tries to give his coworkers directions to his house so they won't use Google Street View. He's embarrassed that he, a 40-ish man, is on a seesaw with his cousin in Street View's picture. When his coworkers find out the truth, Dwight sheepishly says, "They don't warn you when the cameras are coming by."

The scene is hilarious, but the sentiment remains true. Why do we continuously let the same intrusive and uninvited behavior go unchecked? Why should a company be allowed to know so much about us, stuff that puts our livelihoods and personal information at risk, without our explicit consent?

This is the same pattern of behavior we've seen over and over from companies like Google. A big product or feature is released by a company that wrote their own book of ethics. Then, after launch, the problems are exposed. The ethical questions start getting asked. Finally, the public engages in some debate about those questions, at least for a while. Soon, no laws are passed, nothing major about the product has changed, and the company gets to go on to their next big invention which will inevitably raise even more eyebrows among ethical critics.

The US and other governments can put pressure on big technology companies to change their practices. We've seen them do it successfully. However, it seems that the power is only used when those governments' interests are, like military secrets, put at risk. We should be using our Congress's legislative power to force big technology companies to feel that same pressure. Unethical technologies that put the American public at similar risks should be similarly punished and reformed to work in our interests.

## Requiring Regional Differentiation Based on Location

It's also worth mentioning that Google has essentially identified a complicated problem that could have an elegantly simple solution. In their leaked internal slide deck, Google admits that technology firms are struggling with two directly opposing ideologies (freedom vs. control). But if those ideologies are traditionally bound to certain geographical areas (America vs. Europe, respectively) as Google claims,[14] why not just alter the algorithms to respect regional differences?

On top of Google having multiple ways to access to our specific locations, any Internet connection is going to be bound to an IP address which will have an approximate location associated with it. Google, and any other Internet service platform for that matter, can very easily determine from which country a request is coming. If Google is willing to alter my entire Internet experience based on whether or not I'm white or black, straight or gay, Christian or atheist, etc., can't they also change my experience based on the country I live in?

Google has already demonstrated this power: it manipulates its Google Maps results over disputed political areas based on the country a request is coming from. Famously, China and India have disputed borders about who controls certain areas of Tibet. Google Maps essentially plays three sides of the deal: A request coming from China shows the areas under Chinese control, a request from India shows the areas under Indian control, and requests from elsewhere show the region as disputed.

Similarly, in 2014 Russia invaded the Crimean Peninsula, which belonged to Ukraine. Despite a UN resolution ordering no one to recognize Russia's occupation of the region, Google Maps changed its algorithm to show the area as belonging to Russia, if viewed from a Russian domain. And vice versa if the request came from Ukraine.[15]

This shows Google does have the power to change its results on just about anything based on location of users. Why not simply make more of the regulations and censorship rules region-bound? If America as a country sees the freedom of speech as a human right guaranteed by its constitution, and European countries see the freedom of speech as a nice-to-have when people aren't being offensive, then why not change the way those freedoms are experienced on the Internet?

This is a simple solution for a complicated problem, but one that needs to be considered. It's not as if Google's algorithms don't already account for thousands of personal variables before running anyway. Plus, it could be a huge step towards increasing transparency at Google, something of which they are in desperate need.

However, America needs to start doing things for America. If Google refuses under every condition to make software that upholds to our principles, then we must create laws that force software to uphold them. Our values of individualism, freedom, and liberalism are too important to compromise. This will mean goading American companies into understanding the importance of what they're taking from us in their pursuit of profits and power. Samuel Adams, a Founding Father, stated this a day before the Declaration of Independence was signed, August 1, 1776, in Philadelphia: "If ye love wealth greater than liberty, the tranquility of servitude greater than the animating contest for freedom, go home from us in peace. We seek not your counsel, nor your arms."

## Complex Technology's Effect on Law Enforcement

From an education perspective, we have a long way to go to bring everyone up to a reasonable level. Widespread understanding of technology basics is going to be a requirement as our judicial system moves into the digital age. There have already been cases where digital evidence from personal property has been used in a criminal case, and prosecutors dropped the ball for reasons of technical illiteracy.

In a national attention-grabbing case from 2011, a woman named Casey Anthony's daughter was found dead near her home after Ms. Anthony claimed she was missing. Ms. Anthony became a prime suspect due to the strange behavior she had displayed. When examining her home computer for searches regarding any details about the circumstances of her daughter's death, the detectives only looked at the search history for her Internet Explorer browser, which only had 17 total queries recorded. To a fault, they did not examine her Mozilla Firefox browser's search history, which included 1,200 more search queries, some of which were for methods of suffocation, which was how her daughter had died.[16]

Casey Anthony was found to be innocent, which led to national outrage. The detectives misunderstanding of her computer's functionality and intricacies still serves as a shining example of how technological ignorance in the modern era can be majorly impactful to the justice system. If the investigators had simply known that there could have been more than one web browser installed on the computer, they would have found evidence that could've changed the case.

In college, I was given a rare opportunity to speak to an FBI agent about what it's like to go to court with evidence that existed in digital form. He explained that one of the first parts of becoming an FBI investigator is to learn how to speak about technical details in layman's terms, but also in a way that doesn't undermine credibility. Because high-level court cases require a conviction by a jury, he needed to be able to explain to the everyday American how he drew conclusions from the evidence.

For example, if the agent were to argue that he knew that files were deleted from a hard drive in an obstruction of justice case, he would have to argue about how he looked in the backup, found specific data and bytes, and found an entry in the file system log indicating that files had been purged. The defense would always go after terminology, making the agent explain in detail what the words "backup," "data," "bytes," "file system," and "log" meant, in an effort to trip him up or make his conclusion seem shaky. If the defense is successful, the suspect could walk free. In this way, criminals can get off the hook simply because the average American doesn't understand digital evidence and how it is used in 21st century crime.

So, it is not only our legislative branch but also our judicial branch which suffer massively under the general complexities of technical discussions. This leads to a decrease in the quality of our society, because there are simply too few laws which are written for the digital age, and because the judicial branch cannot effectively enforce the ones that do exist. This has, no doubt, aided the extremely ambitious and fast-paced encroachment of big technology corporations into every possible aspect of our lives.

We are at a point in time where it feels like the entire old structure is more tradition and the new structure doesn't exist yet.

## Create an EPA of Tech Ethics

There simply must be a party at the table with the power and resolve to fight for the American people's interests. As a country, we've had this debate many times over. In different industries and contexts, these are the debates that showcase the need for governmental agencies like the EPA, which protects otherwise helpless entities from the ever-powerful corporation and industry.

In regard to the environment, concerns about the effects of human activity had spawned the environmental movement in the post-industrial world. Witnessing the slowly-draining effects that pollution, insecticide, and synthetic substances, as well as catastrophic events such as oil spills, the public demanded governmental action. In 1970, the EPA was created to research these effects of man and to write and enforce regulations that would stop the destructive nature of man on the environment.

There are similarities between where we are now with technology and where we were 60 years ago with industrialization. We can see the negative, slowly-draining effects on the populace: suicide and depression rates increased, more loneliness, lack of trust in technology companies, etc. But we don't know what exactly is causing that, be it screen time itself, the divisive nature of social media, less time spent in physical proximity of other people, the feeling that big technology is slowly taking over more of our lives and there's nothing we can do about it, or any of the other reported causes. This is where the EPA came in for the environment, in research and in regulation. We need to understand the problems as well as regulating them, or else we're writing bad, uninformed policy.

Americans need an EPA for ethics in technology. The reality is that harmful technology is a threat, and the government has a right to regulate it. The reality is that people's lives are being affected by technology elites that wear t-shirts and flip-flops to work. The reality is that these companies will never self-regulate, and they will never rein themselves in. The reality is that these companies will stop making technology for the betterment of human life and start making it purely for corporate goals and bottom lines.

## Diluting Big Tech's Monopoly

We need to provide solutions for other companies to get into the technology game. Across the world of technology only a few companies hold almost all the resources and have established monopolies in all the essential areas. We need to help remove barriers blocking the growth of smaller and startup tech companies, especially those with less popular ideologies.

We need to ensure that companies are treated fairly by other tech providers. As discussed earlier, most tech companies are reliant on other tech companies being willing to work with them. Tech companies need operating systems to build their applications on. Online retailers need to be able to host their websites. We should establish firm antitrust laws that force other tech companies to integrate and be a partner with newer tech companies, and that business privileges cannot be revoked based on ideological, philosophical, and cultural differences.

We also need to encourage that new companies build technologies that compete with the big tech companies on those critical infrastructure pieces. Yes, it's important to force Amazon Web Services to host websites they don't politically agree with, but it's also important to one day have other web hosting providers that are not part of the big tech group. We could also encourage private ownership of servers, although this does increase the workload for smaller tech companies to keep their websites secure, it would help bring down the number of tech companies reliant on cloud computing.

Lastly, we need to make sure that monopolies are not abused. Take Google's location services monopoly. Perhaps the government could pressure Google to lower the costs of location services, which are largely reliant on Global Positioning System (GPS), since the government (through the Air Force) owns and operates GPS via satellites. This would make sure that Google, despite owning a monopoly on location services, was acting in non-abusive ways.

By enforcing that monopolies integrate with others and keep their prices low, we can make sure that their inherent power is not abused to the detriment of other tech companies. By encouraging other tech companies to build critical pieces of infrastructure, we reduce our reliance on a few large companies for Internet stability and introduce more competition which brings prices down and drives innovation. In the end, these are just sample ideas for how we could do it, but the point is that we need to keep an eye on the big tech monopoly and ensure that the market and competition is fair.

## United States Needs to Lead the Charge

In my software development career, I've been faced with tasks to help configure clients so that the products I make are best-suited for them. As my company has grown in customer base, we've been more reluctant to indulge in these efforts. We have a choice to build software and features that work for most clients, instead of dedicating sparse time and resources to help individual client organizations. Sometimes, we have to say "no."

I have a fear that, if individual countries start writing individual mandates imposing individual controls on individual technology companies, that it would massively hurt the industry's engagement to work through these problems. I fear that, at some point, a country is going to impose a rule and be told "no." What would follow would be an upheaval of that companies' services to that country, leaving the user base unhappy, the country unhappy, and the company unhappy.

If the Omaha city council passed a law that required Google and Facebook to stop collecting any data on its citizens, Google and Facebook might not want to remain in that market. Maybe they would, but even then, it would be a massive weight of pros and cons to determine if it was worth it to change their practices so significantly just to appease the city council of America's 40th largest city.

These bittersweet decisions should be avoided. It is absolutely necessary that large, dominant countries like the United States take firm stances and create regulation for the technology industry to follow. This will pave the path forward, setting a precedent that technology companies need to listen and adhere to the countries in which they operate. If any collection of users is going to regain their Internet freedom, it must be established that this is even a possibility and that technology companies are willing to implement those changes. Setting the United States up as the progressive leader of this movement would greatly help this effort.

# XIII

## Evaluating Existing Proposals for Regulation

The threats posed by modern technology have not gone completely unnoticed in the United States. In attempts to fix some of the symptoms of big tech's disease, some Senators have come forward with proposals and the White House has even begun drafting a rewrite of the Communications Decency Act. This chapter is dedicated to examining those proposals, weighing their pros and cons, what each would fix and what problems it would leave behind.

In July 2018, Senator Mark Warner from Virginia outlined 20 proposals for Congress to regulate the technology industry.[1] The ideas aren't meant to be formal policy proposals, but rather talking points and conversation starters. Indeed, in a majority of his points Warner calls out an opposing viewpoint, or why his proposal may not be effective, indicating that the points are genuinely just to kick off the debate and discourse.

Senator Warner's work is by far the most comprehensive official release of research the government is doing to identify and address the threat of big tech. The majority of Warner's propositions represent terrific, solid changes that would greatly benefit our country. There are also a couple of his points that miss the mark of what is truly a priority versus what would simply be extra measures. Lastly, he does propose changes which would be negative and undesirable. We'll go through each point in his release, and evaluate its merits, benefits, and drawbacks.

## Agreeable Points

These are the points that Senator Warner hits on the head, and they should be prioritized:

Increased deterrence against foreign manipulation & Require interagency task force for countering asymmetric threats to democratic institutions

The United States does not do enough to dissuade malicious foreign actors from manipulating our public discourse and political processes. Warner points out that the United States spends ten times the amount on our military compared to Russia, but that "our strategies and our resources have not shifted aggressively to address these new threats in cyberspace and on social media that target our democratic institutions."

The United States needs a "deterrence doctrine" which would make concrete resolutions to stop the cyber aggressions of foreign adversaries. This doctrine would appoint an agency to be in charge of securing the cyber threats and establish protocols that help us respond to these attacks. The protocols should be followed in ways that effectively and preemptively deter malicious foreign actors from engaging in information warfare against us. The doctrine should also take full advantage of the tools at the United States' disposal, including "our own cyber capabilities" and "robust sanctions."

In a very similar but separate suggestion, Warner calls for a "congressionally-required task force" to "bring about a whole-of-government approach to counter asymmetric attacks against our election infrastructure." Warner claims that "the intelligence and national security communities are not as well-positioned to detect, track, attribute, or counter malicious asymmetric threats to our political system." Both of these suggestions are necessary.

## Information fiduciary

An information fiduciary is defined as a service provider which is especially trusted with customer data obtained and stored by the provider. The Yale law professor who formulated the concept, Jack Balkin, would classify "search engines, social networks, ISPs, and cloud computing providers" as information fiduciaries due to "the extent of user dependence on them, as well as the extent to which they are entrusted with sensitive information." This designation would require those service providers to not only "zealously" protect user data, but also to not use that data to benefit solely the provider, with no benefit to the user.

This is essential to securing digital freedoms as it blocks the motive to use user data in bad faith. All applications of user data must actually benefit the user and not benefit the whims of surveillance capitalists. However, as Warner notes, it might drive innovation down and cause the individual technology companies to have "more uniform offerings." But that's a small price to pay. No innovation is better than innovation from surveillance capitalists that simply try to find new ways to collect data on us.

## Comprehensive (GDPR-like) data protection legislation

GDPR is referencing the EU's General Data Protection Regulation laws which took effect in 2018. Some highlighted provisions of the GDPR are "data portability, the right to be forgotten, 72-hour data breach notification, 1st party consent, and other major data protections." A GDPR would also require behavioral data be stored separately from personally identifying data, ensuring data anonymity.

Though there are weaknesses and faults within the GDPR, such as the misclassification of some data as personally identifiable data, it would be great to have it in the United States. Warner points out that a potential negative of a US-GDPR implementation would be the requirement of a central authority to enforce the regulations and fines. This is actually a positive, and the fact that we don't already have such an authority 25 years into the mainstream use of the Internet speaks volumes to how behind we are.

## 1st party consent for data collection

Warner specifically draws attention to this one feature of the GDPR as its exclusive adoption would be a giant step forward for the United States' online data privacy. 1st party consent essentially means that anyone seeking to collect or process user data must get explicit, opt-in permission. This would kill the practice of covertly and meticulously tracking a user's every action. It also slaps a "not for resale" sticker on user data, the data cannot be processed without user consent, and is therefore useless once it leaves the first collector's hands.

As is noted in Warner's proposal, the strong desire for 1st party consent on data collection points to a larger problem where the agreements that users make with service providers are not made in good faith. Because users pay costs of foregoing those services, there is a limitation to which a user can actually consent to be tracked. The "focus on user consent tends to mask greater imbalances in the bargaining power between users and service providers." Regardless, 1st part consent rules would be the single biggest blow (of Warner's propositions, at least) we could make to surveillance capitalism and thus, they should be implemented as soon as possible.

## Statutory determination that so-called "dark patterns' are unfair and deceptive trade practices

In addition to requiring 1st party consent protections, it is also necessary to address the deceiving practices that service providers use to gain consent. Warner includes an example in which Facebook's

Messenger mobile application pushes users to consent to Messenger accessing and importing their phone's contact list. The user interface (UI) constantly directs the user toward consent-giving options, "framing a user *choice* as agreeing with a skewed default option (which benefits the service provider) and minimizing alternative options available to the user." These kind of deceptive UI experiences have been called "dark patterns."

Another example of a dark pattern is during checkout on an online store. When going to a new page, a new product offering is added to the order, and the user is required to manually remove it or unselect it in order to keep their original order. If a website uses confusing language, such as "Click OK to cancel your action. Click Cancel to continue," that is an example of a dark pattern. Any time a website makes the "extra" or "add-on" option appear bright and colorful, while making the default option neutral colored or hard to find, is an example of a dark pattern.

These practices should be regulated and banned, as the agreements that users typically engage in are lopsided very heavily in favor of the service provider. Users deserve to know the truth about those agreements in order to make self-serving decisions.

### Algorithm auditability and fairness

Warner essentially calls out the same problems with artificial intelligence algorithms and comes to the same conclusions as we discussed previously. Warner arrives to the agreeable, nuanced conclusion that "particularly in the context of employment, credit, and housing opportunities, a degree of computational inefficiency seems an acceptable cost to promote greater fairness, auditability, and transparency. Moreover, while complete may not be feasible or preferable, a range of tools and techniques exist to determine whether algorithms align with key values, objectives, and legal rules." The creation of these simple oversights is a necessity to ensuring that our civil freedoms are not under the threat of discrimination.

## Data transparency bill

This is a proposal for laws requiring service providers be more transparent with the personal data they collect and how they use it. "This lack of transparency is an impediment to consumers 'voting with their wallets' and moving to competing services that either protect their privacy better or compensate them for uses of their data." In a free market, this knowledge should not be kept secret.

These laws would also enact restrictions on service providers to expand the scope of their privacy intrusions. Warner notes how Google sold its free email platform, Gmail, on the basis that Google would only use the email data for targeted ads. Once the user base grew, Google started increasing its uses of the data "beyond the terms of the original deal." Similarly, Facebook originally offered its messaging service on smartphones through web browsers, where data collection was limited. Later, Facebook transitioned that service into a standalone application, Messenger, which collects "considerably more data."

Another potential use of these laws would be to "require companies to more granularly (and continuously) alert consumers to the ways their data was being used." The laws could also require companies to disclose the monetary market value of the data given to them by individual users, so that users could make more informed decisions about the services they use. All of these laws are great and every one of them should be a priority to pass and implement.

## Interoperability

Interoperability requirements would force "dominant platforms to blunt their ability to leverage their dominance over one market into complementary or adjacent markets." They would safeguard newer companies from having "to radically reinvent key functions provided by a dominant incumbent." Warner brings up an example when AOL and Time Warner merged in the early 2000s, "the FCC required AOL to make its instant messaging service 'AIM' interoperable with at least one rival immediately, and two more rivals within 6 months."

The goal of this regulation was to avoid a situation where customers would "continue to pay for AOL service despite the existence of more innovative and efficient email and internet connectivity services." Essentially, AIM gave AOL such a large competitive edge that the FCC required AIM be built in a way that other services could integrate with it.

If Google excluded everything about iPhones in their Search algorithm and pushed information about Android phones, this would be a good example of a lack of interoperability due to Google's search monopoly. Services like Amazon Web Services should be forced to integrate and work with hosting a variety of websites, because of their dominance in the cloud hosting market. These anti-monopoly and pro-innovation regulations are essential.

Essential facilities determinations

This proposal echoes the resolution that technology companies shouldn't play favorites and discriminate against who uses their platforms. These proposals would ban technology companies of sufficient size from refusing to integrate with smaller companies looking to take advantage of the already built infrastructure of the Internet. These laws recognize that a vast majority of the Internet functions based on mutual interest and platforms operated by private companies. Following that line of thinking, it would be extremely anti-competitive behavior to give technological advantages and other favors out to certain companies.

These laws would prevent companies like Gab from being bullied away from integrating with certain technologies for not being ideological conformists. Additionally, essential facility determinations would reinforce the notion that it's not the responsibility of the service providers and platforms to practice censorship, but rather that it is virtuous to be neutral in allowing differing and controversial opinions to be platformed. Classifying digital service platforms as privately-owned but essential infrastructure sets the stage for making arguments that those digital service platforms have no right to censor political speech, using decisions such as *Marsh v. Alabama* as a precedent.

## Non-Priority Points

Conversely, Senator Warner also proposed some points which would be positive, but the matter is not pressing:

### Duty to clearly and conspicuously label bots

This proposal would require social media sites to identify accounts that were not being operated by humans. I would agree with that regulation, but it's my understanding that whenever social media platforms identify bots, they simply remove them. At best, this proposed regulation would require social media sites be more diligent about detecting bots. Upon discovering those fake accounts, it's hard to believe that a social media company would choose to label them as bots when they could just remove them. This measure wouldn't be negative, but it's not at all qualified to be a top priority regulation.

### Public Interest Data Access Bill

This set of propositions would allow for "regulators, users, and non-governmental organizations (NGOs)" to get access to anonymized big data that large technology companies have gathered. The goal would be to allow the public to view trends in data by looking at those datasets. It would also grant some transparency into how the large technology companies are using the data and could potentially stop misuse. As it stands, the large technology companies that hold the data guard it "zealously."

Warner cites that the large technology companies do let researchers have access, but only after the researchers sign non-disclosure agreements (which compromises their identity and independence), and that the companies tend to seek "collaboration with researchers whose projects comport with their business goals, while excluding researchers whose work may be adverse to their interests."

It is unjust to be self-serving with those vast amounts of data. Making these datasets available to public research would be positive, but getting access for public research is not a priority. There are more pressing matters about the contents of the data itself, and whether it should exist at all, than to necessarily care about who in the public can see it.

## Disclosure requirements for online political advertisements

This proposal would increase the amount of disclosure political advertisements make online, and to force online services which sell those advertisements to vet them more carefully. Warner claims that "the ease by which our foreign adversaries purchased and targeted politically oriented ads during the [2016 presidential] campaign exposed an obvious threat to the integrity of our democracy." The measure is supportable, but only because it relies on some loose definitions.

Assuming the proposed laws would specifically limit foreign influence on our elections, how would that compare to other means by which foreign governments can make political donations and lobby our politicians? What's the difference between Russia buying a $1000 advertisement on Facebook in support of Candidate A, while

Candidate B's campaign takes $1000 donations from China and spends it on political advertisements? The answers to these questions get into a deeper debate that isn't going to be resolved in a law attempting to regulate Internet advertisement.

Another point to consider is that a lot of online campaign activity is not done through traditional ad-buying. Organizations like ShareBlue and CorrectTheRecord use more advanced tactics, such as creating fake accounts for the sole purpose of pushing politicians and policies. These would not be forced to disclose their affiliation under Senator Warner's proposal, and would need additional thought and policy into regulating them fairly.

## Privacy rulemaking authority at FTC

Warner's big claim in this suggestion is that the FTC has failed to protect user data and prevent "unfair competition in the digital markets" because of a lack of power given to it, and that a restoration of that power would bring some authority back to the lawless hellscape the technology industry has made. We should bolster the abilities of regulators like the FTC and their empowerment to act against evil companies, but the FTC specifically more power to regulate an industry they don't typically acknowledge or oversee might not lead to any change.

I would rather see Internet regulation taken over by a completely separate agency. Since the FCC and the FTC have tossed Internet regulation back and forth to one another like a hot potato, a new agency with the empowerment and willpower to change the industry is required. Of course the creation of this new agency wouldn't necessarily mean that we couldn't also empower the FTC in other areas, but for Internet regulation, the best option is to take it out of the hands of the FTC and FCC.

## Points I Don't Agree With

Lastly, Senator Warner made some propositions that would be negative and require rebuttal:

### Public initiative for media literacy

This suggestion would demand that educational institutions do a better job educating people on media literacy "from an early age." But an initiative of this kind wouldn't work to solve any sort of problem of foreign manipulation in our democracy. It seems to be the case that the media is capable and willing to act in partisan and divisive tactics for views and clicks. In my opinion, that justifies the American people's perception that the media is untrustworthy. It doesn't matter how one educates someone to read if the reader doesn't trust the source.

It is flawed to "pass the buck" like this on such important issues. The responsibility should not fall on the American people to ensure that journalists aren't lying, it should fall on journalist ethics and regulations. It shouldn't be blamed on the American people if a fake news story inserted by Russia makes its rounds on social media, it should be blamed on the social media sites for allowing it to stay in circulation and on the country's cyber security which should be blocking those attacks.

Of course we should support proposals to make sure the American populace is more educated. However, the context of this proposal is different than that of general education. This proposal highlights a misunderstanding of the core problems at the center of America's media trust and fake news crisis.

### Duty to determine the origin of posts and/or accounts

Warner's proposition is that social media platforms ought to disclose the physical location of the accounts posting content. This regulation would fall somewhat in line with my past suggestions for social media to create region or country-based sections of social media that simply don't allow traffic from external entities. While the change would be positive, I think that these regulations would be ineffective. Users could simply use VPNs to change their identifying location. VPNs aren't free, so only a small percentage of users would opt to pay for them, but those seeking to pose as being from another country would certainly have the technical capabilities to do just that.

Also, it's a conscious unmasking of personally identifiable information, all for the purpose of some arbitrary opinion validation. What if someone wanted to seek real-world retaliation for a comment made online and doxx the commenter? In that case commenter's location being exposed puts their safety at risk. And what if it's not a private citizen seeking vengeance, but a government agency? Now the issue is in the realm of free speech violation.

Overall, the founding idea here is okay, but identifiable location data shouldn't be disclosed publicly without the user's consent. It's not the duty of the social media sites to report it. Perhaps hidden filters on the social media's site would be a better solution, meaning that users could have the option to only see posts, accounts, and content originating from their country, but wouldn't be told any specific detail about any specific user.

On the imageboard 4chan, their politics section discloses user location (just the country) which detracts partially from the "you can be anonymous" calling that the website makes. This works to varied effects—it can be used to bolster or discredit a user's argument based on the country from which they are commenting. For example, a Syrian user might gain a lot of credibility if the topic is the Syrian Civil War. But in the end, it doesn't solve any of the astroturfing problems facing the website (due to VPNs) and would be an ineffective ask of social media companies everywhere to disclose country location as it wouldn't solve the core problems.

<u>Duty to identify inauthentic accounts</u>

This proposal is similar to the last one: it would require social media sites to publicly flag accounts and users as "inauthentic." To a fault, Warner continuously uses the word "inauthentic" without giving it a clear definition, despite it being critical to understanding what he's proposing. Let's assume inauthentic means lying under some pretense or assuming an identity that is not one's real world identity. But Warner could simply be talking about any unverified account that has no associated real-world name or data.

To suggest that one must sacrifice their personally identifying information in order to participate online is a gross miscalculation of the importance of one's individual rights to privacy. Reddit is the United States' 4th largest social media platform and it doesn't require any personally identifying information to sign up, just a username, an email (which can be faked), and a password. Are all Reddit accounts inauthentic? Are all US Redditors' opinions to be cast aside?

This isn't some grandstanding case for Reddit's process, but our leaders should understand that we simply don't trust technology companies with our personal information anymore. If we can get away with not providing it, we're going to use those avenues. What's the opposite of "give a man a mask and he'll tell you the truth"? "Take away a man's mask and he'll lie to you"?

<u>Make platforms liable for state-law torts (defamation, false light, public disclosure of private facts) for failure to take down deepfake or other manipulated audio/video content</u>

This suggested regulation is in direct opposition of other positions stated in this book and is a contradiction to other proposed regulations by Senator Warner. The laws under this proposal would restrict the abilities of online services to enact the Communications Decency Act (CDA) as a protection against their slowness to remove content. Early in the book, the claim was made that being too aggressive with removing user content is suppression of their freedom of expression and speech, and that ultimately users should be held liable for the content they post and views they express, not the platform. I called for the opposite: an expansion of the ability of online services to enact the CDA.

Warner's suggestion here is that social media sites should be liable for the lies and salacious content posted to their platforms. But Senator Warner must be warned that the only result of this proposal would be social media platforms abusing their powers to remove content, under the fear of being held liable for it, and those abuses of power will be suppressions of individual freedoms.

Senator Warner is also in open contradiction with other proposals made in this document. Under the proposal to determine essential facilities, Warner made an argument around how important it is that dominant platforms act impartially to those who use them. To turn around and suggest that those platforms be held liable is a double standard for them, where they're essentially being told both to "not care" and "care a whole lot" about the content they host.

Another point to bring up here is the mention of "deepfake" technology. "Deepfake" is a moniker given to faked audio and video content that is so realistic that it is indistinguishable from real audio and video content.[2] So, if real content and deepfake content look and sound the same, how should a social media platform be able to instantly recognize one from the other? Isn't that an impossible standard? We can support laws that regulate the spread of deepfake content, but to hold social media companies liable for not recognizing and removing it is absurd. Deepfake content can't be unrecognizably fake and recognizably fake at the same time.

Data portability bill

Similar to the data transparency bill, a data portability bill would require companies to make data transfers more feasible from service to service. So if Google keeps track of a user's websites visited (and it certainly does), and uses that information to feed its artificial intelligence algorithms to enhance that user's Google experience, then a Google competitor would be entitled to that user data to enhance its own experience. The data would have to be transmittable in a uniform, secure pattern.

These rules are disagreeable for a number of reasons. First, it would almost certainly be used to benefit large technology companies just as much as the small companies. If a small company comes up with a new behavior to track, then Google would be entitled to that data all the same. Second, this data shouldn't be tracked to begin with, much less tossed around like a football for any company to use. Last, it would be directly opposed to any provisions made under 1st party consent laws. Either it's ok for non-primary companies to collect and process user data, or it isn't.

Opening federal datasets to university researchers and qualified small businesses/startups

The proposal here states that the biggest holders of user-generated data are large technology companies and the federal government. "Large platforms have successfully built lucrative datasets by mining consumer data over significant timescales, and separately through buying smaller companies that have unique data sets....The federal government, across many different agencies, maintains some of the most sought-after data in many different fields." Warner claims that these "locked away" resources are causing data scientists to leave the field of academia to do their research for those large companies, which offer more data and higher salaries.

Warner proposes that, by opening up the federal government's databases only to academia and small startups, that a twofold effect could be achieved. First, university data researchers would have a unique set of data to analyze and process, something that large companies couldn't offer, and this would reduce that labor force going to those companies. Second, small technology companies would have access to that large amount of unique data, which could potentially give them a competitive edge to "catch up" to the large tech firms.

This plan deserves opposition on the sole basis of principle. How did the federal government record and store this much user-generated behavior data, given the fact that we citizens have constitutional protections against that kind of surveillance? Non-governmental companies with no real power over me having that data is not okay, so why would we be ok with the government having it? We shouldn't support a plan to start passing that data around, but a plan to throw it in a bonfire might get some traction.

## Summary of Senator Warner's Suggestions

Of Senator Warner's 20 suggestions, half were necessary and should be prioritized. Four were partially agreeable, and six were negative and needed opposition. Hopefully proposals and documents like this will come out more often, as they encourage open discourse and discussion about how we can tackle the issue of tech regulation. However, all of the discussion will be for naught if Congress continues to be self-serving in their own ignorance and determined not to act.

Senator Warner deserves praise for being willing to address these issues publicly. Even if the Senate is controlled by another party, the other chamber of Congress is reportedly brimming with young intellectuals who put people before profits. These issues aren't partisan at all, unless a politician is so aggressively pro-business that they can't see the clear need for regulation in the technology industry.

These are the critical issues of our time. We have plenty of information at our fingertips in order to come to nuanced conclusions about the problems and create regulations that help people. The public massively supports these measures of tech regulation, and Congress might be putting its toes in the water to test what waves it can make.

## Senator Wyden's Proposals

In 2019, Democrat Senator Ron Wyden called for more regulations against big technology companies and protections for the data they take from consumers. His proposal would include jail time for leaders of big technology companies that sell the private data of their customers or jeopardize it by neglecting security. The proposal seemingly takes aim at the leaders of the technology companies who've gained data on us using covert and subversive methods, like Google and Facebook. But it also aims at non-traditionally technology companies like Equifax which have lost extremely private user data via security negligence.

Wyden's bill would also offer technology consumers the ability to be on a "do not share" list, which would block technology companies from tracking and saving behavioral information. But this doesn't necessarily stop the problem, since it would still give companies the ability to save personal identifiable information. For a company like Equifax, their database would be unchanged by the list. They're not tracking user activity, they're just saving personal information in order to report on credit.

Wyden also offered that users could pay to be on the "do not share" list, for a "small fee," although poor users could have that fee waived. To me, it's unclear why this would be proposed – if the practice is unethical, and must be ended, why take a half-measure that allows the corporations to keep profiting? These kinds of technocratic policies are only worse for their details; a universal policy that outright bans or limits behaviors would be preferable.[3]

Wyden's proposal for a "do not share" list misses the point entirely. First of all, it shouldn't be a "do not share" list, it should be a "do share" list. Online behavioral tracking should be opt-in, not opt-out. Secondly, the point of the regulations should be to dismantle surveillance capitalism and the totalitarian ideologies it enables. By encouraging online behavioral tracking, and by offering fees paid by consumers to recoup the losses that technology companies will receive, we'd be affirming that they were at all in the "right" for trying to bring that evil on us.

The essence of Wyden's proposed laws is genius. It is absolutely time to create regulations with the power to send these people to jail. For too long the people have suffered under their invasive and manipulative practices. I'd encourage Wyden, and all members of Congress, to educate themselves on the goals of surveillance capitalism. Simply enough education in identifying and discussing the topic would change their minds on whether we should allow the technology industry to continue their current scheme.

## Response to Trump Administration's Drafted Executive Order

In August 2019, a version of a planned Executive Order by the Trump Administration was reported on by Politico (and other news outlets) and leaked to CNN. The Executive Order, according to CNN (which they did not make available), would have changed the way that the FTC and FCC applied the Communications Decency Act in order to ensure fairness was being applied to all political viewpoints on social media. The order would have been the policy result years in the making by the Trump administration, after the President complained often about censorship and even held a "Social Media Summit" earlier in the year to hear grievances of right-wing personalities being censored online.

The order would have given the FTC and FCC the ability to step in and regulate social media companies to make sure removed content was equal on both sides. Essentially, it would have given the FTC and FCC power to force certain content not be removed from social media, and the power to force other content be taken down. Social media companies who did not abide by the decisions made by the commissions would have to face punishments.[4]

This approach is completely wrong. The foundation of the regulation is solid — there is no oversight into how online platforms can abuse the privileges of the CDA, and that is problematic. However, handing that much power to the FTC and FCC to intervene would be a step in the wrong direction. Giving the power to decide who gets a voice on the Internet over to the government is no better than letting social media companies decide.

Instead of creating a situation where the FTC might tell a social media company to remove content (an easily abusable power), the CDA should be rewritten such that online platforms have no right to remove any content except illegal content. This removes the power of any organization, private or governmental, to dictate what speech is allowed. It facilitates people getting the protections that the Constitution was meant to give them.

Another flawed facet of the Trump administration's plan is that it would give the power of monitoring and regulating the online platforms to commissions which seem to not want to deal with Internet issues. Both the FTC and FCC play hot potato with regulating aspects of the Internet and a lot of abuses have gone to the wayside as a result. The FTC and FCC would essentially be turned into weapons of the executive branch with the capability of forcing the discussion of their talking points while forcing silence out of opposing views and critics.

The Politico article originally talking about the Executive Order also pointed out that Trump's own FCC may not be philosophically on board. In March of the same year, a sitting Trump-Appointed Republican FCC Commissioner named Brendan Carr claimed in a Tweet, "Outsourcing censorship to the government is not just a bad idea, it would violate the First Amendment." This was in response to an op-ed by Mark Zuckerberg, the founder and CEO of Facebook, in which Zuckerberg called for more government involvement in the removal of harmful content.[5] Seemingly, this would mean that one of Trump's own guys at the FCC would be ideologically opposed to regulating online platforms that the draft Executive Order would have wanted.

I proposed earlier that a new commission should be created to deal with Internet-related regulation, and that proposal would work in this case as well. The issue of certain political thoughts being silenced is troubling, but exists in other facets of the Internet like server hosting. A new agency dedicated to ensuring fair practices across all business aspects of the Internet would be the perfect regulator to deal with the issues of social media transparency and perceived bias.

The Trump administration has correctly identified a problem in the lack of regulation and fairness that technology and Internet companies abuse every day. But their proposed Executive Order solution would just make things more imbalanced, shifting power from one unaccountable force in online platforms to another in the FCC. The better solution is just to tell online platforms to stop removing legal speech, as those removal practices are a violation of users' First Amendment rights and because it's the only solution that tackles the issue of uneven censorship without giving any person the power to silence another.

# XIV

## Restoring Power to the People

### The Fight for Freedom on Every Layer of Technology

Net neutrality has been a hard topic to avoid over the past couple of years. Due to regulators trying to axe the regulation, there's been pushes to educate people on its importance, and now 75% of the country supports it. This is good news to me, as I am totally and unashamedly in favor of net neutrality. Everything about it is American, the fact that no one can subversively mistreat users, or deny them access, based on someone else's paying them off. It's the feeling that the individual is as important as the corporation, materialized in writing and law. It is a 21st century Bill Of Rights.

But I do have to criticize those who won't take the next steps. ISPs are only one part of many that have the ability to discriminate, filter, throttle, and modify users' Internet access and experience. We know that our router networks might be configured to act this dastardly. We know that our hardware might be made to do this. We know that our operating systems can. We know that the applications that we use (most importantly social media applications) can filter, discriminate, manipulate the importance of, and mistreat our data.

Why does our care as liberal people (in the classic sense, not as in Republican vs. Democrat), as Americans who care for our rights and freedoms, end when the evildoer changes from ISP to social media company? Perhaps it is because we associate evil-ness with ISPs more freely due to more bad experiences with them. Perhaps it is because it is hard to imagine that evil exists in the social media applications that we interact with practically every five minutes of our lives (actually more often than this according to some studies). Perhaps it is because of some aspects as simple as marketing.

We Americans should make no mistake that evil corporations are behind the wheel of both of these layers equally. In order to fully secure our rights to freedom of speech, freedom of assembly, and freedom to protest, we must not stand down after the fight for Net Neutrality is over. We must continue to fight until every single layer of our Internet transactions is free of corrupt and corporate greed, and is regulated and kept open for all to use equally.

## Wake Up to Declining Privacy Trends

The case of intrusive technologies is only getting worse, despite public pressure for tech companies to act better. Persuing the surveillance capitalist endgame, Facebook filed for patents in the United States for processes and algorithms that seek to predict user movement in late 2018. The algorithms will use the user's location, as well as common routes and paths taken by others, to predict where the user is going physically.

While Facebook's legal team has clarified that patents are not always indicative of future product suites and development,[1] it certainly seems like Facebook could make good use of this. Advertisers, I imagine, would love the opportunity to know exactly where Facebook users are going to be. Additionally, this might open the door for smaller, local businesses to effectively advertise on large scale social media platforms. By using these services, those local businesses could advertise to those who live across town, but happen to be passing through.

One scary process defined in the algorithms is to use environment details other than GPS to locate and track the users. Facebook has now patented the process of determining user location by watching other technical measures, such as WiFi strength, Bluetooth signals, cellular signals, and background noise through the phone's microphone. This would mean that, even if location services (which most smartphones use to connect to GPS) are turned off, Facebook would still be able to determine user location.[2] This would be a clear subversion of user expectations, when a user turns off location services, the expectation should be that they are no longer being tracked for superfluous reasons like advertising. If Facebook were to implement this, it would demand regulation.

While services like this are helpful in some cases, are they ever really necessary for users to have? Or are they just examples of proof that the goal of technological development isn't to improve the human life anymore, but rather to feed the needs of corporations. Predicting where a user is going based on a giant algorithm that watches everybody is not the dream of the average member of the public, it's the dream of a surveillance capitalist who wants to control people's thoughts and actions to make money off them.

The United States is moving headlong into the future. Nothing about the system appears to be changing any time soon, and a corporation with plummeting public trust filing patents to enhance their spying algorithms is the epitome of an out-of-touch ruling class. As the public, we have to realize that the nonchalance about our privacy will never be stopped unless we take action. None of this should be considered acceptable, and we shouldn't let the ignorant technology mob bosses have control over these parts of our lives.

## Social Media Filter Bubbles

Online platforms have gamed our interests, wants, and desires to keep us interacting with their site longer. By tracking our every movement across the entire Internet, companies like Facebook and Google ought to have a pretty good idea of what makes each individual user tick. This can be used to those platforms' advantage, since knowing a user's online behavior is key to modeling a platform that appeals to them.

Americans are spending more time than ever in front of screens, scrolling through social media, playing video games, and watching videos. The American teenager, on average, spends the same amount of time in front of a screen as they do in school, seven-and-a-half hours a day.[3] Still, these historical heights of online entrenchment do not sate the desires of the online platforms to keep users consuming longer. It's a business model to them. It's the essential endgame of surveillance capitalism.

One incredibly effective way that online platforms do this is by serving up content that exclusively matches the end user's opinions. It's safe to say, at this point, that online platforms know every category that every user belongs to, and likely every interest that they have. From political party to race, gender, movie and music preferences, what kinds of partners they've had, etc., online platforms know it all.

With this data, the online platforms can algorithmically decide what kind of content is most interesting to the specific user. Following that logic, online platforms can and do put content in front of users that is specific to their appetite, except the food is social media. Users are shown content they are likely to read and interact with, which extends their stay and activity on the platform, which in turn gives the company more revenue (from advertisement) and more information about the user. Then, the data from the last transaction is accounted for in the next decision, and another post or video appears, this one even more curated to the user's taste.

I, for one, am not always interested in sports. Sure, I catch some Husker games every season, and I'll watch some NHL during the playoffs, but overall, I'm simply not interested in sports. Other topics, like technology and politics, do heavily interest me. Thus, if YouTube were trying to keep me paying attention after I watched a video, it would probably suggest something political over something like a sports highlight reel.

There is a simple rule behind this pervasiveness—all platforms are trying to be the best place to advertise. In the past, advertisers had to rely on group-level demographics in order to sell advertisement. In the past, Nickelodeon and Disney Channel (the two most popular children's cartoon and television networks) might sell advertisements to toy companies. Those same toy companies probably did not buy those same advertisements on NBC and CBS. The theory was simple, children will be watching Nickelodeon and Disney Channel, and this advertisement is geared for children, so we should play it on those channels instead of channels with a higher concentration of adult viewers.

I think Americans would generally be okay with knowing their personal information was used to tell the T.V. network about its audience in a general sense. This kind of data could be seen as invasive, and the American people never truly got to vote and say they were okay with it, but it wasn't too large of a breach of trust. The media machine, however, took this as a form of permission and took off with it, and in a way, started the insane data collection that we know today, even though advertisements targeted at demographics are different than advertisements targeted to individuals.

## The Filter Bubbles Get Tighter

At one point, T.V. networks were learning about the average age and genders of their audiences. In the blink of an eye, online media platforms were finding out every minute detail about every one of their audience members. Then, advertisers bought ads knowing that it was a worthwhile investment due to the concentration of interested parties in the audience. Now, the advertisements watched by two people consuming the same media can be vastly different, as each advertisement is tailored for each user.

YouTube especially has come under a lot of fire for their recommendation engine. Because YouTube tries to distinguish political beliefs to recommend videos to users, it ends up pushing moderate or centrist viewers deep into the extreme side of politics. In a sort of race to the bottom against itself, the YouTube algorithm decides a user's political preferences quickly and then builds up the walls so only that viewpoint is seen.

All of this, from targeted advertisements, to recommended videos, to which post Facebook decides to show you next, culminates in one end result: We all live in an individualized echo chamber. At some point, our political opinions became known to the online platforms. I suppose for most it wasn't hard to decipher, especially if commentary on political topics is available. After the online platforms found out our politics, they began spoon-feeding us content that reinforces those beliefs, again and again.

From a business perspective, it's not inconceivable to believe that people respond better to information that confirms their bias than information that challenges. It's understandable that a negative interaction or experience might cause frustration with the platform, all of which is bad for business. The end result is more terrifying, however, where we have our online tribes and we stick to our own, never venturing out of our caves to see other people's perspective.

## Reusing the Inclusive Model of Online Parasocial Relationships

As our society becomes more digitized, we've had downstream cultural and social impacts that have made us uncomfortable. Parasocial relationships are the relationships that people develop with celebrities when parasocial interaction (interaction that feels personal for one party but not the other) occurs. In a parasocial relationship, the non-celebrity will watch the celebrity, learn personal things about the celebrity, give their money and attention to the celebrity, and put trust into the celebrity, while the celebrity may not ever even learn the other person's name.

Parasocial relationships are not a bad thing, in fact, "[m]ost parasocial relationships are completely harmless." There can be instances where the non-celebrity gets too invested and can be frustrated by the lack of response and attention from the celebrity, but these are outlier cases. While it's true that parasocial relationships are not inherently unhealthy, people engaging in them would rather have fully-reciprocated relationships with mutual interest.[4]

While our real-life friendships and connections are becoming weaker, we should expect to see online parasocial relationships and interactions increase. People are going to give more money to crowdfunding websites like GoFundMe for their idols. They're going to spend more money on subscriptions on websites like Twitch and Patreon to indulge those relationships. People in search of a social outlet are using these as avenues to reach out to the online world in a socially acceptable way.

Online celebrities use these attitudes to gain followers. A study found that YouTube creators, even those with only 100,000 subscribers, use parasocial interactions to bring their fans closer and keep their community tightly knit.[5] Online celebrities use sites like Patreon to offer exclusive access and content to people who pay a monthly subscription fee. Popular video game streamers can set their channel settings such that only paid subscribers can use functions like chatting.

People are spending more time online and trying to figure out acceptable ways to socialize in online mediums. Things are weird, but they're only going to get weirder until we start talking about these social changes. I think that we need to be more open in our invitations to talk and make friends online. Online celebrities are seeing the general cold shoulder of the modern digital world and offering warmth—for a small price, one can join their online community and make friends.

I don't think this model is bad, as I said earlier, parasocial relationships can be healthy outlets. We need to focus on changing Internet culture so that inclusiveness and community don't have price tags, and relationships are reciprocated. We can take the model that online celebrities use with their communities and remove the celebrity-worship aspect of it. We should create ways to make friends and socialize online without the barriers of entry. If we're going to spend all day online with strangers, we might as well not be lonely.

## How to Get Out of the Bubble

Deep down, Americans have thick skin. We know how to face adversity, we know how to overcome our differences, and we know how to work with each other. These are American values, it's what separates us from other countries in the West. We need to be introspective and find our resilience, but we also need to use that introspection to find some humility.

We didn't build a republic by being too offended to talk about issues, and we certainly won't maintain one this way. Americans need to be better about extending the olive branch, online and in person, to come to an understanding. Common ground is very easy to find, it's a shame we don't try harder to find it.

We need to reject business models that support the mentality that we "stick to our own." Yes, this includes most of the media. We need to realize the threat of a segregated American society is at our doorstep. We're tearing down institutions for being offensive instead of building new ones that promote community and understanding. It's never easy to hear that one needs to come out of their room and wear their shame, but America is never going to heal unless we take concrete steps to come together as one again.

The Texas metal band Fit For A King writes beautifully in their 2018 song "The Price Of Agony" that we're "holding on to what we know, too proud to change, too scared to grow." They posit that "[the] heart that beats for hope [and the] voice that fights for reason [... are] closer than you think." We need to break out of our shells, seek out common ground, and find the nearby path towards healing, before that road moves further away. The chorus of the song resonates:

> Every day we're growing colder
> Our divide is growing further and further
> The hands of time are moving faster
> When will we stop paying
> The price of agony?

The media and social media companies would all be content to watch America suffer if it meant people kept using their products. Let's start thinking critically, talk more frequently, and be more open-minded with each other. Let's send a clear message that we are stronger-willed than Facebook thinks. When Google tries to force us into a lane because that's what makes its algorithm easy, we need to recognize what is happening and seek out what Google is trying to keep away from us. Seeking out a second side to the story, a counterargument to the position, and an alternative narrative can go a long way in a country so divided.

If online platforms see Americans intentionally start seeking out different perspectives than those they are familiar with, they might begin to change their algorithms to be more accommodating. If media companies see feedback that their programs' viewers want both sides of the story presented, maybe they will slowly begin to add that in to the production. By being tougher about potential cognitive dissonance and growth-minded, our rejection of the bubble might cause those industries to lose faith in the concept and weaken their grip over our thoughts.

## Youth: Seek Connections, Not Shells

Social media use, phone use, and Internet use among young people has come under a microscope recently as report after report comes out detailing their harmful effects on young minds. Impressionable young people are becoming more isolated and being pushed toward extreme political views. Being on the Internet, be it for video games or social media or whatever, can quickly become an addiction. However, just because there are negatives does not mean that the entire system ought to be rejected.

I am a child of the Internet. The Internet was around all through my education and developmental years. I was taught the dangers of using Wikipedia as a citation source when I was ten. I don't even remember the fabled days of dial-up—as far back as I can remember, my family's home had broadband. I've experienced all the reported negatives of Internet use, at various points and to various degrees.

As young as nine years old, I developed a habit of playing online video games. By the time I was twelve it very well could have qualified as an addiction. Even further, my psychological need to check my social media accounts has become more constant and extreme since

I bought my first smartphone on my 21st birthday, well after my peers. I spent days during summer vacations in middle school and high school sitting behind a computer screen instead of making plans with friends. During the 2016 presidential election, I watched my YouTube recommendations shift from humorous and gaming-related videos to extremely political clips and hours-long political debates.

All of these experiences are backed up by more than my anecdotes. YouTube was noted by the *New York Times* in 2018 to push far-right political content.[6] A 2017 study in the *American Journal of Preventive Medicine* found that people who visit social media over 58 times a week were three times more likely to feel socially isolated than those who kept the visits under nine times a week.[7] An *Atlantic* article from 2017 claimed that 57% more teenagers were sleep deprived in 2015 versus 1991, and that teenagers working for pay dropped from 77% to 55% from the late-1970s to the mid-2010s.[8]

A 2015 Common Sense Media report stated that teens spend nine hours a day consuming media. However, that number is not exclusive to Internet and social media time, it does include music and television time as well. Regardless, that is a higher amount of time than they would spend sleeping, being at school, playing sports, or working a job. Exclusively on screens like smartphones, tablets, and laptops, the hours spent daily drops to 6.5—still a shocking and frightening number.[9] And teenagers know it is a high number, in fact, a majority (54%) of American teenagers say they spend too much time on their cellphones.[10]

The Internet, while at times can be overbearingly addicting and feel overwhelmingly negative, should not be seen as a net negative to America's youth. What may work better is a more nuanced solution for today's youth: use the access provided by technology to branch out. Instead of giving into the effects of becoming isolated, lonely, and reserved, use technology to interact with others. We should defy those who perverted the Internet's benefits for corporate gain, and break out of the shells they built for us—at least the people they think we are.

Facebook, Google, and Twitter want its users to get inside an impenetrable bubble of opinions. Such a tactic might be proven to increase time spent on the platform and decrease frustration, but is it really what we want? Social media networks might try sleight-of-hand tricks to keep us in our echo chambers, but it's not like we don't know the way out. We know where to find opposing viewpoints politically, and we need to make it our duty, not our peril, to risk opening our minds to being persuaded.

As I previously admitted, I spent much of my formative years online. Not just on social networks, but also by playing video games and using forums as well. The most impactful experiences I had online in my youth were gained by talking to people who I would never meet in real life, not the same kids who I went to school with. The Internet is the gift interconnectedness, allowing us to communicate and talk to people from other continents as equals.

Instead of being bound by some social media company's algorithms, which is undoubtedly designed to keep us isolated, why not make the defiant step forward and reject that indoctrination? What's the price of reaching out? There's risk of rejection. There's risk of putting one's opinions and attitudes on the line, at the risk of being opposed. There's a risk to having one's identity compromised.

To each of these, I'd ask for a careful examination of the risk's harms. So one person rejects another person reaching out? Sure, it might sting, but that's no reason to abandon social interaction in general. So one's opinions get critiqued openly? Where's the harm in that? If they are not tenable positions they shouldn't be held, and nothing will shine a light on these more that public discourse.

The only risk I'd say is worth worrying about is one's identity becoming compromised. To this point, I agree that one ought to be worried about the danger that another can inflict solely with this information. However, I also think this kind of power holding and abuse should be illegal (see the chapter on doxxing). Nevertheless, I'd encourage those looking to branch out online to be wary of the personal information they reveal, at least initially.

Would an abolition and outright rejection of the technology industry's products being used by America's youth be beneficial? That is what some are calling for, but it should be a function of the "EPA of Tech Ethics" to research and study such questions. Throwing out the whole system in order to subside negative effects is not necessary. Instead, we should focus on reforming the Internet and social media activity around the original goals of the Internet: connectedness, not isolationism.

## Creating More Open Online Tribes

It's in human nature to be tribalistic. Everything from history to science shows how our need to belong influences our decision to conform. In the information age, in the post-truth world, it's ever so easy to belong to a group, believe in the group's ideology, and isolate oneself from dissenting views and opposing beliefs.

On online forums, there is a practice called "brigading." Its name comes from the act of gathering an army. In an online forum, it's the practice of gathering members of one's own ideological tribe, and commenting in an opposing ideological tribe's space or engaging with their users. In this way, an "invasion" occurs, where a forum ran by a certain ideology gets out represented by members of a directly opposing ideology.

What's surprising to me is that the practice of brigading has a negative connotation. In some cases, even just the accusation of being a "brigader" can derail an online conversation. In some sense, it's correct to label bad actors (people who solely want to disrupt and refuse to participate meaningfully) in an argument, and to not engage with them. However, from my personal experience, it's not so much that a community wants to not engage with bad actors, it's that they fear the cognitive dissonance of hearing opposing viewpoints.

This isn't to say that I don't think communities should police their own content, of course they should have that ability. I simply think that debate and discussion about topics critical to the country and the world should be less focused on keeping true to one's tribe and more focused on finding truth and common ground. Brigading itself might be an act of malicious intent, but to refuse an opportunity to defend one's viewpoints shows ignorance all the same.

This is not to claim that both sides of the proverbial culture war are identical in mentality or behavior, either. But it's true that each side has formed their own enclaves of the Internet, and it's true that most of those enclaves have rules that require a certain level of toeing the line to avoid getting removed or banned. Even enclaves with neutral names, such as Reddit's general "politics" section, is extremely biased towards the mainstream Democratic party, and removes users with opinions that dissent from the mainly held beliefs. The end result is that the user base for the community dedicated to general and neutral politics can't even articulate any other side of a political argument than that of the Democrats.

As feminist Gloria Steinem wrote in 1998: "The truth will set you free, but first it will piss you off." We need to open ourselves up to having some much-needed cognitive dissonance. New information will always be researched and uncovered, so we must not give in to confirmation bias and be dismissive. Be open to listening and understanding. If we encounter information that causes our political views to become inconsistent, we simply must stop being ignorant of it. We have to internalize it and become better, even if it means going through a period of being pissed off.

## Ignoring Political Tribalism to Save Liberty

Too much of our political views and attitudes come from wanting to stand on our opponent's head and laugh, and that's no way to heal. Identity politics and isolating our influences is no way to better understand one another. Both sides have room to understand that despite our miniscule differences in identity and political beliefs, we are all united under one flag and the values associated to it.

This is not a fight against human nature—it's a fight to reshape our thought processes. The true enemy isn't the person on the other side of the keyboard. What kind of power does that person have over anything? Take this versus the technology industry, which repeatedly cuts corners, sacrifices people for profits, uses subversive tactics, has no transparency, and is overseen by an inactive and unrepresentative commission.

Instead of fighting over the values we don't share, let's focus on the biggest threats to the values that we do share. America could be the only country on Earth with as much protection given to individual rights, as our Constitution believes that we're all evil, greedy, and corruptible people that need limits to our power. In this way, the Constitution demands that we take action to defeat the enemies of our freedoms.

There is no greater threat to the American life than the unregulated and unchecked technology industry. Their deceitful tactics, their subversive and wide scale censorship, and their surveillance capitalist economic goals all point to authoritarian control and restrictions on the abilities of the individual to exist freely. In the end, as long as we live under laws that value and protect individual rights and freedoms, we can have disagreements on anything else. The moment that a conspiratorial conglomerate takes over and starts deciding which opinions are valid and which are not is the moment we lose.

Instead of separating into Democrats and Republicans, socialists and liberals, neo-conservatives and libertarians, let's come to one common unifier: We are all American, and we want to work past insignificant ideological differences and find solutions that work for everyone. We can reshape our minds to not see our neighbors as enemies, but as fellow Americans, with the same core values and dreams as everyone else. Our true enemies have been and will continue to be unchecked yet dominant entities, such as corporations, that seek profit and power over their countrymen's livelihoods.

This is the thread that stitched our great country together, and it's the thread we should tighten to fix our division. It was President Ronald Reagan who said, "Freedom is never more than one generation away from extinction. We didn't pass it to our children in the bloodstream. It must be fought for, protected, and handed on for them to do the same." I fear that swift action must be taken, lest this prophecy ring true.

## Ethics in Computing Classes

It is necessary to explore what ethics exist in the world of computing. The short and simple answer is that there are almost no agreed upon ethics which everyone seems to follow. And I mean follow in practice, not in principle. While it seems to be a consensus in the world of computing that there are things technologists *shouldn't* do, rarely are there behaviors that technology companies *don't* do out of a purely ethical stance.

When I was in college, I did have to take an ethics in computing class. I took this class in 2013, in the aftermath of Edward Snowden exiling himself to be a whistleblower. Snowden leaked documents which showed infiltration of privacy done by America's NSA, showing that the NSA had been abusing its power to spy on the country's own citizens. I remember the class was a bit of a breeze, with a fair number of topics to discuss. The professor was intelligent enough about the world of computing, however, it was easy to tell that she was not a programmer and the practical application of any practices we discussed was a bit foreign to her.

The format for the class was always the same. Each day, we would explore a topic and talk about the potential pros and cons of its implementation. Keyloggers on webpages, killer robots, the NSA, etc., were all fair game. What I don't remember, however, was reaching too many conclusions, and this is an understandable outcome from an ethics class. However, when impressionable college students leave the class thinking that there was a middle ground on every issue, when push comes to shove, they are going to agree with whatever moves them along with the least resistance.

If I believe that internet privacy is completely different than any freedoms protected by the Bill of Rights, because the data is being handed over to a private company instead of the government, then I would be against my employer telling me that we need to delete a user's browsing history on our company's website. Conversely, if I absolutely believe that the Constitution guarantees the right of every citizen to not have meaningful information tracked without opt-in consent, whether it's by the government or any private institution, then I would probably be against my employer telling me to set up a click logger on the user's session so the next time they log in, we know how to best capture their attention and retain them longer.

The important thing is to have a stance, and I'm not sure most IT college students leave their ethics classes with a firm grasp on the importance of each one of these ethical issues in the world of computing. Every one of them merits having a strong opinion, yet so few of us do. I think it'll be remarkable to look back on these moments in time when programmers had the chance to say no, because it truly is within our power. If we won't say no to what the business requires, and the business requirements fail to meet the public expectation of the business's practices, then government intervention is inevitable. In fact, we should see the public asking for regulation of the industry as a sign that we've failed to act ethically.

## Internet Freedom Advocates Get Silenced

We need visionaries in the public eye. There have been people with utopian views on how the Internet should work, but often these people were not in positions of power or influence. The very few of those who've had grandiose visions of the Internet and technology are dead or silenced, and I think this has had a negative effect on the ethical stances of technologists.

Aaron Swartz, who founded Reddit and created various other Internet technologies, knew the power at the fingertips of those who create technology. His goals often included the decentralization of information: that information was to be shared, not locked up, and people should use the Internet to connect. Swartz used his power and influence at Reddit and elsewhere online to halt the US Congress's Stop Online Piracy Act (SOPA) of 2011, which was a vast Internet censorship bill. Swartz advocated against censorship at every turn he could, writing statements with titles such as the "Guerilla Open Access Manifesto." Swartz died in 2013, committing suicide after being prosecuted for electronically stealing academic journals from MIT.

Another visionary with power is Julian Assange. Assange is the founder of WikiLeaks, which publishes anonymously provided information on the web. Typically, that information includes incriminating electronic evidence: videos, emails, etc. Assange, in this capacity, has been a huge advocate for the freedom of information. In his own words: "We are obligated…to do something that is meaningful and satisfying…. That is my temperament. I enjoy creating systems on a grand scale, and I enjoy helping people who are vulnerable. And I enjoy crushing bastards."

Assange, despite being just a publisher of material and not participating in hacking or whistleblowing himself, has nevertheless been treated as an international criminal. From 2012 to 2019, he lived under political asylum and could not even leave the Ecuadorian Embassy in London, England, for fear of his life. In April 2019, Ecuador revoked his asylum and gave Assange up to British policeman. Julian will likely spend the rest of his life a prisoner of the U.K. as he is today or in the US, which will try to extradite him as soon as his sentence with the U.K. is completed.

When technologists who advocate for better use of the Internet get silenced, prosecuted, or end up dead, that is hugely discouraging for others. The two perhaps most powerful advocates for Internet freedom suffered this fate, and to my knowledge, no one has tried to pick up the mantle. The movement of embracing the Internet to propel us into a new era of learning, the economy, and individual freedom is largely faceless. The lack of leadership, in my opinion, has led to a lack of unity and direction for technologists interested in advocating for better use of the Internet.

Now, I will commend organizations such as the Electronic Frontier Foundation for their advocacy on issues of Internet freedom. There are groups and organizations which use their voice to promote mainstream tech freedoms, for example, the 150 groups that signed a letter to Congress urging them to save the 2015 Net Neutrality laws in December 2017.[11] Of course, organizations like these exist, but the Internet freedom movement has suffered massive setbacks by seeing our ideological leaders get silenced.

I've seen the abuses of the big tech companies on our country's values and won't sit down any longer. I'll offer to stand up for those values and to offer my perspective as a technologist. I am willing to be a face for a movement that desperately needs life, if the movement will have me. These issues are too important, at a time too critical, to not add my voice and advocacy. The future of our country from every perspective, socially, culturally, and economically, depends on us getting the next few years right.

# Conclusion

In 2011, I was obsessed with the online game League Of Legends. While I had known about and briefly followed the esports scene of some other games like Halo 3, the League Of Legends esports scene was something I had followed practically since its inception. On a weekend shortly following my sixteenth birthday, in the middle of a high school summer, there was a first-of-its-kind League Of Legends tournament that was called the "Season 1 World Championship."

Even though the event was taking place in Sweden, I was glued to my computer watching the event live. This event had everything, it was the best players in the world of the game I was spending every day playing, playing for a gargantuan prize of $100,000. In this era of the game's competitive scene, the biggest personalities, entertainers, and streamers were all on top teams, and they were all at this event.

It was an experience I'll always remember because of how engaged I felt with the event. During the final match, there were fewer than 100 people in the room watching the event in person, but when the stream's concurrent viewers count reached 200,000, that crowd literally cheered. It was a feeling of connectedness with strangers who I didn't know to an event that was taking place 4,500 miles away, and it all happened because of the Internet.

League Of Legends would grow massively from this point. The game had 11.5 million monthly players in 2011, a number that would grow to over 100 million by 2016.[1] This tournament, the Season 1 World Championship, would eventually morph into an event that has taken place every year following. The World Championships would go from fewer than 100 people watching in person to over 40,000 people packed into the famous Beijing National Stadium in 2017. The 200,000 of us watching the championship live would be 100 million by 2018.[2]

I want to chase those feelings I had as a teenager in 2011. I want to seek out people who live half a world away and find what makes us alike and different. Whether those similarities are something as trivial as interest in video games or something more serious like political alignment, it's all important to me. The Internet's purpose is to link us together, is it too idealistic to think that we should use it for that?

## Replacing the Road to Digitization

Throughout this book, I've advocated for a repavement of the road to digitization. Everything—our culture, our social interactions, our economy, our information—is going down a path of becoming more technological and digital. This is undoubtedly the direction that our country will be headed. My main proposal is not to stop or alter the speed at which our nation's vehicle is moving, my main proposal is to fix the road.

The road, right now, is trash. It's got potholes, black ice, and huge chunks of it removed. The road is built by big tech companies that are unethical, profit-greedy, abusive to consumers, and there's no regulators telling them to fix their ways. If we continue down this road, America's vehicle will be broken. We'll have ceded our rights, liberties, freedoms, and unity. There's a way to get to progress without breaking our country, but we can't do it on this path. Let's rebuild how the relationship between the tech industry and the people works.

**Let's do big things, like regulating big tech:**
- Abolish the FTC and FCC's role in Internet regulation and create a new agency that acts as an "EPA of Tech Ethics".
    - a. Make this agency responsible for the regulation of all business aspects of the Internet to ensure practices are fair and ethical.
    - b. Make this agency research the effects of technology use and the technology industry and create regulations based on its findings.
- Rewrite the CDA so online platforms cannot remove legal speech.
- Force online platforms to be transparent about how search results and aggregator lists are compiled and manipulated.
- Ban facial recognition software from being created or owned.
- Ban planned obsolescence.
- Enforce that tech companies are more transparent about how functionality works.

**Let's dismantle surveillance capitalism:**
- Regulate discriminatory artificial intelligence and ban certain data points from being used in algorithms.
- Regulate infrastructure imperialism.
- Regulate data mixing of personal data and behavioral data, as well as cross-platform data.
- Ban saving of data on users who have not explicitly opted in to being tracked.
- Give users the ability to not be tracked and to have their tracked behavioral data deleted.
- Create limits on how long applications can retain opt-in permission to use other functionality and ensure that opt-in messaging is clearer about its use cases.

- Limit rollouts of technologies to give the public time to debate whether the intrusive elements are warranted and wanted.

## Let's make our economy work for us:
- Increase taxes on the entities that will benefit from workforce automation and end the belief in trickle-down economics to pay for social services of displaced workers.
- Research and implement ideas like Universal Basic Income and Robot Taxation to ease economic anxiety with economic security.
- Reinstate Net Neutrality and look to expand similar fairness measures to other aspects of the Internet infrastructure.
- Fund municipal Internet service providers at a national level and make Internet a public utility.
- Make new building codes with fiber optic readiness the national standard.
- Ban government information and identifiers (like SSNs) from being saved and utilized for non-governmental reasons.

## And let's change some fundamentals of our society:
- Change our processes regarding election and voting machine security.
- Create committees with representation from all stakeholders to try to solve the problems with encryption's role in the justice system.
- Increase technical education across the board.
- Ban doxxing by not allowing entities to save the personal information of anyone who has not explicitly submitted that information to that entity.

By implementing these ideas, we can ensure that America will arrive at the finish line of this transition period intact. We need these measures to happen, or else America will be broken: our values will be torn, our division larger, our jobs gone with no means to re-educate and re-enter the workforce, and our privacy completely eroded by surveillance capitalism. The road we're headed down needs to keep us in one piece.

## We Agree on These Issues

The issues that I'm advocating for are not contentious. There may be some, primarily on the economic side I'd imagine, that come with some resistance, but overall these ideas are popular. The people of this country understand what's at stake if there's no protection for them, and they demand regulation.

83% of Americans support Net Neutrality,[3] and that's a result of years of advocacy, awareness, and petitioning. The only reason we don't have Net Neutrality is because Verizon got their own lawyer to head up the regulator and he lied about what the country was telling him. Let's get Net Neutrality and expand the ideology of fair play across all layers of Internet connectivity.

91% of Americans think a free Internet is important.[4] There isn't a single way to split up the American demographic, not by race, sex, or age, that doesn't support the freedom to say controversial things.[5] We need these values enforced on online platforms. Hate speech rules are not valid and put us at odds against each other, instead of letting us focus on discussing the issues.

81% of Americans believe the risks of how tech companies use their data outweigh the benefits, and 79% believe that they are concerned about how their data is being used by those companies. 81% believe that they have little or no control over the data being collected by companies.[6] 79% of voters want Congress to prioritize a privacy protection bill.[7] 75% of Americans wish tech companies would honor their requests to avoid being tracked.[8] Users shouldn't have to game the system to avoid being taken advantage of, not being taken advantage of should be the norm. Let's force companies to give people the tools they want so they can use the Internet how they please.

Even non-technical measures that I've endorsed, such as enacting term limits to ensure Congress is in touch with their constituencies, are massively popular among the American electorate. Polled support for Congressional term limits is in the 75% range.[9] We all agree that the system is broken and legislators are not doing their job.

These are issues of power, freedom, and accountability. We can trace the debates about the values of freedom to the Greek philosophical era, 2500 years ago. Statements about the duty of entities with power to have accountability can be found from over 200 years ago. From a philosophical perspective, these are issues are far from new, and America's stance on them are written into the country's founding documents.

Liberals can support these regulatory measures because they're pro-freedom, people who respect personal liberty can see the value on regulating surveillance and power abuses. Conservatives can support these policies because the tech industry uses their unregulated power against conservatives. People who value our Constitution can support them because the infringements done by the tech industry are extremely comparable to the infringements done by the government that the Constitution protects us from.

We all believe that no entity, governmental or private, should have the power to infringe on our rights to freedom and privacy. Yet we keep letting it happen, all while the American people suffer. I've made a couple speculations as to why, such as the lack of technical knowledge, the average age of legislators, and the disconnected state of the ruling class, but none of these are excuses for the lack of action.

For all the talk I've made about making sure that we're reaching out to people and the other side, about trying to work together to find common ground and create nuanced policy, maybe the best way to get started is to make the changes we already agree on. A few quick wins on issues with bipartisan support would be a good way to get the ball rolling on more regulations and limits that we should place on big tech. A show of unified force to restore some faith in our legislators' ability to fight for us.

## The Stakes of Surveillance Capitalism Are Too High

We can discuss how ISPs abused consumers and made false promises about the Internet infrastructure improvements. We can talk about how terrible the credit reporting industry is for being lazy and compromising government data on half the country. These are all problems caused by modern technology that need to be addressed, debated, and solved. But of all the threats posed by modern technology, by far the biggest is the end goals of surveillance capitalism.

Surveillance capitalism's end goal is to exploit desires and behaviors of people that they don't even understand themselves. Surveillance capitalism will create predictive models for the entire economy, who will get voted into office, and how trustworthy each individual person is. Surveillance capitalism is the reckless desecration of our rights to privacy by putting us under constant surveillance, and of our rights to expression by creating individualized behavior profiles based on how we express ourselves.

We have a right to our own destiny, and to freedom from the shackles of surveillance capitalism's algorithms. We should not have mass surveillance pushed on us as something that will make our lives better, when it will make our lives more controlled. If we allow surveillance capitalism to prevail, we will have ceded our human rights, privacy, and dignity to the ruling class.

We need to push back on surveillance capitalism. We need regulations against the ways that surveillance capitalists monitor us to record behavioral data. We need protections against business offerings and contracts which require constant surveillance. We need laws that allow people to delete tracked data associated to them. We need oversight into the algorithms that surveillance capitalists use to ensure that they are not harmful or discriminatory.

Talking about each of the small instances of the tech industry violating our rights and acting unethically is important, but don't miss the forest for the trees. All these behaviors lead up to the conclusion of surveillance capitalists. We shouldn't get caught up in debating the minor points of certain cases, because the end goal should be to dismantle the anti-American, intrusive, exploitive, and authoritarian system that surveillance capitalism calls for.

Legislators and regulators must act to prevent this. The American public needs to demand action, and vote for people who understand this massive threat and are willing to stand up to it. There are a lot of moving parts in today's political sphere, but the stakes are too high for our government to not protect us from this.

## A Final Call for Unity

I will urge everyone one last time to use the Internet for its purpose of connectivity. Use it to share information and ideas. Use it to make connections with people who are like you and unlike you. Find the humanity in the people you interact with online.

We are a country in despair, and we are running out of hope. We are lonelier and more isolated than ever before, with a declining amount of friends and close connections. The shifting culture and social aspects of our society need to be talked about and controlled. We will never become happier with our country's changes until we make our voices and opinions heard.

Find or make a community. Find friends that spend hours every day doing the same things online as you. Find your 200,000 people watching a competitive video game over an Internet stream. Join the community, be proud of it. Talk about your interests the way older generations talk about sports and reality TV. We are losing our sense of community, but we don't need to return to the culture that we've rejected just to find it, we can find it somewhere much more comfortable for us—the Internet.

There are protections that we need before we can fully achieve these goals online. For example, how can we expect to be fully open when doxxing is legal and prevalent? How can we be sure that voicing our opinion won't lead to us being banned and deplatformed? I recognize that those are problems and advocate against those practices, but they aren't absolute barriers to my proposal of openness.

Don't think that we are too far divided to come back, or that whatever minor disagreement we have over celebrity drama or political positions cannot be overcome. We share a country and with it, its values. Not only are those values under attack, not embracing them will lead to our downfall. America will never lose to an adversary, it can only lose to itself when the belief in its values dies.

We can protect and fight for our individual rights and freedoms all we want. The question is, what will you do to utilize them? Will you say what you truly think, or will you self-censor? Will you talk about your problems openly, or will you suffer in silence? Will you reach out to others online, or will you choose not to reply?

In 2019, years of tension between Hong Kong citizens and the Chinese government erupted into protests. In March, the Chinese government imposed an extradition bill onto Hong Kong, which violated the "one country, two systems [of government]" policy. Hong

Kong is significantly more democratic and freer than the rest of China, its citizens enjoy the freedom of speech and a free press. After blocking the bill from being passed, the protests morphed into anti-Chinese authority and anti-police brutality protests.

The protests continued on for months, picking up steam in June when 2 million (as claimed by organizers) of Hong Kong's 7.5 million citizens protested on June 12. By the end of July, something significant happened: the protestors started waving the American flag. And by early September, they were singing our national anthem.[10]

The world sees America's values of freedom, liberty, individualism, and autonomy as goals to strive for. A comment online encapsulated this book's thesis perfectly: "be the America that Hong Kong thinks you are." The rest of the world looks to our country's founders and ideals for inspiration to remove the shackles placed on them by their government. It's high time we too looked to our past and our ideals for inspiration to remove the shackles placed on us by modern technology.

We live in one of the freest countries in the world, yet we don't defend these freedoms when they are under attack by private companies. We live in the most connected era humans have ever known, yet we don't reach out and talk to each other. Let's break these cycles and change the direction of the situation before us. Let's show the world that we won't stand to let our country's values be subverted and our population die of depression. Let's be the representatives of the change that the entire world needs!

# Notes

## Introduction

1.  Simon Kemp, "Digital trends 2019: Every single state you need to know about the internet," *The Next Web*, January 30, 2019, https://thenextweb.com/contributors/2019/01/30/digital-trends-2019-every-single-stat-you-need-to-know-about-the-internet/.
2.  Ellie Polack, "New Cigna study reveals loneliness at epidemic levels in America," *Cigna Newsroom*, May 1, 2018, https://www.cigna.com/newsroom/news-releases/2018/new-cigna-study-reveals-loneliness-at-epidemic-levels-in-america.
3.  Matthew Walther, "The crisis of American lonelieness," *The Week*, August 7, 2019, https://theweek.com/articles/857296/crisis-american-loneliness.
4.  Jeffrey M. Jones, "Record-High 77% of Americans Perceive Nation as Divided," *Gallup News*, November 21, 2016, https://news.gallup.com/poll/197828/record-high-americans-perceive-nation-divided.aspx.
5.  Bradley Jones, "Majority of Americans continue to say immigrants strengthen the U.S.," *Pew Research Center*, January 31, 2019, https://www.pewresearch.org/fact-tank/2019/01/31/majority-of-americans-continue-to-say-immigrants-strengthen-the-u-s/.
6.  Justin McCarthy, "U.S. Support for Gay Marriage Stable, at 63%," *Gallup News*, May 22, 2019, https://news.gallup.com/poll/257705/support-gay-marriage-stable.aspx.
7.  Aaron Smith, "Public Attitues Toward Technology Companies," *Pew Research Center*, June 28, 2018, https://www.pewresearch.org/internet/2018/06/28/public-attitudes-toward-technology-companies/.

## 1 - Modern Technology Undermines Our Privacy Rights

1.  Tim Cook, "Letter from Tim Cook to Apple investors," *Apple Newsroom*, January 2, 2019, https://www.apple.com/newsroom/2019/01/letter-from-tim-cook-to-apple-investors/.

2.   Samuel Gibbs, "Apple and Samsung fined for deliberately slowing down phones," *The Guardian*, October 24, 2018, https://www.theguardian.com/technology/2018/oct/24/apple-samsung-fined-for-slowing-down-phones.

3.   "Apple investigated by France for 'planned obsolescence'," *BBC News*, January 8, 2018, https://www.bbc.com/news/world-europe-42615378.

4.   Chris Weller, "Silicon Valley parents are raising their kids tech-free — and it should be a red flag," *Business Insider*, February 18, 2018, https://www.businessinsider.com/silicon-valley-parents-raising-their-kids-tech-free-red-flag-2018-2.

5.   Kieran Corcoran, "'F--- you leakers': A former senior Google employee says a frantic quest to stop internal info getting out is now management's 'number one priority'," *Business Insider*, December 8, 2018, https://www.businessinsider.com/jack-poulson-ex-google-says-management-obsessed-with-stopping-leaks-2018-12.

6.   "What is Amazon Rekognition?," Amazon Web Services, accessed December 22, 2019, https://docs.aws.amazon.com/rekognition/latest/dg/what-is.html.

7.   Peter Asaro, Kelly Gates, Woodrow Hartzog, Lilly Irani, Evan Selinger, Lucy Suchman, "Thanks to Amazon, the government will soon be able to track your face," *The Guardian*, July 6, 2018, https://www.theguardian.com/commentisfree/2018/jul/06/amazon-rekognition-facial-recognition-government.

8.   Harini V, "A.I. 'bias' could create disastrous results, experts are working out how to fight it," *CNBC*, December 14, 2018, https://www.cnbc.com/2018/12/14/ai-bias-how-to-fight-prejudice-in-artificial-intelligence.html.

9.   "Fearful of bias, Google blocks gender-based pronouns from new AI tool," *CNBC*, November 27, 2018, https://www.cnbc.com/2018/11/27/fearful-of-bias-google-blocks-gender-based-pronouns-from-new-ai-tool.html.

10.  Jennifer Lynch, "Face Off: Law enforcement use of face recognition technology," Electronic Frontier Foundation, February 15, 2018, https://www.eff.org/files/2018/02/15/face-off-report-1b.pdf.

11.  Sopan Neb, Natasha Singer, "Taylor Swift Said to Use Facial Recognition to Identify Stalkers," *New York Times*, December 13, 2018, https://www.nytimes.com/2018/12/13/arts/music/taylor-swift-facial-recognition.html.

12.  Jessica Guynn, "Facebook must stop ads that exclude races: lawmakers," *USA Today*, November 1, 2016, https://www.usatoday.com/story/tech/news/2016/11/01/congressional-black-caucus-asks-

facebook-to-stop-letting-advertisers-exclude-racial-ethnic-groups-in-housing-ads/93147048/.

13. Stephen Engelberg, "HUD Has 'Serious Concerns' About Facebook's Ethnic Targeting," *Propublica*, November 7, 2016, https://www.propublica.org/article/hud-has-serious-concerns-about-facebooks-ethnic-targeting.

14. Catherine Clifford, "Elon Musk: 'Mark my words — A.I. is far more dangerous than nukes'," *CNBC*, March 13, 2018, https://www.cnbc.com/2018/03/13/elon-musk-at-sxsw-a-i-is-more-dangerous-than-nuclear-weapons.html.

15. Tony Romm, Drew Harwell, Craig Timberg, "Google CEO Sundar Pichai: Fears about artificial intelligence are 'very legitimate,' he says in Post interview," *The Washington Post*, December 12, 2018, https://www.washingtonpost.com/technology/2018/12/12/google-ceo-sundar-pichai-fears-about-artificial-intelligence-are-very-legitimate-he-says-post-interview/.

16. Ibid.

17. Nick Bastone, "Sen. Warner blasts Google for hiden Nest microphone: Federal agencies and Congress 'must have hearings to shine a light on the dark underbelly of the digital economy'," *Business Insider*, February 20, 2019, https://www.businessinsider.com/senator-warner-criticizes-googles-failure-to-disclose-nest-mic-2019-2.

18. Sara Salinas, Jillian D'Onfro, "Google employees: We no longer believe the company places values over profits," *CNBC*, November 27, 2018, https://www.cnbc.com/2018/11/27/read-google-employees-open-letter-protesting-project-dragonfly.html.

19. Elizabeth Dwoskin, "Facebook is rating the trustworthiness of its users on a scale from zero to 1," *The Washington Post*, August 21, 2018, https://www.washingtonpost.com/technology/2018/08/21/facebook-is-rating-trustworthiness-its-users-scale-zero-one.

## 2 - Surveillance Capitalism

1. Shoshana Zuboff, "Big other: surveillance capitalism and the prospects of an information civilization," *Journal of Information Technology* (2015) 30: 75-89, https://cryptome.org/2015/07/big-other.pdf.

2. "Drive Safe & Save Mobile for Your SmartPhone," State Farm, accessed August 20, 2019, https://www.statefarm.com/customer-care/download-mobile-apps/drive-safe-and-save-mobile.

3. "Facebook Profit Margin (Quarterly)," Ycharts.com, accessed June 18, 2019, https://ycharts.com/companies/FB/profit_margin.

4.  Kate Cox, "AT&T Ends Snooping Program, Stops Charging Internet Users Extra For Privacy," *Consumerist*, September 30, 2016, https://consumerist.com/2016/09/30/att-ends-snooping-program-stops-charging-internet-users-extra-for-privacy/.

5.  Thomas M. Lenard, "'Pay-for-privacy' internet actually benefits low-income consumers," *The Hill*, August 16, 2016, https://thehill.com/blogs/pundits-blog/technology/291549-pay-for-privacy-internet-actually-benefits-low-income-consumers.

6.  "AT&T Profit Margin (Quarterly)," Ycharts.com, accessed June 18, 2019, https://ycharts.com/companies/T/profit_margin.

7.  Monica Anderson, "Smartphone, computer, or tablet? 36% of Americans own all three," *Pew Research Center*, Novemer 25, 2015, https://www.pewresearch.org/fact-tank/2015/11/25/device-ownership/.

8.  Vlad Savov, "Isn't it time we declared our independence from bloatware?," *The Verge*, July 4, 2018, https://www.theverge.com/2018/7/4/17533926/windows-ios-android-bloatware.

9.  Shoshana Zuboff, "Big other."

10. Daniel Oberhaus, "The Culture Ware Comes to Linux," *Vice*, September 26, 2018, https://www.vice.com/en_us/article/yw43kj/what-happens-if-linux-developers-remove-their-code.

## 3 - Google: Don't Be Evil, Unless It's Profitable

1.  Peter Bright, "Google isn't the company that we should have handed the Web over to," *Ars Technica*, December 17, 2018, https://arstechnica.com/gadgets/2018/12/the-web-now-belongs-to-google-and-that-should-worry-us-all/.

2.  Gregg Keizer, "Mozilla reports flat revenue from Google-Firefox search deal," *Computerworld*, November 21, 2014, https://www.computerworld.com/article/2850881/mozilla-reports-flat-revenue-from-google-firefox-search-deal.html.

3.  Danny Sullivan, "Google now handles at least 2 trillion searches per year," *Search Engine Land*, May 24, 2016, https://searchengineland.com/google-now-handles-2-999-trillion-searches-per-year-250247.

4.  Brody Mullins, Rolfe Winkler, Brent Kendall, "Inside the U.S. Antitrust Probe of Google," *Wall Street Journal*, March 19, 2015, https://www.wsj.com/articles/inside-the-u-s-antitrust-probe-of-google-1426793274.

5.  "The FTC Report on Google's Business Practices," *Wall Street Journal*, March 24, 2015, http://graphics.wsj.com/google-ftc-report/.

6.  "Google Agrees to Change Its Business Practices to Resolve FTC Competition Concerns In the Markets for Devices Like Smart Phones, Games and Tablets,

and in Online Search," Federal Trade Commission, January 3, 2013, https://www.ftc.gov/news-events/press-releases/2013/01/google-agrees-change-its-business-practices-resolve-ftc.

7.  Camila Domonoske, "EU Hits Google With $5 Billion Fine For Pushing Apps On Android Users," *NPR*, July 18, 2018, https://www.npr.org/2018/07/18/630030673/eu-hits-google-with-5-billion-fine-for-pushing-apps-on-android-users.

8.  Ryan Nakashima, "AP Exclusive: Google tracks your movements, like it or not," *Associated Press*, August 13, 2018, https://apnews.com/828aefab64d4411bac257a07c1af0ecb.

9.  Shannon Liao, "Google still tracks you through the web if you turn off Location History," *The Verge*, August 13, 2018, https://www.theverge.com/2018/8/13/17684660/google-turn-off-location-history-data.

10. Michael Connell, "You are not very incognito in incognito mode," *Computerworld*, April 4, 2017, https://www.computerworld.com/article/3186941/you-are-not-very-incognito-in-incognito-mode.html.

11. April Glaser, "Youtube's Search Results for "Abortion" Show Exactly What Anti-Abortion Activists Want Women to See," *Slate*, December 21, 2018, https://slate.com/technology/2018/12/youtube-search-abortion-results-pro-life.html.

12. "Google Data Collection." *C-SPAN* Video, 3:35:18. December 11, 2018. https://www.c-span.org/video/?455607-1/google-ceo-sundar-pichai-testifies-data-privacy-bias-concerns.

13. Tucker Carlson, "Tucker EXCLUSIVE: Email Reveals Google Exec's Effort to Help Hillary Clinton in 2016," *Fox News*, September 11, 2018, https://insider.foxnews.com/2018/09/11/tucker-carlson-reports-google-helped-hillary-clinton-turnout-2016-election.

14. Caroline Tanner, "Voto Latino aims to register 1 million new Latino voters by 2020," *USA Today*, June 14, 2018, https://www.usatoday.com/story/news/politics/onpolitics/2018/06/14/voto-latino-wants-register-1-million-new-latino-voters-2020/695344002/.

15. Julia Angwin, "Google has quietly dropped ban on personally identifiable web tracking," *TNW*, February 4, 2019, https://thenextweb.com/google/2019/02/05/google-has-quietly-dropped-ban-on-personally-identifiable-web-tracking/.

16. Nick Statt, "Leaked Google research shows company grappling with censorship and free speech," *The Verge*, October 10, 2018, https://www.

theverge.com/2018/10/10/17961806/google-leaked-research-good-censor-censorship-freedom-of-speech-research-china.

## 4 - Facebook: The Ongoing Privacy Disaster

1.  Rob Price, "How Facebook employees react to latest scandals: 'Why does our company suck at having a moral compass'," *Business Insider*, November 16, 2018, https://www.businessinsider.com/facebook-employees-react-nyt-report-leadership-scandals-2018-11.

2.  Paige Leskin, "Facebook employees are reportedly so paranoid they're buying burner phones 'to talk s--t about the company with each other'," *Business Insider*, December 8, 2018, https://www.businessinsider.com/facebook-employees-paranoid-burner-phones-2018-12.

3.  Katie Rogers, "Mark Zuckerberg Covers His Laptop Camera. You Should Consider It, Too.," *New York Times*, June 22, 2016, https://www.nytimes.com/2016/06/23/technology/personaltech/mark-zuckerberg-covers-his-laptop-camera-you-should-consider-it-too.html.

4.  Kasia Anderson, "WikiLeaks Accuses Facebook of Censorship in Hillary Clinton Email Release," *Truthdig*, March 19, 2016, https://www.truthdig.com/articles/wikileaks-accuses-facebook-of-censorship-in-hillary-clinton-email-release/.

5.  Bruce Golding, "Facebook admits to blocking Wikileaks links in DNC email hack," *New York Post*, July 24, 2016, https://nypost.com/2016/07/24/facebook-admits-to-blocking-wikileaks-links-in-dnc-email-hack/.

6.  Tim Hains, "CNN's Chris Cuomo: Remember, It Is Illegal To Download WikiLeaks Emails," *Real Clear Politics*, October 16, 2016, https://www.realclearpolitics.com/video/2016/10/16/cnns_chris_cuomo_remember_it_is_illegal_to_download_wikileaks_emails.html.

7.  Gillian B. White, "When Algorithms Don't Account for Civil Rights," *The Atlantic*, March 7, 2017, https://www.theatlantic.com/business/archive/2017/03/facebook-ad-discrimination/518718/.

8.  Max Jaeger, "Facebook accused of enabling gender bias in job ads," *New York Post*, September 18, 2018, https://nypost.com/2018/09/18/facebook-accused-of-enabling-gender-bias-in-job-ads/.

9.  Samuel Gibbs, "Women less likely to be shown ads for high-paid jobs on Google, study shows," *The Guardian*, July 8, 2015, https://www.theguardian.com/technology/2015/jul/08/women-less-likely-ads-high-paid-jobs-google-study.

10. Gillian B. White, "When Algorithms Don't Account for Civil Rights."

11. Helena Horton, James Cook, "Facebook accused of targeting young LGBT users with 'gay cure' adverts," *Telegraph*, August 25, 2018, https://www.telegraph.co.uk/news/2018/08/25/facebook-accused-targeting-young-lgbt-users-gay-cure-adverts/.

12. Justin Lafferty, "Facebook Privacy Settings Lead To The Outing Of Sensitive Secrets," *AdWeek*, October 16, 2012, https://www.adweek.com/digital/facebook-groups-wall-street-journal-gay/.

13. Teo Armus, "Facebook can tell whether you're gay based on a few 'likes,' study says," *NBC News*, November 22, 2017, https://www.nbcnews.com/feature/nbc-out/facebook-can-tell-if-you-re-gay-based-few-likes-n823416.

14. Daizhuo Chen, Samuel P. Fraiberger, Robert Moakler, Foster Provost, "Enhancing Transparency and Control When Drawing Data-Driven Inferences About Individuals," *Big Data* Vol. 5, No. 3 (2017), https://www.liebertpub.com/doi/full/10.1089/big.2017.0074.

15. Hafsa Quraishi, "Under Employers' Gaze, Gen Z Is Biting Its Tongue On Social Media," *NPR*, April 13, 2019, https://www.npr.org/2019/04/13/702555175/under-employers-gaze-gen-z-is-biting-its-tongue-on-social-media.

16. Tom McKay, "Facebook Is Paying Teens to Install a 'Research' App That Lets It Monitor Their Phones [Updated]," *Gizmodo*, January 30, 2019, https://gizmodo.com/facebook-is-paying-teens-to-install-a-research-app-that-1832182370.

17. Christine Wang, Julia Boorstin, "Sheryl Sandberg defends Facebook data-collecting app: Users 'knew they were involved and consented'," *CNBC*, January 30, 3019, https://www.cnbc.com/2019/01/30/facebooks-sheryl-sandberg-defends-research-app-says-users-opted-in.html.

18. Tom McKay, "Facebook Is Paying Teens to Install a 'Research' App."

19. Alex Hern, "Facebook shared private user messages with Netflix and Spotify," *The Guardian*, December 19, 2018, https://www.theguardian.com/technology/2018/dec/19/facebook-shared-user-data-private-messages-netflix-spotify-amazon-microsoft-sony.

20. Alfred Ng, "Facebook's 'proof' Cambridge Analytica deleted that data? A signature," *CNET*, May 16, 2018, https://www.cnet.com/news/facebook-proof-cambridge-analytica-deleted-that-data-was-a-signature/.

21. Sarah Berger, "Mark Zuckerberg could be 2018's biggest loser — he's already down nearly $20 billion," *CNBC*, December 21, 2018, https://www.cnbc.com/2018/12/21/facebooks-zuckerberg-on-track-to-end-2018-losing-the-most-money.html.

## 5 - Censorship in the Digital Age

1.  *Brandenburg v.* Ohio, 395 U.S. 444 (1969).

2.  "Section 230 of the Communications Decency Act," *Electronic Frontier Foundation,* accessed July 25, 2019, https://www.eff.org/issues/cda230.

3.  Hannah Fingerhunt, "In 'political correctness' debate, most Americans think too many people are easily offended," *Pew Research Center,* July 20, 2016, https://www.pewresearch.org/fact-tank/2016/07/20/in-political-correctness-debate-most-americans-think-too-many-people-are-easily-offended/.

4.  Ryan Gaydos, "Twitter apologizes after conservative commentator Candace Owens was briefly locked out of her account," *Fox News,* August 6, 2018, https://www.foxnews.com/entertainment/twitter-apologizes-after-conservative-commentator-candace-owens-was-briefly-locked-out-of-her-account.

5.  Natasha Lomas, "Twitter grilled on policy approach that reinforces misogyny," *TechCrunch,* May 1, 2019, https://techcrunch.com/2019/05/01/twitter-grilled-on-policy-approach-that-reinforces-misogyny/.

6.  Felix Kjellberg (PewDiePie), "We broke a world record! LWIAY - #0062," *YouTube* video, 15:15, December 30, 2018, accessed January 6, 2019, https://www.youtube.com/watch?v=x5mlFY7XuOA.

7.  Felix Kjellberg (@pewdiepie), "petition to turn YouTube's "trending" page into YouTube's "staff picks"," Twitter, December 28, 2018, 2:13 P.M. Archived December 30, 2018. https://web.archive.org/web/20181230072238/https:/twitter.com/pewdiepie.

8.  Patricia Hernandez, "YouTube Is Failing Its Creators," *The Verge,* September 21, 2018, https://www.theverge.com/2018/9/21/17879652/youtube-creator-youtuber-burnout-problem.

9.  April Glaser, "Youtube's Search Results for "Abortion" Show Exactly What Anti-Abortion Activists Want Women to See."

10. Michael Nunez, "Former Facebook Workers: We Routinely Suppressed Conservative News," *Gizmodo,* May 9, 2016, https://gizmodo.com/former-facebook-workers-we-routinely-suppressed-conser-1775461006.

11. Kevin Collier, "Tech Companies Are Gathering For A Secret Meeting To Prepare A 2018 Election Strategy," *Buzzfeed News,* August 23, 2018, https://www.buzzfeednews.com/article/kevincollier/tech-companies-are-gathering-for-a-secret-meeting-to.

12. Sarah Wells, "Here are the platforms that have banned Infowars so far," *TechCrunch,* August 8, 2018, https://techcrunch.com/2018/08/08/all-the-platforms-that-have-banned-infowars/.

13. Peter Kafka, "Elizabeth Warren says Apple, Amazon and Google are trying to 'lock out' the competition," *Vox*, June 29, 2016, https://www.vox.com/2016/6/29/12060804/elizabeth-warren-apple-google-amazon-competition.

14. Mike Masnick, "Newt Gingrich: Merely Visiting An ISIS Or Al Qaeda Website Should Be A Felony," *Techdirt*, July 15, 2016, https://www.techdirt.com/articles/20160715/07492134980/newt-gingrich-merely-visiting-isis-al-qaeda-website-should-be-felony.shtml.

15. Ted Lieu, Interview with Brianna Keiler, *CNN Right Now with Brianna Keilar*. CNN, December 12, 2018. https://www.realclearpolitics.com/video/2018/12/12/dem_rep_lieu_i_would_love_to_regulate_free_speech_but_its_better_in_the_long_run_not_to.html.

16. Aaron Smith, "Public Attitues Toward Technology Companies."

17. Richard Wike, "Americans more tolerant of offensive speech than others in the world," *Pew Research Center*, October 12, 2016, https://www.pewresearch.org/fact-tank/2016/10/12/americans-more-tolerant-of-offensive-speech-than-others-in-the-world/.

# 6 - Doxxing

1. Casey Newton, "People older than 65 share the most fake news, a new study finds," *The Verge*, January 9, 2019, https://www.theverge.com/2019/1/9/18174631/old-people-fake-news-facebook-share-nyu-princeton.

2. Fernando Alfonso III, "After 4chan manhunt, cat-kicker slapped with animal cruelty charges," *The Daily Dot*, August 21, 2013, https://www.dailydot.com/news/walter-easley-cat-kicker-animal-cruelty/.

3. Traci G. Lee, "The Real Story of Sunil Tripathi, the Boston Bomber Who Wasn't," *NBC News*, June 22, 2015, https://www.nbcnews.com/news/asian-america/wrongly-accused-boston-bombing-sunil-tripathys-story-now-being-told-n373141.

4. Burgess Everett, Kyle Cheney, "Ex-Democratic staffer charged with posting senators' private info," *Politico*, October 3, 2018, https://www.politico.com/story/2018/10/03/gop-senators-doxxing-arrest-868122.

5. "What is Doxxing?," Panda Security, August 20, 2018, https://www.pandasecurity.com/mediacenter/panda-security/what-is-doxxing/.

6. Meagan Flynn, "WikiLeaks publishes identities and information about ICE employees amid intensifying anger," *The Washington Post*, June 22, 2018, https://www.washingtonpost.com/news/morning-mix/wp/2018/06/22/wikileaks-publishes-identities-and-information-about-ice-employees-amid-intensifying-anger/.

7.  Trump, Donald J. (@realDonaldTrump). "#FraudNewsCNN #FNN." Twitter. July 2, 2017, 6:21 A.M. https://twitter.com/realDonaldTrump/status/881503147168071680.

8.  Andrew Kaczynski, "How CNN found the Reddit user behind the Trump wrestling GIF," CNN, July 5, 2017, https://www.cnn.com/2017/07/04/politics/kfile-reddit-user-trump-tweet/index.html.

9.  Liam Stack, "Alt-Right, Alt-Left, Antifa: A Glossary of Extremist Language," New York Times, August 15, 2017, https://www.nytimes.com/2017/08/15/us/politics/alt-left-alt-right-glossary.html.

10. Minyvonne Burke, Marianna Sotomayor, "James Alex Fields found guilty of killing Heather Heyer during violent Charlottesville white nationalist rally," NBC News, December 7, 2018, https://www.nbcnews.com/news/crime-courts/james-alex-fields-found-guilty-killing-heather-heyer-during-violent-n945186.

11. Abby Ohlheiser, Cleve R. Wootson Jr., "A man clobbered protesters with a bike lock at a Berkeley rally, police say. The Internet went looking for him.," The Washington Post, June 3, 2017, https://www.washingtonpost.com/news/the-intersect/wp/2017/05/29/a-man-clobbered-trump-supporters-with-a-bike-lock-the-internet-went-looking-for-him/.

12. Doug Bock Clark, "Meet Antifa's Secret Weapon Against Far-Right Extremists," Wired, January 16, 2018, https://www.wired.com/story/free-speech-issue-antifa-data-mining/.

13. Sarah Mervosh, "Viral Video Shows Boys in 'Make America Great Again' Hats Surrounding Native Elder," New York Times, January 19, 2019, https://www.nytimes.com/2019/01/19/us/covington-catholic-high-school-nathan-phillips.html.

14. Sarah Mervosh, Emily S. Rueb, "Fuller Picture Emerges of Viral Video of Native American Man and Catholic Students," New York Times, January 20, 2019, https://www.nytimes.com/2019/01/20/us/nathan-phillips-covington.html.

15. Robby Soave, "The Media Wildly Mischaracterized That Video of Covington Catholic Students Confronting a Native American Veteran," Reason, January 20, 2019, https://reason.com/2019/01/20/covington-catholic-nathan-phillips-video/.

16. Tapper, Jake (@jaketapper). ".@reason: "Video footage strongly contradicts Native American veteran Nathan Phillips' claim that Covington Catholic High School boys harassed him. The media got this one completely wrong,"

writes @robbysoave." Twitter. January 20, 2019, 1:31 P.M. https://twitter.com/
jaketapper/status/1087100286433402881.

## 7 - Dangers of the Digital Economy

1.  "State of Remote Work 2017," OWL Labs, accessed July 25, 2019, https://www.
    owllabs.com/state-of-remote-work/2017.
2.  Ibid.
3.  Ibid.
4.  Yuki Noguchi, "Freelanced: The Rise Of The Contract Workforce," *NPR*,
    January 22, 2018, https://www.npr.org/2018/01/22/578825135/rise-of-the-
    contract-workers-work-is-different-now.
5.  Henry R. Hyatt, James R. Spletzer, "The Shifting Job Tenure Distribution,"
    *IZA DP* No. 9776 (February 2016), http://ftp.iza.org/dp9776.pdf.
6.  Cameron Keng, "Employees Who Stay In Companies Longer Than Two Years
    Get Paid 50% Less," *Forbes*, June 22, 2014, https://www.forbes.com/sites/
    cameronkeng/2014/06/22/employees-that-stay-in-companies-longer-than-2-
    years-get-paid-50-less/#33455840e07f.
7.  "Why Tenure Metrics Matter: The Value of a Stable Workforce," *Digitalist
    Magazine*, August 3, 2017, https://www.digitalistmag.com/future-of-work/
    2017/08/03/tenure-metric-matter-value-of-stable-workforce-05250332.
8.  Yuki Noguchi, "1 In 10 Workers Is An Independent Contractor, Labor
    Department Says," *NPR*, June 7, 2018, https://www.npr.org/2018/06/07/
    617863204/one-in-10-workers-are-independent-contractors-labor-
    department-says.
9.  Mark Bergen, Josh Eidelson, "Inside Google's Shadow Workforce," *Bloomberg*,
    July 25, 2018, https://www.bloomberg.com/news/articles/2018-07-25/inside-
    google-s-shadow-workforce.
10. Carl Benedikt Frey, Michael A. Osborne, "The Future of Employment: How
    Susceptible are Jobs to Computerisation?," University of Oxford (September
    2013),      https://www.oxfordmartin.ox.ac.uk/downloads/academic/The_
    Future_of_Employment.pdf.
11. Jason Gastrow (videogamedunkey), "I'm Done With League of Legends,"
    *YouTube* video, 7:23, September 12, 2015, https://www.youtube.com/
    watch?v=VjzgbZL12VI.
12. Mike Emanuel, "Census figures show more than one-third of Americans
    receiving    welfare    benefits,"    *Fox    News*,    August    29,    2014,
    https://www.foxnews.com/politics/census-figures-show-more-than-one-
    third-of-americans-receiving-welfare-benefits.

13. "The Employment Situation," U.S. Department of Labor's Bureau of Labor Statistics, accessed August 8, 2019, https://www.bls.gov/news.release/pdf/empsit.pdf.

14. Nicki Lisa Cole, Ph.D., "The Truth About Welfare Recipients," *ThoughtCo*, September 28, 2019, https://www.thoughtco.com/who-really-receives-welfare-4126592.

15. Tom Davenport, "Advancing the Debate on Taxing Robots," *Forbes*, June 13, 2019, https://www.forbes.com/sites/tomdavenport/2019/06/13/advancing-the-debate-on-taxing-robots/#18daa00225a4.

16. Kimberly Amadeo, "US Federal Government Tax Revenue," *The Balance*, accessed September 3, 2019, https://www.thebalance.com/current-u-s-federal-government-tax-revenue-3305762.

17. "Chart Book: The Legacy of the Great Recession," Center for Budget and Policy Priorities, June 6, 2019, https://www.cbpp.org/research/economy/chart-book-the-legacy-of-the-great-recession.

18. "All Employees, Manufacturing," Federal Reserve Economic Data, accessed September 3, 2019, https://fred.stlouisfed.org/series/MANEMP.

19. "Reports, Trends & Statistics," American Trucking Associations, accessed July 25, 2019, https://www.trucking.org/News_and_Information_Reports_Industry_Data.aspx.

20. "Occupational Employment and Wages, May 2018: 43-5081 Stock Clerks and Order Fillers," U.S. Bureau of Labor Statistics, May 2018, https://www.bls.gov/oes/current/oes435081.htm.

21. "Occupational Employment and Wages, May 2018: 43-3031 Bookkeeping, Accounting, and Auditing Clerks," U.S. Bureau of Labor Statistics, May 2018, https://www.bls.gov/oes/current/oes433031.htm.

22. "Occupational Employment and Wages, May 2018: 43-9061 Office Clerks, General," U.S. Bureau of Labor Statistics, May 2018, https://www.bls.gov/oes/current/oes439061.htm.

23. "Secretaries and Administrative Assistants," U.S. Bureau of Labor Statistics, accessed July 25, 2019, https://www.bls.gov/ooh/office-and-administrative-support/secretaries-and-administrative-assistants.htm.

24. "Occupational Employment and Wages, May 2018: 43-4171 Receptionists and Information Clerks," U.S. Bureau of Labor Statistics, May 2018, https://www.bls.gov/oes/current/oes434171.htm.

25. Bill Chappell, Laurel Whamsley, "Amazon Sets $15 Minimum Wage For U.S. Employees, Including Temps," *NPR*, October 2, 2018, https://www.npr.org/

2018/10/02/653597466/amazon-sets-15-minimum-wage-for-u-s-employees-including-temps.

26. Isobel Asher Hamilton, "People are horrified by an Amazon patent that puts workers in cages — but an Amazon exec said even 'bad ideas' get submitted," *Business Insider*, September 11, 2018, https://www.businessinsider.com/amazon-defends-worker-cage-patent-that-was-recently-unearthed-2018-9.

27. Lindsey Bever, "Bear repellent accidentally discharges in Amazon warehouse, sickening dozens of workers," *The Washington Post*, December 5, 2018, https://www.washingtonpost.com/business/2018/12/05/dozens-amazon-workers-sickened-after-bear-repellent-accidentally-discharged-warehouse/.

28. Carl Benedikt Frey, Michael A. Osborne, "The Future of Employment."

29. Paul Krugman, "What happened to the Great Divergence?," *New York Times*, February 28, 2016, https://krugman.blogs.nytimes.com/2016/02/28/what-happened-to-the-great-divergence/.

30. "Share of the Nation's Income Earned by the Top 1 Percent," *New York Times*, October 25, 2011, https://archive.nytimes.com/www.nytimes.com/interactive/2011/10/26/nyregion/the-new-gilded-age.html?ref=politics.

31. Christopher Ingraham, "The richest 1 percent now owns more of the country's wealth than at any point in the past 50 years," *The Washington Post*, December 6, 2017, https://www.washingtonpost.com/news/wonk/wp/2017/12/06/the-richest-1-percent-now-owns-more-of-the-countrys-wealth-than-at-any-time-in-the-past-50-years.

32. Diana Hembree, "CEO Pay Skyrockets To 361 Times That Of The Average Worker," *Forbes*, May 22, 2018, https://www.forbes.com/sites/dianahembree/2018/05/22/ceo-pay-skyrockets-to-361-times-that-of-the-average-worker.

33. "Cost Of College Degree In U.S. Has Increased 1,120 Percent In 30 Years, Report Says," *Huffington Post*, August 15, 2012, https://www.huffpost.com/entry/cost-of-college-degree-increase-12-fold-1120-percent-bloomberg_n_1783700.

34. Quoctrung Bui, "50 Years Of Shrinking Union Membership, In One Map," *NPR*, February 23, 2015, https://www.npr.org/sections/money/2015/02/23/385843576/50-years-of-shrinking-union-membership-in-one-map.

35. "Union Members — 2013," U.S. Bureau of Labor Statistics, January 24, 2014, https://www.bls.gov/news.release/archives/union2_01242014.pdf.

36. Timothy Noah, "The Great Divergence," *Slate*, January 29, 2013, http://img.slate.com/media/3/100914_NoahT_GreatDivergence.pdf.

37. "The Foreign-Born Population in the United States," United States Census Bureau, November 30, 2011, https://www.census.gov/newsroom/pdf/cspan_fb_slides.pdf.

38. "The Productivity–Pay Gap," Economic Policy Institute, accessed July 23, 2019, https://www.epi.org/productivity-pay-gap/.

39. "Historical Highest Marginal Income Tax Rates," *Tax Policy Center*, January 18, 2019, https://www.taxpolicycenter.org/statistics/historical-highest-marginal-income-tax-rates.

40. "The Rise in Dual Income Households," *Pew Research Center*, June 18, 2015, https://www.pewresearch.org/ft_dual-income-households-1960-2012-2/.

41. Tom Harper, "Timeline: The ATM's history," *ATMmarketplace*, October 24, 2004, https://www.atmmarketplace.com/news/timeline-the-atms-history/.

42. Thom File, "Computer and Internet Use in the United States," United States Census Bureau, Report Number P20-569, May 2013, https://www.census.gov/library/publications/2013/demo/p20-569.html.

43. Greg Sargent, "`There's been class warfare for the last 20 years, and my class has won'," *The Washington Post*, September 30, 2011, https://www.washingtonpost.com/blogs/plum-line/post/theres-been-class-warfare-for-the-last-20-years-and-my-class-has-won/2011/03/03/gIQApaFbAL_blog.html.

44. Ben Sasse, *Them: Why We Hate Each Other—and How To Heal* (New York: St. Martin's Press, 2018), 31.

45. Ibid., 227-228.

46. "Most popular mapping apps in the United States as of April 2018, by monthly users," Statista, April 2018, https://www.statista.com/statistics/865413/most-popular-us-mapping-apps-ranked-by-audience/.

47. Kate Abrosimova, "Building an App Like Uber: What Is the Uber App Made From?," *Medium*, May 22, 2014, https://medium.com/yalantis-mobile/uber-underlying-technologies-and-how-it-actually-works-526f55b37c6f.

48. "Company Info," Uber, accessed July 20, 2019, https://www.uber.com/newsroom/company-info/.

49. Cristina Vargas, "Cloud Market Share 2019: AWS vs Azure vs Google – Who's Winning?," McAfee Skyhigh Labs, October 25, 2019, https://www.skyhighnetworks.com/cloud-security-blog/microsoft-azure-closes-iaas-adoption-gap-with-amazon-aws/.

50. Frank Konkel, "The Details About the CIA's Deal With Amazon," *The Atlantic*, July 17, 2014, https://www.theatlantic.com/technology/archive/2014/07/the-details-about-the-cias-deal-with-amazon/374632/.

51. Naomi Nix, "Inside the Nasty Battle to Stop Amazon From Winning the Pentagon's Cloud Contract," *Bloomberg*, December 20, 2018, https://www. bloomberg.com/news/features/2018-12-20/tech-giants-fight-over-10-billion-pentagon-cloud-contract.

52. "Introducing Instacart's New Earnings Structure for Shoppers," Instacart Shopper News on *Medium*, October 10, 2018, https://medium.com/shopper-news/introducing-instacarts-new-earnings-structure-for-shoppers-26a11df53581.

53. Khanna, Ro. Interview with Tucker Carlson. "Are progressive billionaires exploiting their workers?," *Tucker Carlson Tonight*. Fox News, February 9, 2019. https://video.foxnews.com/v/6000199293001#sp=show-clips.

54. Kevin Roose, "After Uproar, Instacart Backs Off Controversial Tipping Policy," *New York Times*, February 6, 2019, https://www.nytimes.com/2019/02/06/technology/instacart-doordash-tipping-deliveries.html.

55. Lauren Kaori Gurley, "Instacart Cuts 'Quality' Bonus After Workers Go on 3-Day Strike," *Vice*, November 8, 2019, https://www.vice.com/en_us/article/j5y3q7/instacart-cuts-quality-bonus-after-workers-go-on-3-day-strike.

## 8 - Internet Service Providers

1. Ernesto Falco, "The Big Lie ISPs Are Spreading in State Legislatures Is That They Don't Make Enough Money," *Electronic Frontier Foundation*, May 4, 2018, https://www.eff.org/deeplinks/2018/05/big-lie-isps-are-spreading-state-legislatures-they-dont-make-enough-money.

2. Bruce Kushnick, "Time Warner Cable's 97 Percent Profit Margin on High-Speed Internet Service Exposed," *The Huffington Post*, February 2, 2015, https://www.huffpost.com/entry/time-warner-cables-97-pro_b_6591916.

3. Ernesto Falco, "The Big Lie ISPs Are Spreading in State Legislatures Is That They Don't Make Enough Money."

4. Eric Griffith, "The Fastest ISPs of 2018," *PCMag*, June 18, 2018, https://www.pcmag.com/article/361765/the-fastest-isps-of-2018.

5. Sam Lounsberry, "More than half of Longmont has signed up for NextLight, and private internet providers have reacted," *The Times-Call*, October 31, 2018, http://www.timescall.com/longmont-local-news/ci_32243114/more-than-half-longmont-has-signed-up-nextlight.

6. James O'Toole, "Chattanooga's super-fast publicly owned Internet," *CNN Business*, May 20, 2014, https://money.cnn.com/2014/05/20/technology/innovation/chattanooga-internet/.

7.   Nick Coltrain, "$900,000 spent on failed fight against Fort Collins broadband," *Coloradoan*, December 8, 2017, https://www.coloradoan.com/story/news/2017/12/08/fort-collins-broadband-vote-spending/934967001/.

8.   Cohen Coberly, "Massachusetts town votes to build their own municipal fiber network over Comcast alternative," *TechSpot*, December 12, 2018, https://www.techspot.com/news/77819-charlemont-residents-vote-municipal-fiber-network-over-comcast.html.

9.   Ernesto Falco, "The Big Lie ISPs Are Spreading in State Legislatures Is That They Don't Make Enough Money."

10.  Bruce Kushnick, "The Book Of Broken Promises: $400 Billion Broadband Scandal And Free The Net," *The Huffington Post*, September 17, 2014, https://www.huffpost.com/entry/the-book-of-broken-promis_b_5839394.

11.  Ibid.

12.  Ibid.

13.  Ibid.

14.  Ibid.

15.  Patrick McGeehan, "New York City Sues Verizon, Claiming Broken Promises of Fios Coverage," *New York Times*, March 13, 2017, https://www.nytimes.com/2017/03/13/nyregion/ny-sues-verizon-fios.html.

16.  Maria Farrell, "Quietly, symbolically, US control of the internet was just ended," *The Guardian*, March 14, 2016, https://www.theguardian.com/technology/2016/mar/14/icann-internet-control-domain-names-iana.

17.  Richard Wike, "Broad support for internet freedom around the world," *Pew Research Center*, February 23, 2016, https://www.pewresearch.org/fact-tank/2016/02/23/broad-support-for-internet-freedom-around-the-world/.

18.  Kieren McCarthy, "The internet's very own Muslim ban continues: DNS overlord insists it can freeze dot-words," *The Register*, July 30, 2018, https://www.theregister.co.uk/2018/07/30/icann_muslim_ban/.

19.  Karl Bode, "It's Now Clear None of the Supposed Benefits of Killing Net Neutrality Are Real," *Vice*, January 24, 2019, https://www.vice.com/en_us/article/gyab5m/its-now-clear-none-of-the-supposed-benefits-of-killing-net-neutrality-are-real.

20.  Klint Finley, "A Straightforward Timeline of the FCC's Twisty DDoS Debacle," *Wired*, August 18, 2018, https://www.wired.com/story/fcc-net-neutrality-investigation/.

21.  Harper Neidig, "Poll: 83 percent of voters support keeping FCC's net neutrality rules," *The Hill*, December 12, 2017, https://thehill.com/policy/

technology/364528-poll-83-percent-of-voters-support-keeping-fccs-net-neutrality-rules.

22. Mike Snider, "ISPs can now collect and sell your data: What to know about Internet privacy rules," *USA Today*, April 4, 2017, https://www.usatoday.com/story/tech/news/2017/04/04/isps-can-now-collect-and-sell-your-data-what-know-internet-privacy/100015356/.

23. Joseph Cox, "I Gave a Bounty Hunter $300. Then He Located Our Phone," *Vice*, January 8, 2019, https://www.vice.com/en_us/article/nepxbz/i-gave-a-bounty-hunter-300-dollars-located-phone-microbilt-zumigo-tmobile.

## 9 - Security

1. Nadav Avital, "The State of Web Application Vulnerabilities in 2018," *Imperva*, January 9, 2019, https://www.imperva.com/blog/the-state-of-web-application-vulnerabilities-in-2018/.

2. Paul Lewis, Paul Hilder, "Leaked: Cambridge Analytica's blueprint for Trump victory," *The Guardian*, March 23, 2018, https://www.theguardian.com/uk-news/2018/mar/23/leaked-cambridge-analyticas-blueprint-for-trump-victory.

3. Sara Salinas, "Zuckerberg on Cambridge Analytica: 'We have a responsibility to protect your data, and if we can't then we don't deserve to serve you'," *CNBC*, March 21, 2018, https://www.cnbc.com/2018/03/21/zuckerberg-statement-on-cambridge-analytica.html.

4. "Starting Point: U.S. Election Systems as Critical Infrastructure," United States Election Assistance Commission, January 6, 2017, https://www.eac.gov/assets/1/6/starting_point_us_election_systems_as_Critical_Infrastructure.pdf.

5. J. Alex Halderman, "Hacking Democracy," *MIT Technology Review*, September 13, 2018, https://events.technologyreview.com/video/watch/halderman-michigan-hacking-democracy/.

6. Kim Zetter, "Top Voting Machine Vendor Admits It Installed Remote-Access Software on Systems Sold to States," *Vice*, July 17, 2018, https://www.vice.com/en_us/article/mb4ezy/top-voting-machine-vendor-admits-it-installed-remote-access-software-on-systems-sold-to-states.

7. J. Alex Halderman, "Hacking Democracy."

8. Andrew Flowers, "More Evidence James Smith Is The Most Common Name In The U.S.," *FiveThirtyEight*, November 24, 2014, https://fivethirtyeight.com/features/more-evidence-james-smith-is-the-most-common-name-in-the-u-s/.

9.  Brian Fung, "Equifax's massive 2017 data breach keeps getting worse," *The Washington Post*, March 1, 2018, https://www.washingtonpost.com/news/the-switch/wp/2018/03/01/equifax-keeps-finding-millions-more-people-who-were-affected-by-its-massive-data-breach/.

10. Lisa Weintraub Schifferle, "Equifax's free credit monitoring - time is ticking …," Federal Trade Commission, January 18, 2018, https://www.consumer.ftc.gov/blog/2018/01/equifaxs-free-credit-monitoring-time-ticking.

11. "Former Equifax employee sentenced for insider trading," Department of Justice-U.S. Attorney's Office: Northern District of Georgia, June 27, 2019, https://www.justice.gov/usao-ndga/pr/former-equifax-employee-sentenced-insider-trading.

12. "Equifax to Pay $575 Million as Part of Settlement with FTC, CFPB, and States Related to 2017 Data Breach," Federal Trade Commission, July 22, 2019, https://www.ftc.gov/news-events/press-releases/2019/07/equifax-pay-575-million-part-settlement-ftc-cfpb-states-related.

13. "The Equifax Data Breach," U.S. House of Representatives Committee on Oversight and Government Reform, December 2018, https://republicans-oversight.house.gov/wp-content/uploads/2018/12/Equifax-Report.pdf.

14. Ron Miller, "Why the Pentagon's $10 billion JEDI deal has cloud companies going nuts," *TechCrunch*, September 15, 2018, https://techcrunch.com/2018/09/15/why-the-pentagons-10-billion-jedi-deal-has-cloud-companies-going-nuts/.

15. "General Data Protection Regulation," Official Journal of the European Union, April 27, 2016, https://eur-lex.europa.eu/legal-content/EN/TXT/PDF/?uri=CELEX:32016R0679.

16. Nick Statt, "Amazon sent 1,700 Alexa voice recordings to the wrong user following data request," *The Verge*, December 20, 2018, https://www.theverge.com/2018/12/20/18150531/amazon-alexa-voice-recordings-wrong-user-gdpr-privacy-ai.

17. Lauren Feiner, "Amazon exposed customer names and emails in a 'technical error'," *CNBC*, November 21, 2018, https://www.cnbc.com/2018/11/21/amazon-exposed-customer-names-and-emails-in-a-technical-error.html.

18. Joseph Cox, "The FBI's 'Unprecedented' Hacking Campaign Targeted Over a Thousand Computers," *Vice*, January 5, 2016, https://www.vice.com/en_us/article/qkj8vv/the-fbis-unprecedented-hacking-campaign-targeted-over-a-thousand-computers.

19. Robert Lemos, "Home Computers Connected to the Internet Aren't Private, Court Rules," *eWeek*, June 28, 2016, https://www.eweek.com/security/home-computers-connected-to-the-internet-aren-t-private-court-rules.

20. Mark Rumold, "Federal Court: The Fourth Amendment Does Not Protect Your Home Computer," *Electronic Frontier Foundation*, June 23, 2016, https://www.eff.org/deeplinks/2016/06/federal-court-fourth-amendment-does-not-protect-your-home-computer.

21. Abraham Lincoln. Abraham Lincoln to Henry L. Pierce and others, Springfield, IL, April 6, 1859, http://www.abrahamlincolnonline.org/lincoln/speeches/pierce.htm.

22. Molly Price, "New antiphishing features come to Google G Suite," *CNET*, March 21, 2018, https://www.cnet.com/news/new-anti-phishing-features-come-to-google-g-suite/.

23. Jenna Sargent, "Report: Careless end users are an organization's biggest security threat," *IT Ops Times*, March 21, 2019, https://www.itopstimes.com/itsec/report-careless-end-users-are-an-organizations-biggest-security-threat/.

24. Izhar Bar-Gad, "Identifying the 10 most common application-level hacker attacks," *TechRepublic*, August 21, 2001, https://www.techrepublic.com/article/identifying-the-10-most-common-application-level-hacker-attacks/.

25. Zach Whittaker, "Millions of bank loan and mortgage documents have leaked online," *TechCrunch*, January 23, 3019, https://techcrunch.com/2019/01/23/financial-files/.

26. "The most vulnerable players of 2017," GFI Labs Team on *TechTalk*, March 29, 2018, https://techtalk.gfi.com/the-most-vulnerable-players-of-2017/.

27. Josh Fruhlinger, "What is WannaCry ransomware, how does it infect, and who was responsible?," *CSO*, August 30, 2018, https://www.csoonline.com/article/3227906/what-is-wannacry-ransomware-how-does-it-infect-and-who-was-responsible.html.

28. Jordan Robertson, Michael Riley, "The Big Hack: How China Used a Tiny Chip to Infiltrate U.S. Companies," *Bloomberg*, October 4, 2018, https://www.bloomberg.com/news/features/2018-10-04/the-big-hack-how-china-used-a-tiny-chip-to-infiltrate-america-s-top-companies.

29. Jordan Robertson, Michael Riley, "The Big Hack: Statements From Amazon, Apple, Supermicro, and the Chinese Government," *Bloomberg*, October 4, 2018, https://www.bloomberg.com/news/articles/2018-10-04/the-big-hack-amazon-apple-supermicro-and-beijing-respond.

30. Jacob Applebaum, Judith Horchert, Christian Stöcker, "Catalog Advertises NSA Toolbox," *Spiegel*, December 29, 2013, https://www.spiegel.de/international/world/catalog-reveals-nsa-has-back-doors-for-numerous-devices-a-940994.html.

31. Glenn Greenwald, "Glenn Greenwald: how the NSA tampers with US-made internet routers," *The Guardian*, May 12, 2014, https://www.theguardian.com/books/2014/may/12/glenn-greenwald-nsa-tampers-us-internet-routers-snowden.

32. Sean Gallagher, "Photos of an NSA "upgrade" factory show Cisco router getting implant," *Ars Technica*, May 14, 2014, https://arstechnica.com/tech-policy/2014/05/photos-of-an-nsa-upgrade-factory-show-cisco-router-getting-implant/.

33. Matthew J. Schwartz, "Router Hacks: Who's Responsible?," *BankInfoSecurity*, May 18, 2015, https://www.bankinfosecurity.com/compromised-routers-whos-responsible-a-8233.

34. Paul Wagenseil, "Russians Hack Wi-Fi Routers: What to Do Right Now," *Tom's Guide*, May 29, 2018, https://www.tomsguide.com/us/russian-router-malware,news-27288.html.

35. William Largent, "New VPNFilter malware targets at least 500K networking devices worldwide," Cisco Talos Intelligence, May 23, 2018, https://blog.talosintelligence.com/2018/05/VPNFilter.html.

36. Darrell Etherington, Kate Conger, "Large DDoS attacks cause outages at Twitter, Spotify, and other sites," *TechCrunch*, October 21, 2016, https://techcrunch.com/2016/10/21/many-sites-including-twitter-and-spotify-suffering-outage/.

37. Chris Baynes, "Entire country taken offline for two days after undersea internet cable cut," *Independent*, April 10, 2018, https://www.independent.co.uk/news/world/africa/mauritiana-internet-cut-underwater-cable-offline-days-west-africa-a8298551.html.

38. Tom Parfitt, "Georgian woman cuts off web access to whole of Armenia," *The Guardian*, April 6, 2011, https://www.theguardian.com/world/2011/apr/06/georgian-woman-cuts-web-access.

## 10 - Encryption

1. "HIPAA Encryption Requirements," HIPAA Journal, accessed July 25, 2019, https://www.hipaajournal.com/hipaa-encryption-requirements/.

2. "Lawmakers back spy bill dubbed 'French Patriot Act'," *France 24*, May 5, 2015, https://www.france24.com/en/20150505-lawmakers-back-spy-bill-dubbed-french-patriot-act.

3. Scarlet Kim, "The snooper's charter is flying through parliament. Don't think it's irrelevant to you," *The Guardian*, March 14, 2016, https://www.

theguardian.com/commentisfree/2016/mar/14/snoopers-charter-apple-fbi-bill-hacking-gagging.

4.  Abelson et al., "Keys Under Doormats: Mandating insecurity by requiring government access to all data and communications," MIT Computer Science & Artificial Intelligence Lab, July 6, 2015, https://dspace.mit.edu/bitstream/handle/1721.1/97690/MIT-CSAIL-TR-2015-026.pdf.

5.  "White Paper - Presidential Candidates," U.S. Chamber of Commerce National Security and Emergency Preparedness Department, October 28, 2016, https://www.uschamber.com/sites/default/files/national_security_2016_presidential_candidate_white_paper.pdf.

6.  "Going Dark, Going Forward: A Primer on the Encryption Debate," House Homeland Security Committee Majority Staff, June 2016, https://www.hsdl.org/?abstract&did=795726.

## 11 - The Difficulty of Regulatory Change

1.  Ariane de Vogue, "Hawaii judge blocks Trump's latest travel ban," *CNN*, October 18, 2017, https://www.cnn.com/2017/10/17/politics/travel-ban-3-0-blocked/index.html.

2.  Jennifer Valentino-DeVries, Natasha Singer, Michael H. Keller and Aaron Krolik, "Your Apps Know Where You Were Last Night, and They're Not Keeping It Secret," *New York Times*, December 10, 2018, https://www.nytimes.com/interactive/2018/12/10/business/location-data-privacy-apps.html.

3.  Alex Johnson, "'Post-Truth' Is Oxford Dictionaries' Word of the Year for 2016," *NBC News*, November 16, 2016, https://www.nbcnews.com/news/us-news/post-truth-oxford-dictionaries-word-year-2016-n685081.

4.  Adi Robertson, "Google's CEO had to remind Congress that Google doesn't make iPhones," *The Verge*, December 11, 2018, https://www.theverge.com/2018/12/11/18136377/google-sundar-pichai-steve-king-hearing-granddaughter-iphone-android-notification.

5.  Jeff Stein, "The FBI report on Hillary Clinton's private email server, explained," *Vox*, September 6, 2016, https://www.vox.com/2016/9/6/12774948/fbi-hillary-clinton-report.

6.  "Rep. Louie Gohmert questions Peter Strzok about Hillary Clinton's emails." *C-SPAN* Video, 3:17. July 18, 2018. https://www.c-span.org/video/?c4740875/user-clip-gohmert-strzok.

7.  Maggie Haberman, Annie Karni, "The Use of Private Email and Chats, This Time by Trump's Family, Comes Under Fire," *New York Times*, March 22, 2019,

https://www.nytimes.com/2019/03/22/us/politics/jared-kushner-ivanka-trump-private-emails.html.

8. Niraj Chokshi, "Older People Shared Fake News on Facebook More Than Others in 2016 Race," *New York Times*, January 10, 2019, https://www.nytimes.com/2019/01/10/us/politics/facebook-fake-news-2016-election.html.

9. "Amazon selects New York City and Northern Virginia for new headquarters," Amazon, November 13, 2018, https://blog.aboutamazon.com/company-news/amazon-selects-new-york-city-and-northern-virginia-for-new-headquarters.

10. Ibid.

11. Jillian Jorgensen, Clayton Guse, Denis Slattery, Noah Goldberg, "Amazon cancels plans to open headquarters in New York, citing opposition from local politicians," *New York Daily News*, February 14, 2019, https://www.nydailynews.com/new-york/ny-metro-amazon-cancels-new-york-20190214-story.html.

12. Matt Mosley, "Jones building a legacy with $1.3 billion Cowboys stadium," *ESPN*, September 15, 2008, https://www.espn.com/nfl/columns/story?columnist=mosley_matt&page=hotread1/mosley.

## 12 - Regulating Big Tech

1. "13 Reasons Google Deserves Its 'Best Company Culture' Award," Forbes Technology Council in *Forbes*, February 8, 2018, forbes.com/sites/forbestechcouncil/2018/02/08/13-reasons-google-deserves-its-best-company-culture-award/.

2. Nick Statt, "Leaked Google research shows company grappling with censorship and free speech."

3. Bradford Richardson, "Alliance Defending Freedom removed from AmazonSmile after 'hate group' designation," *The Washington Times*, May 4, 2018, https://www.washingtontimes.com/news/2018/may/4/alliance-defending-freedom-removed-amazonsmile-aft/.

4. *Marsh v. Alabama*, 326 U.S. 501 (1946).

5. Chris Hrapsky, "The Target app price switch: What you need to know," *11Alive*, January 27, 2019, https://www.11alive.com/article/money/consumer/the-target-app-price-switch-what-you-need-to-know/.

6. "'Tracking every place you go': Weather Channel app accused of selling user data," Associated Press in *The Guardian*, January 4, 2019, https://www.theguardian.com/technology/2019/jan/04/weather-channel-app-lawsuit-location-data-selling.

7. James Vincent, "Facebook ordered to stop combining WhatsApp and Instagram data without consent in Germany," *The Verge*, February 7, 2019, https://www.theverge.com/2019/2/7/18215143/facebook-whatsapp-instagram-third-party-user-data-combined-banned-germany-fco-competition.

8. Makena Kelly, "Facebook plans to let Messenger, Instagram, and WhatsApp users message each other," *The Verge*, January 25, 2019, https://www.theverge.com/2019/1/25/18197228/facebook-instagram-whatsapp-merge-messaging-services-mark-zuckerberg.

9. Shannon Liao, "Google still tracks you through the web if you turn off Location History," *The Verge*, August 13, 2018, https://www.theverge.com/2018/8/13/17684660/google-turn-off-location-history-data.

10. Keith Collins, "Google collects Android users' locations even when location services are disabled," *Quartz*, November 21, 2017, https://qz.com/1131515/google-collects-android-users-locations-even-when-location-services-are-disabled/.

11. "The "Do Not Track" Setting Doesn't Stop You from Being Tracked," DuckDuckGo, accessed July 23, 2019, https://spreadprivacy.com/do-not-track/.

12. Mariella Moon, "Apple is withdrawing Safari's Do Not Track feature," *Engadget*, February 7, 2019, https://www.engadget.com/2019/02/07/apple-removes-safari-do-not-track/.

13. Riley Panko, "The Popularity of Google Maps: Trends in Navigation Apps in 2018," *The Manifest*, July 10, 2018, https://themanifest.com/app-development/popularity-google-maps-trends-navigation-apps-2018.

14. Nick Statt, "Leaked Google research shows company grappling with censorship and free speech."

15. Human Interests, "Google Maps is Different in Other Countries," YouTube video, 6:48, March 1, 2018, https://www.youtube.com/watch?v=q9ZMub2UrKU.

16. "Casey Anthony detectives missed 'suffocation' search," *Associated Press* on *CBS News*, November 25, 2012, https://www.usatoday.com/story/news/nation/2012/11/25/casey-anthony-suffocation-google/1725253/.

# 13 - Evaluating Existing Proposals for Regulation

1. David McCabe, "Scoop: 20 ways Democrats could crack down on Big Tech," *Axios*, July 30, 2018, https://www.axios.com/mark-warner-google-facebook-regulation-policy-paper-023d4a52-2b25-4e44-a87c-945e73c637fa.html.

2.  James Vincent, "Why we need a better definition of 'deepfake'," *The Verge*, May 22, 2018, https://www.theverge.com/2018/5/22/17380306/deepfake-definition-ai-manipulation-fake-news.

3.  Farron Cousins, "Democrat Proposes Jail Time For Tech Companies Who Steal Your Data," *The Ring of Fire*, February 8, 2019, https://trofire.com/2019/02/08/democrat-proposes-jail-time-for-tech-companies-who-steal-your-data/.

4.  Margaret Harding McGill, Daniel Lippman, "White House drafting executive order to tackle Silicon Valley's alleged anti-conservative bias," *Politico*, August 7, 2019, https://www.politico.com/story/2019/08/07/white-house-tech-censorship-1639051.

5.  Carr, Brendan (@BrendanCarrFCC). "Facebook says it's taking heat for the mistakes it makes in moderating content. So it calls for the government to police your speech for it. Outsourcing censorship to the government is not just a bad idea, it would violate the First Amendment. I'm a no." Twitter, March 30, 2019 5:31 P.M. https://twitter.com/brendancarrfcc/status/1112150281066819584?lang=en.

## 14 - Restoring Power to the People

1.  Nicole Nguyen, "Facebook Filed A Patent To Calculate Your Future Location," *BuzzFeed News*, December 10, 2018, https://www.buzzfeednews.com/article/nicolenguyen/facebook-location-data-prediction-patent.

2.  Ibid.

3.  Kristen Rogers, "US teens use screens more than seven hours a day on average -- and that's not including school work," *CNN*, October 29, 2019, https://www.cnn.com/2019/10/29/health/common-sense-kids-media-use-report-wellness/index.html.

4.  Lauren Young, "How Our Make-Believe Relationships With Celebrities Shape Our Social Lives," *Atlas Obscura*, September 23, 2016, https://www.atlasobscura.com/articles/how-our-make-believe-relationships-with-celebrities-shape-our-social-lives.

5.  Leslie Rasmussen, "Parasocial Interaction in the Digital Age: An Examination of Relationship Building and the Effectiveness of YouTube Celebrities," *The Journal of Social Media in Society* Vol. 7, No. 1 (Spring 2018). Pages 280-294. https://thejsms.org/index.php/TSMRI/article/viewFile/364/167.

6.  Max Fisher, Katrin Bennhold, "As Germans Seek News, YouTube Delivers Far-Right Tirades," *New York Times*, September 7, 2018, https://www.nytimes.com/2018/09/07/world/europe/youtube-far-right-extremism.html.

7.   Katherine Hobson, "Feeling Lonely? Too Much Time On Social Media May Be Why," *NPR*, March 6, 2017, https://www.npr.org/sections/health-shots/2017/03/06/518362255/feeling-lonely-too-much-time-on-social-media-may-be-why.

8.   Jean M.Twenge, "Have Smartphones Destroyed a Generation?," *The Atlantic*, September 2017 Issue, https://www.theatlantic.com/magazine/archive/2017/09/has-the-smartphone-destroyed-a-generation/534198/.

9.   Kelly Wallace, "Teens spend a 'mind-boggling' 9 hours a day using media, report says," *CNN*, November 3, 2015, https://www.cnn.com/2015/11/03/health/teens-tweens-media-screen-use-report/index.html.

10.  Jingjing Jiang, "How Teens and Parents Navigate Screen Time and Device Distractions," *Pew Research Center*, August 22, 2018, https://www.pewresearch.org/internet/2018/08/22/how-teens-and-parents-navigate-screen-time-and-device-distractions/.

11.  "150 Groups Call on Congress to Support Net Neutrality," American Civil Liberties Union, December 12, 2017, https://www.aclu.org/letter/150-groups-call-congress-support-net-neutrality.

## Conclusion

1.   Paul Tassi, "Riot Games Reveals 'League of Legends' Has 100 Million Monthly Players," *Forbes*, September 13, 2016, https://www.forbes.com/sites/insertcoin/2016/09/13/riot-games-reveals-league-of-legends-has-100-million-monthly-players.

2.   Annie Pei, "This esports giant draws in more viewers than the Super Bowl, and it's expected to get even bigger," *CNBC*, April 14, 2019, https://www.cnbc.com/2019/04/14/league-of-legends-gets-more-viewers-than-super-bowlwhats-coming-next.html.

3.   Harper Neidig, "Poll: 83 percent of voters support keeping FCC's net neutrality rules."

4.   Richard Wike, "Broad support for internet freedom around the world."

5.   Hannah Fingerhunt, "In 'political correctness' debate, most Americans think too many people are easily offended."

6.   Brooke Auxier, Lee Rainie, Monica Anderson, Andrew Perrin, Madhu Kumar, Erica Turner, "Americans and Privacy: Concerned, Confused and Feeling Lack of Control Over Their Personal Information," *Pew Research Center*, November 15, 2019, https://www.pewresearch.org/internet/2019/11/15/americans-and-privacy-concerned-confused-and-feeling-lack-of-control-over-their-personal-information/.

7.   Sam Sabin, "Most Voters Say Congress Should Make Privacy Legislation a Priority Next Year," *Morning Consult*, December 18, 2019, https://

morningconsult.com/2019/12/18/most-voters-say-congress-should-make-privacy-legislation-a-priority-next-year/.

8. "The "Do Not Track" Setting Doesn't Stop You from Being Tracked," DuckDuckGo.

9. "More Voters Than Ever Want Term Limits for Congress," *Rasmussen Reports*, October 26, 2016, https://www.rasmussenreports.com/public_content/politics/general_politics/october_2016/more_voters_than_ever_want_term_limits_for_congress

10. Tara John, "Why Hong Kong is protesting: Their five demands listed," *CNN*, August 30, 2019, https://www.cnn.com/2019/08/13/asia/hong-kong-airport-protest-explained-hnk-intl/index.html

www.ingramcontent.com/pod-product-compliance
Lightning Source LLC
LaVergne TN
LVHW092010050326
832904LV00002B/46